PEACE AND THE COLD WAR

Part One: 1945-1951
Labour in Government

Ernie Trory

HOVE, EAST SUSSEX
Crabtree Press
4 Portland Avenue
1996

© Ernie Trory 1996

First Published 1996
by Crabtree Press

Printed in Great Britain
by BPC Books and Journals Ltd. (TU) Exeter

Cover Design by Steve Lawton

ISBN 0 9515098 5 3

**Cover Photograph: Harry Pollitt addressing a mass
demonstration in Cranbourne Street, London, on May Day 1949.**

To the Memory of William Gallacher M.P.

By the same author

BETWEEN THE WARS
Recollections of a Communist Organiser

IMPERIALIST WAR
Further Recollections of a Communist Organiser

WAR OF LIBERATION
Recollections of a Communist Activist

Erratum: Page 225, Line 17. For North Korea, read South Korea.

Contents

Author's Introduction		7
Chapter I	The End of the War	9
Chapter II	Problems of Peace	33
Chapter III	Labour and Bread	54
Chapter IV	The 1946 TU Congress	80
Chapter V	The Communist View	117
Chapter VI	Manpower Crisis	129
Chapter VII	The Role of Social Democracy	149
Chapter VIII	Economic Disaster	158
Chapter IX	Moving to the Right	185
Chapter X	The 1950 General Election	210
Chapter XI	The Invasion of North Korea	225
Chapter XII	The Return of Churchill	235
Bibliography		251
Index		255
Catalogue		273

A part of the bourgeoisie is desirous of redressing social grievances in order to secure the continued existence of bourgeois society. To this section belong economists, philanthropists, humanitarians, improvers of the conditions of the working class, organisers of charity, members of societies for the prevention of cruelty to animals, temperance fanatics, hole-and-corner reformers of every imaginable kind.

Manifesto of the Communist Party, Marx and Engels, 1848.

When I say a country is a democracy I mean that it is not a Communist country.

Christopher Mayhew, Parliamentary Under-Secretary for Foreign Affairs, in an address to the Conference of Education for World Citizenship, 30th December, 1948.

As capitalism all over the world sinks deeper and deeper into its crisis, it places its dependence more and more upon such right-wing social-democrats to shield it from the attacks of the working class.

The Twilight of World Capitalism, William Z. Foster, 1949.

As long as there is exploitation of men by robber landlords and capitalists we shall have to fight for Communism. Even if Russia were out of the picture, I would still be fighting for Communism, and more and more of the masses of the workers would listen to my plea for the support of Communism.

Rise Like Lions, William Gallacher, 1951.

Historians ... are the professional remembrancers of what their fellow-citizens wish to forget.

Age of Extremes (p.103), Eric Hobsbawm, 1994.

Author's Introduction

SOME PEOPLE have the idea that the "cold war" was started by the Soviet Union and that since the collapse of socialism in that country the "cold war" has come to an end. Nothing could be further from the truth. Those of you who have read my *War of Liberation* will know that the "cold war" was started covertly by Churchill and his friends well before the end of the Second World War and that it can be dated back at least to the accession to power of Harry S. Truman as President of the USA after the death of Franklin D. Roosevelt on the 12th April, 1945.

Overtly, it began with Churchill's infamous "iron curtain" speech at Fulton, Missouri, on the 5th March, 1946. The details are to be found in Chapter II of this book. The fact is that every aggressive move in the "cold war" right from the start was made by Britain and America, either jointly or severally.

Nor has the "cold war" ended yet. While the vultures of Anglo-American imperialism are picking over the bones of the collapsed socialist countries and savaging the suffering bodies of their peoples, the aggressors are now targeting the remaining socialist countries, as well as any other anti-imperialist states that dare to take an independent line in this troubled world.

Another misconception is that the "cold war" as far as this country is concerned has been waged exclusively from the right by the conservative hierarchy. This is not the case. The right-wing leaders of the Labour Party and of some trade unions have been just as active in peddling their anti-Soviet and anti-communist propaganda as the Tories. The chapter on *The Role of Social Democracy* may, nevertheless, come as a shock to some readers.

It has to be realised that the propaganda levelled against the Soviet Union and the rest of the socialist countries has been directed, not so much against any particular country or group of countries as against the working class of the whole world. And that includes the British working class. The "cold war" was, and is, an integral part of the class war that will not cease until the last capitalist surrenders his power.

It is also important to remember that the collapse of socialism in the Soviet Union and elsewhere was preceded by the collapse of socialism in the British Labour Party and in the Euro-Communist Parties.

What we are now witnessing, in fact, is not so much the collapse of socialism as the collapse of capitalism. The reversion of the Soviet Union and of the other former socialist countries in Europe to a market economy is proving every day that capitalism no longer works. It has outlived its usefulness and needs to be replaced by a more equitable system of society wherein working people are able to secure the full fruits of their labour and control their own destinies.

The collapse of the Soviet Union and the erstwhile socialist countries of central and eastern Europe can be traced not to the socialist content of their governments but to the concessions to capitalism that were made in increasing measure, both internally and externally, after the death of Stalin. That, however, is not the subject of this volume. It is a subject that will have to be addressed in a future work, though a start has been made in my two booklets: *The Social Wage* and *How Did It Happen?*

If you have already seen a copy of my *Churchill and the Bomb*, you will find some duplication in the final chapters of this book. This is inevitable since it was necessary to cover some of the same ground again. That I do still stand by what I wrote in 1984 gives me, and I hope my readers, some cause for satisfaction.

As in my earlier volumes I have included a few autobiographical notes where I have thought them to be of interest. I can promise you that they are not obtrusive.

25th June, 1995.

I had intended withholding publication of this book until after the next General Election in order to prevent the Tories from using it to their own advantage; but changed circumstances now dictate that it should be published as soon as possible.

Whether or not the next Labour government lives up to the expectations of its electors will depend upon the amount of pressure exerted upon it by those who vote for it.

Inevitably the ultimate choice will be either to go forward to socialism, or to be dragged down by capitalism. All previous Labour governments have chosen subservience to capitalism, and it may well be that history will repeat itself in this respect. In any case the final say will rest with the workers in the fields, factories and offices.

7th November, 1995.

Chapter One
THE END OF THE WAR

IN THE CLOSING DAYS OF 1945, the world stood on the threshold of great changes. The military defeat of fascism in Italy, Germany and Japan, by the armies of the anti-facist coalition, was an event of great historical significance, bringing with it a radical shift in the balance of world forces in favour of socialism.

Revolutionary and social changes were started in a number of countries, both in Europe and in Asia, which eventually led to the creation of a world socialist system in which the Soviet Union and Mongolia were no longer alone. Already, in the first few months of peace, the peoples of Albania, Bulgaria, Hungary, Czechoslovakia, Poland, Rumania and Yugoslavia, as well as the peoples of China, Korea and Vietnam, were advancing along the road to socialism.

The presence of the Soviet Army in central and eastern Europe, and in parts of Asia, inhibited the plans of the imperialist powers for a return to the old system that had been found wanting. It prevented the revival of the forces of militarism and enabled the peoples it had freed from fascism to consolidate their independence.

The end of the Second World War also saw the growth of the national liberation movement, leading to the eventual collapse of the colonial system. The struggle for independence was raised to new high levels in India, Burma, Ceylon, the Philippines, Cambodia and Laos. In Indonesia and in Vietnam, republics were proclaimed before the end of the year

Within the imperialist camp, the balance of power had also radically changed. Of the five great pre-war imperialist countries, Germany and Japan had been defeated while Britain and France had been considerably weakened. The USA, on the other hand, had grown rich on war profits; and having acquired the most important spheres of investment, it had become the main bastion of world reaction.

The Second World War was at an end but victory over the axis powers had still to be consolidated. The peace treaties had not yet been drawn up. Already differences between the victorious powers were beginning to surface, eagerly seized upon by the neo-fascists emerging as a result of these differences. In addition, atomic diplomacy now threatened the unity of the anti-fascist coalition. Everywhere economic prospects were uncertain. In a victory broadcast on the 9th May, Stalin said: "Henceforth the great banner of people's freedom and of peace among the peoples will fly over Europe." But in an article written ten days later and published in the June, 1945 issue of *Labour Monthly*, Palme Dutt, its long-serving editor, warned:

> The unconditional surrender of Hitler's armies is not the end, but the beginning. Already a thousand new questions are arising; and the decision on every one of them is fateful for the future. History teaches us that the hour after victory is often more difficult and dangerous than the winning of victory. Victories, won with infinite toil and sacrifice, have been thrown away by division of the victors, by relaxation of effort or by infirmity and confusion of purpose. Decisions taken during these coming months, when the fate of nations is thrown into the melting pot, will govern the future for generations.... We shall need to ensure that liberation is not frittered away through wrangles on the manifold forms of democracy and new expressions of popular freedom arising from the struggle against fascism. We shall need to ensure that the old black forces do not creep back in thinly altered disguises.

These were prophetic words indeed. Even before the war had ended, the "old black forces" were already creeping back, openly encouraged by the imperialist powers, now led by the United States of America. The old imperialist rivalries still existed, of course, but for the time being these were subordinated to the urgent task of stemming the rising tide of socialism that threatened to engulf the whole of Europe.

Nevertheless, on the 24th October, 1945, the United Nations Organisation formally came into being, a union of 51 nations including the Soviet Union, pledged to a policy of peace and friendship. Despite its many weaknesses, the formation of the United Nations Organisation represented a step in the right direction. It was an attempt, if a somewhat half-hearted one on the part of some of its members, to convert the wartime anti-fascist coalition into a permanent organisation for the preservation of peace.[1]

A meeting of the Foreign Ministers of Britain, the USA and the USSR, was held in Moscow from the 16th to the 26th December. There agreement was reached on a number of issues, not least among them a recommendation that a commission of the United Nations on the control of atomic energy be established. An *Associated Press* cable from Moscow, dated the 27th December, reported that James Byrnes, the American Secretary of State had declared that the conference had been "very constructive," not only because of the settlement of many problems but because of "the cordial relations between the three countries represented."

On the following day, the *Daily Express* reported Ernest Bevin, the British Foreign Secretary, as having described the conference as "a most important step towards a solution of the world's problems." In an editorial, *The Times* declared: "The Christmas conference of the three Foreign Ministers at Moscow has been a striking success and has gone far to redeem the breakdown of the preceding conference in London." [2]

Meanwile, history had not been standing still in Europe. Elections were held in Yugoslavia in November, 1945, when, for the first time, the right to vote and be elected was given to all citizens over the age of 18 irrespective of sex, nationality, religious or social position. Women, youths between the ages of 18 and 21, and members of the armed forces had never before been allowed to vote. Every party was given the right to put up candidates; the ballot was secret; and seats were allotted by proportional representation. Only former quislings and collaborators were deprived of the right to vote.

The allocation of seats by proportional representation always favours the weaker parties but in spite of this the opposition decided to boycott the elections. So, in order to give everyone the right to register disapproval of the policy of the candidates of the National Liberation Front, special boxes were installed in the polling booths.

The electors were asked to choose candidates for two chambers - for the Parliament of the Federal State, on a basis of one deputy for every 50,000 inhabitants, and for the Parliament of Nationalities, in which all six Federal States: Slovenia, Croatia, Bosnia-Herzegovina, Montenegro, Serbia and Macedonia, were each represented by an equal number of

---

[1] For a detailed account of the drawing up of the United Nations Charter, see Chapter VIII of *War of Liberation* by Ernie Trory.
[2] See Chapter IX of the same book.

deputies; and in which the autonomous province of Vosvodina and the autonomous region of Kosovo-Metohiba were also represented.

Despite the attempted boycott by the opposition parties, over 90 per cent of the electorate voted, and over 90 per cent of the votes were cast for the candidates of the National Liberation Front. The first session of the newly-elected Constituent Assembly opened on the 29th November, 1945, and immediately abolished the monarchy in favour of a republic. On the 3rd December it made public a draft Constitution, which was discussed during the following two months in trade union branches, youth and women's organisations, children's clubs and orphanages, organised bodies of old age pensioners and civil servants, as well as in Catholic, Orthodox, Moslem and Jewish communities, and in army, navy and air force groups and village gatherings.

After considering thousands of suggestions and amendments and incorporating a large number of them in the draft, the Constitution was unanimously adopted in both Chambers of the Constituent Assembly on the 31st January, 1946. The Constitution laid down that "all authority of the Federative People's Republic of Yugoslavia derives from the people and belongs to the people" and that "it is the duty of every citizen to work according to his abilities; he who does not contribute to the community cannot receive from it." A new democratic state had been born.

In Albania, a Constituent Assembly was elected on the 2nd December, 1945. In the first democratic elections ever held in Albania, 93 per cent of the votes were cast for the candidates of the Democratic Front. On the 11th January, 1946, the Constituent Assembly unanimously proclaimed the People's Republic of Albania. A draft Constitution was drawn up and presented to the people for their judgment. After two months of discussion, on the 14th March, 1946, the Constituent Assembly adopted the new Constitution, which confirmed the changes that had been made in the political and economic order of the country after the establishment of people's power. The Constitution proclaimed the principle that the main means of social production were the common property of the people, and that the private sector was subject to state control.

The alliance of the working class with the labouring peasantry was embodied in the Democratic Front, which was led by the Communist Party of Albania. While in the first stage of the revolution the strategic objective of the Party had been to ensure national independence and the establishment of the order of people's democracy, in the second stage the

THE END OF THE WAR (1945)

strategic objective, after reinforcing the state of people's democracy, was to eliminate the economic base of capitalism and to build a socialist society.

In May, 1946, the law on Agrarian Reform was given "a deeper revolutionary content." Vineyards, olive groves, gardens and agricultural buildings owned by those who did not cultivate the land themselves were expropriated. The elimination of large-scale ownership swept away the remnants of feudalism and limited the scope for the development of capitalism in the countryside. Small private ownership of the land by working peasants was preserved though these peasants were encouraged to collectivise and set up agricultural co-operatives.

The educational reform of August, 1946, provided for universal, free, secular education in the mother tongue. Tuition fees were abolished and primary education became obligatory.

Throughout that year, the process of nationalisation went on. The power stations, the construction materials industry, all the existing light industries and the food-processing industries became state property. By the end of 1946, 87 per cent of the total volume of industrial output in Albania was contributed by the state sector.

The post-war development of Czechoslovakia was marked by a struggle for power between the workers and the reactionary bourgeoisie. The government that emerged in 1945 comprised a National Front of Czechs and Slovaks. The defeated invaders and the traitors from the ranks of the financiers, landlords and industrialists were deprived of power; but the working class had still to engage in a bitter struggle to decide whether the country was to go forward to socialism or back to some form of bourgeois social democracy.

The Eighth Congress of the Communist Party of Czechoslovakia (CPCz), which for the first time in the history of the country had become the dominant party, met from the 28th to the 31st March 1946. It was attended by 1,166 delegates, representing more than a million members from the Czech lands, and 50 guests from the Communist Party of Slovakia (CPS), which at the time was organisationally independent. The main report was delivered by Klement Gottwald, who characterised the most important tasks of the party as maintaining and strengthening the programme "begun by our national and democratic revolution." This included the decrees on nationalisation, by which all the banks and insurance companies, all the mines and the iron and steel industry, the electric power companies and big enterprises in other industrial branches were nationalised. He reminded his listeners that "small-scale and medium-scale private enterprise would be a part of our new economic system and would be accorded the full support of the National Front."

Klement Gottwald warned that reactionary forces were concentrating in several political parties and that this represented a threat to the National Front. To combat this, the Congress enjoined the party "to strengthen the National Front from below." It set two main tasks: to complete the restoration of the economy ruined by the war and to elaborate a new constitution into which would be written the results of the democratic development of the republic, including nationalisation.

Elections to the National Assembly were held on the 26th May, 1946, and resulted in an overwhelming political victory for the Communists who took 38 per cent of the votes. For the first time in the history of the Czechoslovak Republic, a communist, Klement Gottwald, became Prime Minister. In the National Assembly the CPCz and the CPS had a total of 114 seats. Together with the Social Democrats, who had 38 seats, this made a total of 152 seats for the National Front out of a total of 300 - a majority of four seats. The actual voting figures were as follows:

Party:	Seats:	Votes:
Czech Communist Party	93	2,205,658
Czech National Socialist Party	55	1,298,917
Czech People's Party	47	1,110,920
Slovak Democratic Party	43	988,275
Czech Social Democratic Party	36	855,771
Slovak Communist Party	21	490,257
Slovak Freedom Party	3	67,575
Slovak Labour Party (Soc. Dem.)	2	49,983
Blank Voting Papers		32,055
	300	7,099,411

On the 2nd July, 1946, just a week after the Czechoslovak elections, A British all-party, parliamentary delegation arrived in Czechoslovakia. It consisted of Lord Amherst of Hackney, William R. Blyton, Lt.-Col.

THE END OF THE WAR (1945)

W. Corbett DSO, Edgar Grierson, Margaret Herbison, Kenneth Lindsay, Ellis Smith and Barnett Stross. They spent a full fortnight in Czechoslovakia and on their return to England produced a comprehensive report, which was published by the British-Czechoslovak Friendship League. The following extracts make interesting reading:

> No one in Czechoslovakia questions that there must be a close permanent relationship with the Soviet Union, the power that played so prominent a part in the liberation.
> It is stated that the press is uncensored and free, but newspapers may be published only by consent of the government on behalf of political, cultural and social organisations, and not on behalf of or by individual citizens. The Ministry of Information has great influence. Some of the delegates found this alien to their conception of a free press and others considered that the citizen was in this way better served than in Britain.
> When Dr. Benes, the President of the Republic, and Mr. Masaryk, the Minister of Foreign Affairs, invited us to meet them, they made it clear that the very close relationship enjoyed with the Soviet Union met with common approval. One section of the present government had worked in Britain throughout the war, and another section in Moscow. Although united in many of their views they had been compelled to arrive at a synthesis on other aspects of their opinion. A common policy was now offered in a two-year plan. Mr. Gottwald had stressed that the external security of the republic depended upon permanent alliance and universal co-operation with the Soviet Union. The alliance must be a sincere political and military one, with expansion of economic links. The government would, however, continue to develop and intensify its political, economic and cultural relations with Great Britain and America, as well as with France. On the 26th May, 1946, general elections were held in Czechoslovakia. [See previous page for results.] The British Ambassador has assured us that in his opinion the elections were secret and free.

The following view of the political situation was added by William Blyton, speaking as an individual member of the delegation:

> After close observation and study, my opinion is that

Czechoslovakia is going over to the Communist Party. I believe that in the next elections, the Communist Party will considerably increase its strength.... My contact with the many people I met on the tour has led me to the above conclusions. I may say that if I had been a Czech, I would have followed the same policy towards Russia as the Czechoslovak government has done. The betrayal of Czechoslovakia at Munich has brought about that policy, coupled with the fear of a resurrected Germany. I must clearly indicate, however, that the Communist Party, Social Democrats and others all believe in maintaining the traditional friendly relationship with Great Britain.

On the 8th July, 1946, while the British all-party parliamentary delegation was still in Czechoslovakia, Klement Gottwald introduced the Programme of Construction of the National Front government to the National Assembly. This programme conformed to the demands made by the Communist Party in its election manifesto, including a two-year economic plan for the regeneration of the republic.

Reactionaries in the National Front, about whom Gottwald had warned the Communist Party at it Eighth Congress, only agreed to the Programme of Construction after it had become evident that if they had refused they would have seriously compromised themselves in the eyes of the public. They held out as long as they could but on the 25th October, 1946, they had finally to agree to approve a law on the Two-Year Plan.

In Hungary, the liberation of the country by troops of the Soviet Army was completed by April, 1945, after six months of heavy fighting. During the time it had taken to free Hungary from the Nazis, agriculture had lost more than half its livestock and a third of its machines and equipment; mining and industry had lost half its productive capacity; and 36 per cent of the railway system had been destroyed. All large bridges had been blown up and a quarter of all the houses in the country had been seriously damaged. Production had come to a standstill and there was no organised administration.

As early as December 1944, however, representatives of the Communist Party, the Social Democratic Party, the National Peasant Party, the Smallholders' Party and the trade unions had come together and formed the Hungarian National Independence Front. This had demanded a complete break from Germany and full support for the Soviet Army; it had demanded government control of the banks, large factories, power stations and oil wells, as well as radical land reform. It had also called for the setting up of local committees of representatives of the coalition parties to function as local organs of the Independence Front. On the 22nd December, 1944, a provisional National Assembly had been convened under the premiership of General Miklos, with ministers from all four coalition parties. It had immediately adopted the programme proclaimed by the Independence Front.[3]

On the 20th January, 1945, the new Hungarian government signed an armistice with the Allied powers and undertook to play an active part in the war against Germany, to disband all fascist organisations and to bring its war criminals to justice. An Allied Control Commission, under the chairmanship of a representative of the Soviet High Command, had been appointed to supervise the implementation of the armistice provisions.

But even before the signing of the armistice, on the 4th January, 1945, the goverment had dissolved the hated gendarmerie and had begun to organise a democratic police force. People's courts were set up soon afterwards, charged with the task of bringing to justice all who had committed war crimes and crimes against the civilian population. On the 30th January, the government appealed for volunteers for a new democratic army.

A few weeks later, on the 17th March, the government issued a decree expropriating the land of all big estates. It made no distinction between secular and clerical owners. Land belonging to the banks and to big businesses was also taken over. Land owned by small and middle peasants, however, was not affected by the decree; and grants of land were made to 371,000 former agricultural labourers and to 214,000 holders of plots of land not considered large enough to give them a living. Altogether about 60 per cent of the expropriated land was redistributed. The rest, largely forest land, became the property of the state.

The land reform completely transformed the countryside. Assisted with grants of sowing seed, livestock and fuel, the newly-landed peasants went to work with confidence in the new system. Under the impact of the land reform, the Communist Party and other left-wing forces greatly increased their influence among the formerly conservative small and

---

[3] For more details of this period of Hungarian history, see *Hungary 1919 and 1956* by Ernie Trory.

middle peasants.

In the late spring and early summer of 1945, however, differences between the Soviet Union and the Western powers had begun to sharpen. This gave encouragement to the reactionary forces that had gone to ground in Hungary. Differences between the parties comprising the Independence Front, which had been subordinated to the need for unity in the critical days of the liberation, began to appear again. The Smallholders' Party, supported by the right wings of the National Peasant Party and the Social Democratic Party, attempted to restrict the economic and political changes necessary to consolidate the advances that had been made in Hungary.

At its national conference in May, 1945, the Hungarian Communist Party declared itself in favour of economic reconstruction but the Smallholders' Party, with the help of well-to-do peasants, various groups of small capitalists and the Hungarian clergy, countered by calling for a revision of the land reform and a halt to the revolutionary transformation of the economy. Fortunately, at its congress in August, the Social Democratic Party adopted progressive resolutions and came out in support of co-operation with the Communist Party.

Exploiting the difficulties of democratic development in Hungary, as well as the remaining vestiges of nationalism, anti-semitism and anti-Sovietism, the Smallholders' Party rallied every known reactionary to its cause, and, in the parliamentary elections of the 7th November, 1945, succeeded in obtaining an absolute majority with 57 per cent of the votes. In spite of this majority, however, the Smallholders' Party did not dare to try to turn back the clock. Nearly two million workers had voted for the left-wing parties in the elections and they could not be ignored.

In the aftermath of the war, the disruption of normal economic relations and the consequent decline of production strengthened the hopes of the reactionaries for the restoration of capitalism and made it necessary for the state to intervene in economic affairs. Accordingly, in December, 1945, a Supreme Economic Council was set up under left-wing leadership with the responsibility for distributing state credits and the limited stocks of raw materials. This council became an effective instrument for state supervision of the capitalists. The coal mines were placed under direct state control; and factory committees were given a stronger voice in the activities of enterprises still under private ownership. Such was the position in Hungary at the end of 1945.

On the 1st February, 1946, a republic was proclaimed and a law

THE END OF THE WAR (1945)

passed giving effective legal protection to the democratic advances that had been achieved since the end of the war. The election successes of the right-wing parties during the previous November had caused the Communist and Social Democratic Parties to strengthen their alliance and, on the 5th March, 1946, on the initiative of the Communist Party, a Left-Wing Bloc was formed in which the National Peasant Party and the trade unions also participated. In this climate, the currency was stabilised and an equitable tax system introduced. Prices and wages were controlled and, by the end of the year, productivity was increasing by leaps and bounds. The improved situation increased the influence of the Communist Party in Hungary and consolidated its position in the vanguard of the left-wing movement. On the 7th March, 1946, at the call of the Left-Wing Bloc, 400,000 Budapest workers demonstrated against the reactionaries in Heroes Square.

Justice, in the name of the new democratic republic, was seen to be done on the 12th March, 1946, when Ferenc Szalasi and several members of the fascist Arrow-Cross, having been tried and sentenced by the people's tribunal, were executed as war criminals. Szalasi, leader of the Arrow-Cross from the 1st October, 1940, had been appointed Prime Minister by the dictator, Admiral Horthy. Designating himself "the nation's leader," he had lost no time in establishing a regime of total fascism. In the reign of terror that followed, all political prisoners, most of them communists, had been handed over to the Germans who had carried them off to concentration camps where the majority had perished through torture and privation. In addition, some 80,000 Jews, including many old people and children, had been driven on foot to extermination camps in Germany and German-occupied territories. Others had been herded into a hurriedly-constructed ghetto in Budapest, only to be tortured and then executed on the Danube embankment. It has been estimated that 10,000 Jews were disposed of in this way on the orders of Szalasi.

In April, 1946, a Hungarian government delegation visited Moscow to negotiate questions of economic co-operation between the two countries; and in June a similar delegation travelled to Washington, London and Paris. At its third Congress, in September, the Communist Party of Hungary put forward plans for a conscious advance along the road to socialism. This was to be accomplished through nationalisation and the gradual transformation of private small-scale farming into large-scale socialist forms of agricultural production. In striving for these fundamental changes, the Communist Party stressed that it would be relying on the alliance of the working class with the peasants and with the middle sections of the population. A start was made on the 22nd November, 1946, when the Council of Ministers adopted a resolution to nationalise the country's three major iron works with effect from the 1st December.

In planning the advance to socialism, the Communist Party of Hungary had taken into account its common border with the Soviet Union and the presence of Soviet Army units in the country, which, while guaranteeing freedom to the democratic processes taking place inside Hungary, prevented interference from the external imperialist forces that were then regrouping under the leadership of the United States.

In Poland also, the presence of Soviet troops had created favourable conditions for a relatively peaceful development of the struggle to build a new life along democratic lines. Under the guidance of the Polish Workers' Party, the popular authorities of the Polish republic had initiated an agrarian reform and had ended the domination of the industrialists by nationalising key branches of industry. The Provisional Government had also tackled the difficult task of settling and developing the recovered western territories that had given Poland access to the sea again through the ports of Gdansk (formerly Danzig) and Szczecin (formerly Stettin).

On the 28th June, 1945, A Polish Provisional Government of National Unity was set up. This had included members of the former Provisional Government, and some of the more democratic elements from among the Poles living abroad. The Polish Provisional Government of National Unity was recognised by the USSR, the USA, Britain and China. On the insistence of the Soviet Union at the Potsdam Conference, Britain and the USA had also agreed to terminate diplomatic relations with the Polish "government" in London. A treaty of friendship, mutual assistance and post-war co-operation had been signed between the Soviet Union and Poland on the 21st April, 1945. By the end of the year, a new democratic Poland was beginning to arise on the ruins of the old.

On the 6th March, 1945, following the overthrow of the bourgeois government of Generals Sanatescu and Radescu, a People's Democratic Government, headed by Petru Groza, had come to power in Rumania;

and the Soviet military authorities had rendered it fraternal assistance and support in normalising economic and political activity in the country. Economic agreements were signed with the government of the Soviet Union in Moscow on the 8th May, and, as a result, Rumania had received supplies of cotton, non-ferous metals, coke, coal, equipment for its timber and paper industries and, above all, aid in food. This had been of particular importance in view of the serious crop failure in 1945. As in other countries liberated by the Soviet Army, these economic agreements had paved the way for an advance towards socialism.

Led by the Bulgarian Workers' Party, the people of Bulgaria had risen against the royal fascist regime on the 9th September, 1944. The uprising, which had started in Sofia, had soon spread to the rest of the country and it had not been long before a Fatherland Front government, including four communists, had been installed. On the day of the uprising, the Soviet Army in Bulgaria had advanced 120 kilometres, but following the victory of the uprising, and the declaration of war on Germany by the Fatherland Front government, there had been no need for the Soviet Army to continue its operations in Bulgaria.

The formation of a new Bulgarian People's Army had been begun immediately after the victory of the armed uprising, incorporating, where practical, sections of the old army made up of revolutionary soldiers and progressive officers. Elsewhere, whole divisions of the old army had been disbanded. Pro-fascist officers, who had taken part in repressive activities against the people, had been arrested and court-martialled. On the 22nd September, 1944, it had been decreed that commanders of all units should have deputies on political affairs.

Within three weeks of the successful uprising, noticeable changes had begun to take place in Bulgaria, despite the opposition of anti-national forces. The Bulgarian people and their local organs of power had been helped in the normalisation of economic and political activity by the Soviet military commandants in the country, and in March 1945, the USSR and Bulgaria signed a commodity exchange agreement under which Bulgaria received enormous supplies of petroleum products, ferreous and non-ferreous metals, textile raw materials, chemicals, railway rolling stock, locomotives, farm machines and thousands of tons of food. Later, Georgi Dimitrov, general secretary of the Bulgarian Communist Party, was to write: "The Bulgarian people will always remember that Russian troops once liberated their country from the

Turkish pashas and beys; and that the brave sons of the Russian and other peoples of the Soviet Union had now helped to liberate Bulgaria for the second time from foreign conquerors." It was on the basis of this friendship that Bulgaria set out firmly on the road to socialism.

When Finland had entered the war on the side of Germany in 1941, the prospects of extending Finland's territory at the expense of the Soviet Union had looked good. By 1943, however, after 37,000 officers and men of the Finnish army had been killed in action on the Soviet front without the consolation of any significant advances, the dream of establishing a Greater Finland reaching as far as the Ural mountains had turned sour; and by January, 1944, General Erfurth, the German liaison officer at the headquarters of the Finnish General Staff had been overheard speaking of the possibilities of a separate peace. Large sections of the civilian population, rallied by the illegal Communist Party of Finland, had begun to demand Finland's withdrawal from the war. In these circumstances, the Finnish government had been compelled to enter into negotiations with the Soviet Union and, on the 19th September, 1944, an armistice agreement had been signed in Moscow between the Soviet Union and Britain on the one side and Finland on the other.

The armistice agreement had not been reached without opposition from some fascist and para-military organisations that had established secret arms caches in various parts of the country. But the Finnish working class and other progressive sections of the Finnish people had given full support to the firm line taken by the Allied Control Commission in Finland under the chairmanship of Colonel-General A.A. Zhdanov, a member of the Military Council of the Leningrad Front, who dissolved the fascist organisations and put their leaders on trial as war criminals. As a result, favourable conditions were created for the development of Finland along democratic lines.

In October, 1944, on the initiative of the Communist Party of Finland, a Democratic Union of the People of Finland had been formed. Five months later, this body had won 25 per cent of the votes in a parliamentary election; and by the end of 1945, a new era in Finnish-Soviet relations had begun on a basis of peace and friendship.

In Norway, which had been under the control of the Nazis since the 9th April, 1940, a resistance movement had been operative from the earliest days of the occupation. It had been considerably stimulated by news of

THE END OF THE WAR (1945)

the entry of the Soviet Union into the war in June, 1941, and had continued its activities throughout 1942 and 1943. At the beginning of 1944, when a plan to call up 75,000 men for active service against the Soviet Army on the Eastern Front had been announced, the Communist Party of Norway had called for a boycott of the mobilisation. The Quisling government had replied with mass arrests but in spite of this only 300 men, instead of the expected 75,000, had reported at the induction centres.

In October, 1944, Soviet troops had entered Norway, where they had been joyously welcomed by the Norwegian people. There had been fierce fighting in northern Norway, where the Nazis and their local collaborators had spread rumours alleging that the people living in the areas liberated by Soviet troops were to be driven to Siberia, where the men were to be conscripted into the Soviet Army. The Norwegian guerrillas, however, had ignored this crude propaganda effort and had co-operated with the Soviet troops. The Central Committee of the Norwegian Communist Party had called upon the Norwegian government in London to instruct the underground patriotic organisations in Norway to intensify their sabotage of German military installations throughout the country; but the emigré government in London had not responded to this appeal. Nevertheless, the Norwegian guerrillas, as well as large numbers of escaped Soviet prisoners of war, had stepped up their opposition to the German occupying forces.

In the liberated areas, the civilian population had begun to form military units; and on the 9th November, 1944, a Norwegian military detachment of 234 men had arrived in northern Norway from Britain. On the same day, two police platoons, totalling 307 men, had arrived from Sweden.

From February, 1944, until the following April, more Norwegian units continued to arrive from Britain and Sweden. By the end of the war, the total number of Norwegian troops in the northern part of the country had risen to 2,735. The Soviet Union had supplied them with machine guns, ammunition, motor vehicles and medical equipment. The Soviet Union had also sent food to the populations in the liberated areas, without which they would not have survived the rigorous Arctic winter. And when epidemics of diphtheria and dysentery had broken out, the Soviet Command had opened six additional hospitals for the Norwegians.

All the Soviet troops had been withdrawn from northern Norway by the end of September, 1945, their mission having been fulfilled. In the course of the fighting for the liberation of Finland and northern Norway, 15,773 Soviet officers and men had been killed or wounded. According to the Norwegian newspaper *Aftenposten*: "The Russians were the first to come to us and they were the first to leave us. Norwegians will always remember what the Russians have done for them and for the common victory over the enemy."

Austria had ceased to exist as an independent state on the 12th March, 1938, when the Nazi forces of Hitler's government had invaded the country, proclaiming its incorporation in the German Reich on the following day. The *Anschluss* had been accepted by right-wing socialists but the Communist Party of Austria had rejected it and organised resistance to it from the first day. In the years that followed, the Nazis had turned Austria into an arsenal. By 1945, the number of arms factories in Austria had reached 600, manufacturing 9,000 aircraft and 850 panzers and armoured vehicles annually, as well as 1,000 artillery pieces monthly.

At the instigation of the Communist Party of Austria, an underground organisation called the Austrian Freedom Front was set up on the 31st March, 1945; but this was not strong enough to throw off the Nazi yoke without outside help. Many thousands of Austrian patriots who had opposed the Nazi "new order" had already been sent to death camps.

After completing the liberation of Hungary in March, 1945, Soviet troops crossed into Austria, where, on the 13th April, after bitter fighting, they liberated Vienna. On the 9th April, while the fighting was still continuing, the Soviet government issued a statement to the effect that it had no intention of interfering in the internal affairs of Austria and would assent to the wishes of the Austrian public to entrust the formation of a provisional government to the social-democratic leader, Karl Renner. On the 27th April, within a fortnight of the liberation of Vienna, a provisional goverment consisting of representatives of the Communist, Socialist and People's Parties was formed.

Pending the final solution of the problem of Austria's independence, the government of the anti-Nazi coalition established four zones of occupation in Austria. In the Soviet zone, troops of the Soviet Army repaired two of the most important bridges across the Danube in Vienna

THE END OF THE WAR (1945)

while sailors of the Danube Flotilla cleared the river of mines, salvaged 128 ships and restored 30 per cent of the cranes and other equipment in the ports of the Danube. Soviet Army engineers also helped the Austrian people to repair railways and highways. In addition, in the five months following the liberation of the Austrian capital, the Soviet Union provided Austria with as much food as had the USA, Britain and France together.

Nevertheless, Austria did not take the revolutionary path that was to lead to socialism in twelve other European and Asian countries at the end of the war. Nor did Finland, Norway, Denmark or Iran, all of them countries where Soviet troops had been in occupation, to a greater or lesser degree, in the process of carrying out their liberation mission. On the other hand, the peoples of Albania and Vietnam did take the path to socialism although no Soviet troops had been in their countries at all.

The decisive factor in determining whether or not a country was to strike out along the road to socialism was not the presence of Soviet troops but the existence of the internal prerequisites for revolution. In all cases, the basic causes of revolutionary change in those countries that took the progressive road, whether or not they had been liberated by Soviet troops, sprang from the general, democratic, national-liberation struggle conducted by the people against the foreign invaders.

On this basis, the class struggle of the workers and peasants against the wealthy capitalists and landowners who had sold themselves to the Nazi invaders, matured and developed according to the demands of history. And in all cases the progressive movement was led and guided by a Marxist-Leninist party. The presence of Soviet troops in some countries did facilitate the development of the democratic forces by reducing the possibilities of interference from the major imperialist states, but it was the will of the people themselves that provided the basic motivation.

At the end of the war, the people of Germany were also confronted with the problem of choosing which path to tread. Even before the war, the Communist Party of Germany had begun to work out a general line of struggle for a democratic revival. At its conference in Brussels in 1935, it had already laid down guidelines for the formation of an anti-fascist Germany; and by the time of its Berne conference in 1939, the conditions had been created for a broad union of all the democratic forces, both inside the country and outside of it. Communists, social-democrats and other anti-fascists had begun to collaborate in underground organisations and groups - in factories, in concentration camps and in exile.

On the outbreak of war with Britain, on the 3rd September, 1939, the Central Committee of the Communist Party of Germany had taken an uncompromising stand, declaring that it built its hopes "neither on Chamberlain's and Daladier's bayonets nor on a 'liberal wing' of the German bourgeoisie," but on the united power of the people, on the international solidarity of the working class and "on the help of the strong and great Soviet Union."

Fascism in Germany, with its dual policy of repression at home and aggression abroad, had created an economic situation in which the contradictions between the class interests of the industrialists and financiers, on the one hand, and the interests of all the other classes and sections of the German people, on the other hand, had been considerably sharpened. The constant demand for sacrifices to meet the insatiable appetite of the Nazi war machine, particularly after the attack on the Soviet Union in 1941, had brought additional hardships to the German people. On the 24th June, 1941, two days after the German invasion of the USSR, the Communist Party of Germany, through its clandestine press, had called upon the German people and the German armed forces to overthrow Hitler.

Soviet victories in the winter of 1942-43, especially at Stalingrad, which had involved the loss of 147,000 German soldiers killed and another 91,000 taken prisoner, had led to a crisis in Germany and the proclamation of "total mobilisation." An important feature of the internal crisis in Germany had been the increase in the anti-fascist activity by patriotic groups led by the German Communist Party.

In mid-1943, German prisoners-of-war and anti-fascist exiles in the Soviet Union had met near Moscow to form the Free Germany National Committee. The Communist Party of Germany, which had continued to operate in Berlin, Leipzig and Thuringia despite arrests, had attempted to unite all the anti-fascist forces within the country on the programme of this committee.

The establishment of the Free Germany National Committee had been the logical consequence of the struggle waged by the Communist Party of Germany for a broad united front against fascism after the tide of war had turned in favour of the Allies. In the September 1943 issue of *Labour Monthly*, Palme Dutt, its editor, had stated that "the changed psychology among the German prisoners-of-war" had illustrated that the

THE END OF THE WAR (1945)

time was ripe for the formation of the Free Germany National Committee, and that "critics in the west who fail to understand the significance of this development as a powerful additional weapon for the defeat of Hitler, would do better to turn their attention to the urgent necessity of a corresponding policy on the side of Britain and the United States.... It is vitally important that there should be a co-ordinated and unified policy of the United Nations in relation to the encouragement and stimulation of a mass opposition movement in Germany against Hitler for peace and freedom."

After the opening of the Second Front on the 6th June, 1944, the political crisis inside Germany had deepened and on the 20th July there had been an attempt on the life of Hitler by a group of army officers and some civilians who had wanted to come to terms with the Allies and make peace with them while there was still time. The attempt had failed and the leaders of the conspiracy had either been shot out of hand or hanged.

A few days later, sixteen German generals captured in Byelorussia had published an appeal calling upon generals and other officers of the German armed forces to make a resolute break from Hitler and to stop fighting forthwith. In agreement with the other signatories to the appeal, four of these generals had then asked for a meeting with Erich Weinert, President of the Free Germany National Committee, and with General von Seydlitz, President of the German Officer's League. A meeting had been held and full agreement reached on questions relating to the immediate tasks of the freedom movement in its fight against Hitler.

The main weakness of this movement, unfortunately, had been that it had failed to find ways of acting with members of such underground organisations as the National Peace Movement; with those who had been participating in the People's Councils of East Prussia; with those who had demonstrated for peace in Eisenach; or with those who had risked their lives to take strike action in Hamburg and Kiel.

It had become clear, at that stage, that in spite of the heroism of the German anti-fascist fighters, the defeat of Nazism would not be brought about by the democratic forces inside Germany but rather as a result of the military blows struck from without by the armies of the anti-fascist coalition.

In 1944, the Central Committee of the Communist Party of Germany had nevertheless drawn up a "programme of struggle to achieve the end of the war" and a "programme of action" that had laid down guidelines for activities on the part of the democratic forces in the final stages of the war and in the post-war period. The latter had called for the building of a mass popular movement capable of stamping out the last vestiges of Nazism and creating a new democratic Germany in the conditions of an Allied occupation.

On the 19th January, 1945, while Soviet troops were still fighting on the Vistula and on the Oder, Stalin issued instructions that the German population was not to be treated harshly. The Soviet Army would be entering Germany as a liberating army and not as a conquering army. Despite the fact that almost everyone in the Soviet Union had lost a near relative in the fighting, the cause of humanity demanded that a distinction be made between the common people of Germany and their fascist rulers. The Soviet government could not be indifferent to the suffering of the German people and would do everything in its power to supply them with food and help them return to normal life. This was especially important with regard to Berlin, where the food shortage was more acute than in any other part of Germany.

In February, 1945, with the end of the war in sight, the Political Bureau of the Communist Party of Germany (still in exile) set up a commission, under the chairmanship of Walter Ulbricht, to draft directives for anti-fascists in specific areas occupied by the Soviet Army.

On the 28th April, some days before hostilities ended, Colonel-General Bazarin, in whose hands the administrative and political power for the whole of Berlin was to be placed, issued an order to the effect that all communal enterprises and all other vital institutions should start operating again. Two days later, on the day that Hitler committed suicide, a large group of German functionaries, including Walter Ulbricht, returned to their homeland.

A new, democratic administration was set up in Berlin on the 17th May with Dr. Arthur Werner, a non-party man, as Lord Mayor. It held its first meeting on the 20th May and decided to put anti-fascist trustees in charge of all enterprises that had been run by active Nazis; to remove Nazi elements from the administration, from schools and other institutions; and to build up an anti-fascist police force. Trade union and factory councils started to clear fascist elements out of places like the Thyssen and Daimler-Benz works. By the end of the month, 73 fascist economic organisations had been disbanded.

On the 5th June, three important documents were issued by the four occupying powers. The first of these proclaimed the assumption of supreme authority in Germany by the governments of the four occupying powers; the second gave "supreme authority in Germany" to the British, United States, Soviet and French Commanders-in-Chief, "each in his own zone of occupation, and also jointly in matters affecting Germany as a whole;" the third defined the zones of occupation as allocated to their respective powers. The third document also stated that "the area of Greater Berlin will be occupied by forces of each of the four powers." and that "an Inter-Allied Governing Authority consisting of the four commandants appointed by their respective commanders-in-chief, will be established to direct its administration."

As there were to be only four zones, Berlin clearly lay in the Soviet zone and was an integral part of it under the "supreme authority" of the USSR. In accordance with this interpretation, the railways throughout Berlin and the entire Berlin waterways network were placed under the control of the Soviet Command. The western powers had the right to participate in the occupation and to co-operate in the joint administration of Berlin only through the Allied Control Council. This was confirmed at the first meeting of that body on the 11th July, when it had unanimously approved all the measures taken up to that date for the Soviet City Commandant.

The Soviet Military Administration in Germany assumed supreme authority in the Soviet zone of occupation on the 9th June, 1945. On the following day, Marshal Zhukov issued an order permitting the establishment of "all anti-fascist parties working for the complete eradication of Nazism and the strengthening of democratic foundations and civil liberties in Germany." By the same order, Marshal Zhukov also granted the working population in the Soviet zone "the right to unite into free trade unions and organisations for the purpose of upholding the interests and rights of the working people."

In the British and American zones of occupation, however, the authorities very quickly banned all political activity so far as the German population was concerned. The attitude of the Americans to this issue had been made clear by President Truman a full month earlier when, on the 10th May he had sent a directive to the Commander-in-Chief of the United States Forces of Occupation stating categorically: "Germany will not be occupied for the purpose of liberation but as a defeated nation."

On the 11th June the Political Bureau of the Communist Party of Germany, relying on the support of the Soviet Military Command, issued an appeal to the working people in the towns and villages for the confiscation of property belonging to Nazi leaders and war criminals; the abolition of large landed estates and the distribution of the land to the poor peasants and farm hands; the transfer of all key utilities (transport, gas, water, power etc.) to self-government bodies; and recognition of the need to compensate for the war damage caused by Germany to other countries.

By drawing all the democratic forces in the country into political activity around these issues, the Communist Party of Germany was able to create a united People's Front, which included, besides the Communist Party, the Social Democratic Party and the Liberal Democratic Party. All this was achieved by the middle of July, when a committee comprising five from each party had been set up to co-ordinate activity.

On the 2nd August, the final agreement of the Potsdam Conference was signed in Berlin by Truman, Attlee and Stalin.[4] Although acclaimed in democratic circles as the foundation stone of a new, democratic Europe from which war would be banned for evermore, its terms did not meet with the approval of everyone. On the 5th August the *Sunday Express* announced that "the Potsdam deal is not liked." *The Times* cautiously suggested that "the Potsdam plan does not meet every expectation," while the *New York Herald-Tribune* frankly described the agreement as "awesome." On the 11th August, the *Economist* declared bluntly: "The Potsdam settlement will not last ten years."

In the September 1945 issue of *Labour Monthly*, Palme Dutt warned that a dangerous situation had already arisen in the first phase after the armistice "owing to the divergence of policy between the British, American and Russian zones" of Germany. He noted that whereas in the Soviet zone the Nazis had been "sternly dealt with," while democratic political parties and working-class organisations had been "given scope," in the British and American zones Nazi officials had been maintained in power; close economic relations had been resumed between British and American monopoly interests and their German partners; while democratic anti-fascist expression and working-class organisation has been suppressed as "political."

In a further article on Germany, in the November 1945 issue of *Labour Monthly*, Peter Field, a contributor, reported that in the Soviet

---

[4] For a detailed study of this agreement, see Chapter IX of *War of Liberation* by Ernie Trory.

THE END OF THE WAR (1945)

zone of occupation "the whole Junker class" had been expropriated and deprived of their influence, and that there were now no "trust magnets and monopolists" to contend with; but that in the British, French and American zones "the role of the big landowners and trust magnets in Germany had obviously not been understood."

On the 26th February, 1946, it was stated before the US Senate Military Affairs Committee, by Russel A. Nixon (Deputy Head of the Decartelisation Department of the United States Military Government in Germany), that: "at every level of the hierarchy of the US military government from one end of the US zone in Germany to the other, responsible officers are resisting denazification on the grounds that we must set up a bulwark against Bolshevism and Russia." Nixon was also to complain that decartelisation was being resisted for the same reason. He was to tell the US senators that US officers in command in Hesse, Bavaria and Württemburg had taken sides with the German heads of trusts on the grounds that they were "our allies in the struggle against Bolshevism."

On the 5th October, 1945, Konrad Adenauer, then Mayor of Cologne, but later to become West German Chancellor, was asked by Barbara Page, a representative of the *News Chronicle* and the *Associated Press*, what he thought of the Franco-Belgian proposal for a separate Rhine-Ruhr state. He replied that in his opinion it would be wrong to separate a Rhine-Ruhr state from the rest of the non-Russian occupied regions of Germany and that it would be necessary to link the economy of the whole of the non-Russian occupied regions of Germany with the economies of France and Belgium, so that common economic interests would arise.

At that time the four-power administration had been functioning reasonably well and most Germans believed that the unity of Germany had to be preserved at all costs. Adenauer realised, however, that as long as the Soviet occupation authorities were in a position to influence the whole of Germany, through the framework of the four-power administration, German imperialism could not be re-established. In such a situation, the reforms carried out in the Soviet-occupied zone represented a real threat to the future of Germany - as envisaged by the western imperialists.

Adenauer was much encouraged by Churchill's speech at Fulton in March 1946, which clearly signalled the opening of the overt stage of the cold war against the Soviet Union. The covert stage had already commenced long before the war had ended, at least as far back as the

12th April, 1945, when Truman had become President of the USA on the death of Roosevelt.

In the autumn of 1946, the American Secretary of State, James Byrnes, paid a visit to the western zone of Germany, stating in a speech made in Stuttgart on the 6th September that it was the intention of his government "to unite the economy in its own zone with one or all of the others who were ready to do so." The British Labour government had already agreed to this.

Chapter Two
PROBLEMS OF PEACE

THE YEAR 1946 CAME IN full of promise. It was the first New Year's Day on which people could look back to the end of the war rather than forward to it. It was to be a year of mixed blessings, however, in which the problems of peace were to prove almost as difficult to solve as the earlier problems of the war.

The General Assembly of the United Nations met on the 24th January in the Central Hall, Westminster, and the opening session was addressed by Prime Minister Clement Attlee who said:

> The United Nations Organisation must become the overriding factor in foreign policy. After the First World War there was a tendency to regard the League of Nations as something outside the ordinary range of foreign policy. Governments continued on the old lines, pursuing individual aims and following the path of power politics, not understanding that the world had passed into a new epoch.... Looking back on past years we can trace the origins of the late war to acts of aggression, the significance of which was not realised at the time. Failure to deal with the Japanese adventure in the Far East and with the acts of aggression of the fascist rulers of Germany and Italy led inevitably to the breakdown of the rule of law and to the Second World War.

The United Nations Organisation adopted all the proposals of the conference of Foreign Ministers held in Moscow during the previous December, including the proposal for the establishment of a commission on the control of atomic energy; the proposal that a provisional Korean democratic government be set up by a joint commission representing the United States command in the south and the Soviet command in the north; and other proposals affecting China and Japan and the Balkans. This was a promising start.

Less promising, however, was the reaction to the Soviet notes sent to the Security Council of the United Nations, questioning the involvement of British troops in Greece and Indonesia. In Greece, these were being used for the maintenance of a regime of former collaborators and pro-fascists that had been installed in power by military action against the National Liberation Movement of the Greek people.[5] In Indonesia, British troops had been used, in collaboration with Japanese forces, against the republic established by a nationalist movement of the Indonesian people and for the re-imposition of colonial rule.

These notes provoked an outburst from Ernest Bevin in the Security Council on the 1st February against the Communist Parties of the world. Referring to this in an article on *Mr. Bevin and British Foreign Policy* in the March 1946 issue of *Labour Monthly*, Konni Zilliacus, a left-wing Labour MP, said that it had "aroused the utmost enthusiasm in the press of Franco Spain and fascist Argentine, not to mention the Greek royalists, General Anders's Polish army in Italy, the Hearst press and the *Chigago Tribune* in the USA, the Kemsley and Rothermere papers here and the whole rag-tag and bobtail of the fascist and reactionary down-and-outers throughout Europe." Summing up at the end of his article, Zilliacus wrote:

> Mr. Bevin's outlook on Europe, the Middle East and the Soviet Union, it will be observed, does not differ by a hair's breadth from that of Lord D'Abernon twenty years ago, in the days when we lost the last peace. Our Foreign Secretary stands with one foot in the Crimean Conference and the other in the Crimean War.

In the House of Commons on the 21st February, during a two-day debate on international affairs, H.L. Hutchinson, MP, declared:

> We are the unfortunate heirs to the traditional policy which dates back to Castlereagh after the Napoleonic wars and Curzon after the last war. We have not entirely broken away from it. That policy is one of bolstering up reactionary monarchs and decaying regimes wherever we can find them. In that policy I believe we can find the explanation for the antagonism between ourselves and Soviet Russia. It is an antagonism, not of peoples but of policies.

---

[5] For details of the British invasion of Greece, after the defeat of the German forces in that country by the National Liberation Movement of the Greek people, see Chapter VII of *War of Liberation* by Ernie Trory.

PROBLEMS OF PEACE (1946)

We are suspected of pursuing a policy of bolstering up reaction in Europe while the Soviets are supporting the policy of revolutionary forces in Europe. I believe that is the explanation of our armed intervention in Indonesia, Indo-China and Greece. It is the explanation of the maintenance, at the expense of the British taxpayer, of General Anders's anti-Soviet army in Italy. I believe it is behind the refusal to give Russia those vital scientific secrets to which she is entitled as a fighting Ally. I also think it is behind the abuse that is showered on Russia because of her attempt to obtain that information by other means. All this suspicion and antagonism result from a misconceived policy.

Speaking in the same debate, Anthony Eden said:

I believe the Soviet Union is sincere when they say to us that they want to collaborate with ourselves and the United States, their two great partners in the mortal conflict from which we have only just emerged. I think also that the Soviet Union is sincere in wishing that the United Nations Organisation should function. It can only function if there is a measure of understanding between the three great powers. That far we are agreed. But here comes the rub. While Russia wants this collaboration ... she appears only to want it on her terms.

Winding up the debate for the government, Ernest Bevin expressed a measure of agreement with Eden and went on to say: "It is said we are drifting into war with Russia. I cannot conceive any circumstances in which Britain and the Soviet Union should go to war."

The debate was widely reported in the British press on the following day. This comment from *The Times* is typical of the line taken by most of the dailies:

Relations with the Soviet Union were the general theme both of Mr. Eden's and Mr. Bevin's speeches last night. Both reiterated the desire to see these relations on a firmer and more cordial footing. Both observed, in slightly different language, that the Soviet government sincerely desired co-operation with Great Britain and the United States, but desired it on their own terms. The converse is no doubt equally and, provided the "terms" are reasonable, properly true of the British attitude towards the Soviet Union.

On the 5th March, Churchill made his infamous "iron curtain" speech at Fulton, Missouri, in the USA. It was not an original phrase, having been first used in the same context by Dr. Goebbels in an editorial in *Das Reich*, dated the 25th February, 1945. The particular paragraph that seems to have caught Churchill's eye at the time read as follows:

> If the German people lay down their arms, the whole of eastern and south-eastern Europe, together with the Reich, would come under Russian occupation. Behind the iron curtain, mass butcheries of people would begin, and all that would remain would be a crude automation, a daily fermenting mass of thousands of proletarians and despairing slave animals knowing nothing of the outside world.

This warning had obviously had a profound effect upon Churchill, but he had not deemed it expedient to repeat it while the Western Allies still had need of the Soviet Army in Europe and of the sacrifices it had yet to make in what its soldiers still believed to be a common cause. After a three-month period of gestation, however, Churchill had considered it appropriate to incorporate both the sentiments and the terminology of Dr. Goebbels in a telegram addressed to President Truman on the 12th May, 1945, as the following extract clearly shows:

> What will be the position in a year or two ... when we may have a handful of divisions, mostly French, and when Russia may choose to keep two or three hundred on active service? An iron curtain is drawn down upon their front. We do not know what is going on behind.

Churchill had used the phrase again on the 4th June, 1945, when he had tried to persuade Truman to postpone the withdrawal of American troops from the line they had gained in the fighting to the zone prescribed in the occupation agreement. Then he had written:

> I view with profound misgivings the retreat of the American army to our line of occupation in the central sector, thus bringing Soviet power into the heart of western Europe and the descent of an iron curtain between us and everything to the eastward.

PROBLEMS OF PEACE (1946)

Churchill was to use the phrase so many times during the following months that the majority of people eventually came to believe that Churchill himself had originated it. It was at Fulton, however, that the "iron curtain" of Dr. Goebbels was finally immortalised by Churchill in the following lines:

> From Stettin in the Baltic to Trieste in the Adriatic, an iron curtain has descended across the continent. Behind that line lie all the capitals of the states of central and eastern Europe ... and all are subject, in one form or another, not only to Soviet influence but to a very high and increasing measure of control from Moscow.

During the course of his speech, Churchill also said, disparagingly, that he did not believe that "Soviet Russia" desired war; but only "the fruits of war and the indefinite expansion of their power and doctrines." Warming to his subject, he went on to say:

> Our difficulties and dangers will not be removed by closing our eyes to them. They will not be removed by mere waiting to see what happens.... From what I have seen of our Russian friends and allies during the war, I am convinced there is nothing they admire so much as strength and there is nothing for which they have less respect than military weakness.

This was to become almost as familiar a theme as General Goering's "guns before butter" theme of the middle and late 'thirties. And it bore a certain resenblance, be it noted, to the pre-war calls for sacrifices, on the part of the German people, in the interests of a strong Germany, equipped to do battle with the Soviet Union.

On the 6th March, the day after Churchill's Fulton speech, the London *Evening News* quoted the *New York Herald Tribune* as having said: "Mr. Churchill seems quite plainly to mean that Russia is today a menace comparable with that of Nazism a decade ago, that can be met only by such a show of strength as Churchill once called for in vain against Germany, and that this strength can only be provided by an Anglo-American military alliance."

In India, the *Morning Standard* remarked that "Britain's post-war aim, according to Churchill, appears to be to prepare for a new war - against the Soviet Union." On the following day, the 7th March, the

PEACE AND THE COLD WAR I

London *Daily Herald* issued the following statement:

> There is speculation all over the world about the origin of Mr. Churchill's speech at Fulton. He declared that he was speaking as a private individual, but clearly there are many who believe that the speech was composed in collaboration with the British government. We can say with authority that its contents were neither known to nor influenced by the government.

Nevertheless, when a few days later 105 MPs signed a motion "that this House considers that proposals for a military alliance between the British Commonwealth and the United States for the purpose of combating the spread of communism, such as were put forward in a speech at Fulton ... by the right honourable gentleman the Member for Woodford ... are inimical to the cause of world peace," the leader of the House of Commons, Herbert Morrison, stated that the government could not find time to debate it. On the 11th March, Attlee closed the matter by informing the House that "His Majesty's Government is not called upon to express any opinion of a speech delivered in another country by a private individual."

In the Soviet Union there was an immediate reply to Churchill's speech in the form of a long article in *Pravda* headed: *Churchill Rattles His Sabre*. The following extracts are of special significance:

> While the war was on, while mortal danger threatened Britain and Europe, Churchill in his speeches repeatedly pointed to the outstanding role of the USSR. At that time he pretended to be a friend of the Soviet people, and took an oath of loyalty to Soviet-British friendship as to the entire Anglo-American-Soviet coalition. But the danger has passed. The mortal danger that threatened Europe and Britain has sunk into oblivion - and Churchill has become his own self. Now he can give vent to his true sentiments, which he hid through all those years of war, painstakingly concealing his hostile intentions and plans towards the Soviet Union.

After commenting on Churchill's attitude towards the newly-formed democratic republics of eastern Europe, the article continued:

Churchill finds his only comfort in Athens. In Churchill's conception, the prototype of liberated Europe is Greece, where, under the protection of British troops, the fascist-monarchist reaction is doing its job; where the Greek X-ites, these last Hitlerite offsprings, are with impunity terrorising the Greek patriots. Yet just as one swallow does not make a summer, one "democratic" Greece is unable to turn Churchill's ire from the whole of eastern Europe.

Just as after the First World War, so now after the Second World War, Churchill fancies himself the saviour of Europe from communism.... He puts forward the proposal of creating an Anglo-American military alliance. He adds quite openly that this military alliance must be directed against the USSR - against the power that bore on its shoulders the brunt of the war and played a decisive role in the rout of Hitlerite Germany....

Churchill forgets that the freedom-loving peoples have during the years of war acquired tremendous political experience, and the know-how to differentiate between genuine friends of peace and imperialists who, under the false banner of "defence of peace," are preparing plans to unleash a new imperialist war.

In his Presidential Address to the Annual Conference of the Labour Party on the 10th June, about which more in the next chapter, Harold Laski referred to the hostility that had grown up between Britain and the Soviet Union since the end of the war and went on to add, amid loud cheers, that no small part of the responsibility for Russian suspicions must be borne by those who decided on secrecy in relation to the atom bomb. Laski had no illusions about Bevin and had on more than one occasion accused him of treating the Soviet Union as if it were "a breakaway from the Transport and General Workers' Union."

The first meeting of the Atomic Energy Commission, set up in response to the resolution adopted by the General Assembly of the United Nations, was held in New York on the 14th June. At this meeting, Bernard Baruch, on behalf of the US government, put forward a number of proposals, which afterwards became known as the "Baruch Plan." The first of these was to create an International Atomic Development Authority, to which would be entrusted all phases of the development and use of atomic energy potentially dangerous to world security, as well as power to control, inspect and license all other atomic activities. Then, as Baruch outlined in his speech:

> When an adequate system of control of atomic energy, including the renunciation of the bomb as a weapon, has been agreed upon and put into effective operation; and condign punishments set up for the violations of the rules of control, which are to be stigmatised as international crimes, we propose that: 1. manufacture of atom bombs shall stop; 2. existing bombs shall be disposed of pursuant to the terms of the treaty; 3. the Authority shall be in possession of full information as to the know-how for the production of atomic energy.

Baruch assured the Atomic Energy Commission, so as to avoid misunderstanding, that "my country [the USA] is ready to make its full contribution towards the end we seek, subject, of course, to our constitutional processes." These "constitutional processes" were important. Observers in Washington believed that if the other nations had accepted the Plan, the US Congress would not have ratified it.

On the subject of violations, Baruch suggested that "penalties of as serious a nature as the nations may wish and as immediate and certain in their execution as possible, should be fixed for: 1. illegal possession or use of an atomic bomb; 2. illegal possession or separation of atomic material suitable for use in an atomic bomb; 3. seizure of any plant or any other property belonging to or licensed by the Authority; 4. wilful interference with the activities of the Authority; 5. creation or operation of dangerous projects in a manner contrary to, or in the absence of, a licence granted by the international control body."

The Atomic Energy Commission was, of course, subject to the Security Council, which was in turn subject to the General Assembly. Under the Charter of the United Nations, penalties for violations would be permitted only by the unanimous decision of the five great powers: the USSR, Britain, China, France and the USA. But Baruch wanted to do away with the principle of unanimity of the five permanent members of the Security Council, insofar as it affected this particular problem. "There must be no veto to protect those who violate their solemn agreements not to develop or use atomic energy for destructive purposes," he had said.

If this had been agreed, the International Atomic Authority would have become a law unto itself, even having the power to declare war without reference to the Security Council or to the General Assembly. Andrei Gromyko, the Soviet delegate, was quick to point out that this would run counter to the Charter of the United Nations. Dorothy Thompson, a widely-read American commentator, reminded her readers that only one nation, the United States, possessed atomic power and that because of this the power of the Authority would be delegated power only. Because of its anti-Soviet majority, the Authority would, in practice, have to approve almost any action the USA cared to take. It could even be made to declare war on the Soviet Union without appeal to the Security Council.

On the 19th June, Gromyko called upon the countries represented at the Atomic Energy Commission to consider the question of concluding an international convention "prohibiting the production and employment of weapons based on the use of atomic energy for the purpose of mass destruction." Such a convention would also call for the destruction of existing stocks of atomic weapons and the condemnation of all activities undertaken in violation of the said convention. In introducing the Soviet Plan, Gromyko stated quite clearly:

> The activity of the Atomic Energy Commission can bring about the desired results only when it is in full conformity with the principles of the Charter of the United Nations, which are laid down as the basis of the activity of the Security Council, because the Commission is an organ of this organisation, working under the instructions of the Security Council and responsible to the same. Attempts to undermine the principles, as established by the Charter, of the activity of the Security Council, including the unanimity of the members of the Security Council in deciding questions of substance, are incompatible with the interests of the United Nations, who created the international organisation for the preservation of peace and security. Such attempts must be rejected.

The basic difference between the US plan and the Soviet plan was that under the US plan a majority of members of the International Atomic Development Authority would have supreme power, and would be able to declare war against any member of the United Nations which, in the opinion of the majority, was defaulting. Under the Soviet plan, the powers of the General Assembly and the Security Council would remain intact as laid down in the Charter of the United Nations.

PEACE AND THE COLD WAR I

On the 24th September, the Soviet news agency *Tass* published an interview with Stalin during the course of which the interviewer, Alexander Werth, asked: "Do you believe that virtual monopoly by the United States of America of the atomic bomb constitutes one of the main threats to peace?" To this Stalin replied:

> I do not believe the atomic bomb to be as serious a force as certain politicians are inclined to regard it. Atomic bombs are intended for intimidating the weak-nerved, but they cannot decide the outcome of war since atomic bombs are by no means sufficient for this purpose. Certainly monopolist possession of the secret of the atomic bomb does create a threat, but at least two remedies exist against it: (a) monopolist possession of the atomic bomb cannot last long; (b) use of the atomic bomb will be prohibited.

The relative merits of the Baruch Plan and the Soviet Plan were discussed at length in all quarters of the globe but on the 20th December the Atomic Energy Commission accepted the Baruch Plan with ten countries voting for and only the Soviet Union and Poland voting against. The Soviet Union was criticised in many places for voting against the Baruch Plan and thus effectively vetoing it; but the *Manchester Guardian* thought that "Mr. Baruch" had not been "entirely realistic" and sought to justify this conclusion in a leading article, which read in part as follows:

> If the international inspectorate discovers that some country (say Russia if need be) is violating the treaty by manufacturing atom bombs, what happens? Then, says Mr. Baruch, Russia must be "punished" by "sanctions" and no government should have the right to prevent it. This is fair enough in theory, but it has very serious implications. Sanctions against a great power mean war, and it is highly doubtful whether nations will bind themselves to go to war automatically with a great power no matter how just the cause.... The truth is that no government can pledge itself to go to war in any particular circumstances unless it is quite sure that public opinion will support it. And it is one thing to declare war on an aggressor, which has already invaded the country of an ally, and quite another to declare war on Russia (or any other country) whose guilt is to have made certain weapons which she has not yet used.

On the same subject, the *New Statesman and Nation* had this to say:

> The Americans claim the right to retain exclusive possession of the atomic bomb until the USSR has been internationally "inspected and controlled" - a process which could reveal the location of all Russia's carefully concealed munition plants and defences. The Russian reply is to say: "if you want to be sure that we are not making atom bombs, we must first be sure that you will not use your bombs against us when you have discovered where they can most effectively be dropped." This is the real crux of the matter; and, until it is solved, it is academic to argue whether agreement on automatic sanctions against "atomic violations" would in practice be more effective than the provisions embodied in the Covenant of the old league for automatic sanctions against aggression in general.

It should be emphasised that the Soviet government was prepared to agree to the establishment of a supervision and control commission, of which the rules of work would have been drawn up by the Security Council on a basis of the unanimous support of the five major powers. Once the rules had been drafted and agreed, of course, there would be no further question of a veto. Obviously, however, there could be no inspection until all had agreed to destroy their atomic bombs and had, in fact, declared that they had done so. Subsequent events were to justify the principled stand taken by the Soviet Union on this issue.

In the autumn of 1946 the American Secretary of State, James Byrnes, paid a visit to west Germany and, in a speech made in Stuttgart on the 6th September, announced that it was the intention of his government "to unite the economy in its own zone with one or all of the others who are ready to do so." The British Labour Government had already agreed to this.

On the 2nd December, an "Agreement on Joining the British and American Occupation Zones" was signed in New York. It came into force on the 1st January, 1947 and established the so-called "Bi-zone" as the first step towards a separate West German state. Six months later, a "bizonal economic council" was formed in Frankfurt-on-Main.

Meanwhile, in the Soviet zone, events were proceeding in full accord with the Potsdam agreement and other decisions taken by the four powers. As a result of united action, the working class and the anti-fascist forces everywhere were creating democratic organs of self-administration that were recognised by the Soviet military authorities as organs of power. Based on relevant decrees passed by the provisional administration in September 1945, tens of thousands of farm workers, peasants, resettlers and craftsmen of varying political tendencies, received a total of 3,298,082 hectares of land expropriated from 7,136 large landowners, active Nazis and war criminals.

In Saxony, in the Soviet zone, a draft law was published on the 25th May, 1946, expropriating "the entire property of the Nazi Party and its organisations, and the enterprises and undertakings of war criminals, leaders and active champions of the Nazi Party and the Nazi State." In a plebiscite held on the 30th June, this draft received 77.62 per cent of all votes cast. Similar laws were passed by other provincial administrations, both in the Soviet zone and in the western zones.

Side by side with the struggle for land reform and for the nationalisation of "cartels, syndicates, trusts and other monopolistic arrangements" as a means of "eliminating the present excessive concentration of economic powers," to quote from the text of the Potsdam Agreement, there developed in all zones a struggle for the unification of the working class. In carrying through the land reform and in building up democratic administrative organs, communists and social-democrats drew closer together and in April 1946, as a result of this unity of action, a single Marxist-Leninist party of the working class was formed. Speaking at the unifying congress, Wilhelm Pieck, representing the Communist Party of Germany, said:

> The closing of the rift in the German working class and the merger of both parties into the Socialist Unity Party of Germany is an event of enormous historical importance for the German working-class movement and for the entire German people.

Unfortunately, the unification was only possible in the Soviet zone of Germany. In the western zones, the right-wing social democrats, led by Dr. Kurt Schumacher, broke away from their fellow social democrats in the Soviet zone and formed a separate party.

Meanwhile events were also on the move in Britain. On the 1st January, 1946, the *Daily Worker* proudly annouced: "Our readers are owners." The People's Press Printing Society (PPPS) had been launched on the 12th

PROBLEMS OF PEACE (1946)

September, 1945, after having been duly registered under the Industrial and Provident Societies Act. Within six months the membership had reached 14,513, of which 426 were organisations. Among them were 266 trade union and co-operative organisations. During the six months the sum of £95,000 had been raised in share capital. In addition the PPPS had received an interest-free loan of £56,000 from the trustees of the old *Daily Worker* Fighting Fund. An application for affiliation to the Co-operative Union, however, had been rejected on the grounds that the PPPS might one day find itself in competition with the Co-operative press.

The formal document, transferring ownership of the *Daily Worker* to the PPPS, was handed to the editor of the paper, William Rust, by the leader of the London busmen, Bill Jones, at the 16th birthday celebrations in the Albert Hall on the 6th January, 1946, amid scenes of great enthusiasm. On that date the *Daily Worker* came under the control of a committee of management elected by the shareholders of the PPPS on the basis of one vote per shareholder regardless of his or her shareholding.

A commercial survey of the readership of all national daily newspapers carried out at the time revealed that 69 per cent of the readers of the *Daily Worker* were trade unionists, the highest percentage of any of them. The next highest was the *Daily Herald* with 45 per cent. The survey also revealed that the *Daily Worker* had a younger readership than any of the other national newspapers, two-thirds of it being in the 21 to 49 age group.

In a New Year survey in the *Daily Worker* on the 1st January, William Rust had warned of "a revival of fascist activity in numerous countries including Britain, where Mosley and his thugs have reappeared." The National Council of Labour considered this question on the 26th February as a result of numerous resolutions it had received from its constituent bodies. The council agreed that "It would be intolerable if any fascist group were permitted to resume its threat either to peace and order or to the liberties, political and economic, racial or religious, of any residents in Great Britain" and proposed "to watch carefully for any signs of a significant fascist revival." But it did not believe that special legislation was required to deal with it. A letter to this effect was sent to Chuter Ede, the Labour Home Secretary, who replied agreeing with the view expressed by the National Council of Labour, and suggesting that "the greatest service in combating fascism" would be rendered by "ensuring that fascist arguments do not go unanswered, and by stimulating informed discussion of democratic principles, institutions and policies."

This proved to be typical of the attitude of the leadership of the Labour Party and of the Labour Government to the many problems that had to be faced in the coming months and years - both at home and abroad. William Rust, in the survey mentioned above, laid out the options clearly and optimistically:

> The good things of life are rooted in prosperous industry, and the success of Labour's social programme is dependent on the unbending carrying through of its nationalisation proposals and the breaking of the power of the vested interests.... The coming year should, however, bring positive results providing steel as well as mining comes under state ownership and providing the country is not saddled with new burdens in the shape of fantastically high rates of compensation to idle employers and redundant bankers....
>
> Against Labour's programme the Tories intend to wage a ding-dong battle. It is true that the Tory Party today is demoralised... But it would be a sorry mistake to write the Tories off.... This cunning, canting crowd are biding their time. They will strike again when they see a chance to turn the clock back.

The hopes and fears expressed by William Rust were underlined by Jim Gardner, general secretary of the National Union of Foundry Workers, in an article in the January 1946 issue of *Labour Monthly*, in which he expressed the opinion that "at no time in British history" had there been "greater hope and expectancy" than in the months that had followed the General Election of 1945 and the return of a Labour Government to power. "But expectancy has to be satisfied and, while hope continues, it is tempered by a growing uneasiness, as revealed in the widespread demand for a speed-up of demobilisation, and in the growing unrest, of which the strikes of dockers and gas workers, and the demonstrations of building workers, were manifestations."

Not the least of the government's worries were the associated problems of housing and manpower. Confidential Cabinet documents, released for public inspection in 1977, under the 30-year rule, revealed that the Cabinet had held several discussions on the squatters' movement. During 1946 nearly a thousand army camps had been occupied by Britain's homeless.

PROBLEMS OF PEACE (1946)

On the 7th February, George Isaacs, Minister of Labour, announced that the government's promise of a million and a half releases from the armed forces by the end of 1945 had been fulfilled but this still left substantial bodies of men in the forces overseas who were sorely needed at home. We now know that there were widespread strikes of RAF personnel in India, Ceylon and the Middle East demanding speedier demobilisation.

Early in 1946 the failure of the Siamese and Burmese rice crops and the world shortage of cereals, particularly wheat, arising out of war damage in some of the producing countries, and weather disasters in others, had brought about a food crisis of immense proportions.

On the 5th February Sir Ben Smith, Minister of Food, had announced the decision of the government to increase the flour extraction rate to 85 per cent and so return to the wartime loaf as a means of conserving supplies of cereals. This had meant a reduction in the volume of animal feeding stuffs and had lowered the supply of bacon, poultry and eggs as a consequence.

In a debate in the House of Commons on the 14th February, Sir Ben Smith warned that sacrifices might have to be made in certain, as yet unspecified, directions. The Chancellor of the Exchequer explained to the House, during the course of the debate, that besides the world food shortage there were other problems. Restrictions on import programmes were governed now, not by lack of shipping but by lack of finance. As long ago as the 25th August, 1945, the Prime Minister had announced that the President of the United States had cancelled all outstanding lease-lend contracts, and that stocks and deliveries secured under the Lease-Lend Act would now have to be paid for either in cash or through negotiated credit arrangements.

An American loan was negotiated but was prematurely exhausted as a result of the cynical cancellation of controls in the United States which sent prices rocketing by some 40 per cent. At that time Britain was importing a large amount of goods from America with little or no reciprocal trade, leaving Britain with a serious adverse trade balance. Towards the end of the year, the situation was aggravated by a demand from Canada for payment in dollars instead of in sterling. Canada needed the dollars to meet her own debts to America.

The British government could, of course, have imported food from the Soviet Union and from the food-producing countries of eastern Europe in exchange for much-needed agricultural and industrial machinery. But this source was ignored until 1949 when Argentina also began demanding payment in dollars as a condition of the meat agreement then being negotiated. Desperate for a solution to its problems in this field, the Labour government was compelled to make a deal with the Soviet Union for the supply of cattle feed to enable Britain to extend its own herds and thus increase its own meat supplies. But this trade with the Soviet Union was not developed, probably for fear of upsetting the USA.

On the 12th February, 1946, Sir Hartley Shawcross, Attorney-General, moved the second reading of the Trades Disputes and Trade Unions Bill, effectively repealing the Trades Disputes Act of 1927. No longer would sympathetic strikes be illegal; no longer would there be any limits to the practice of peaceful picketing when a strike was in progress; no longer would the Civil Service trade unions be debarred from affiliation to the TUC and the Labour Party; no longer would local authorities and other public bodies be prohibited from making membership of a trade union a condition of employment; and no longer would it be necessary to "contract in" before individual members of trade unions could pay the political levy to the Labour Party.

The Conservatives fought a stubborn rearguard action against the Bill during the committee stage on the 27th February, and on the 1st April tried to exclude from repeal each section of the 1927 Act in turn. But the House sat through the night and, at 5.24 a.m. on the 2nd April, after 12 divisions, the Bill finally became law.

This complemented the setting up of the World Federation of Trade Unions that had taken place in October, 1945, establishing a representative, international trade union body of more that 66 million organised workers in 56 countries. It is sometimes forgotten that it was on the initiative of the TUC that this was made possible; and that it was in recognition of this that Sir Walter Citrine was unanimously elected its first President. On the industrial front there was working-class unity of an order never before experienced in the developed world.

In the absence of Palme Dutt, who was touring in India, the *Notes of the Month* for the May, 1946 issue of *Labour Monthly* were written by Robin Page Arnot who described the founding of the World Federation of Trade Unions as "one of the most notable gains of the war and of the victory over fascism."

The unity of the working class in Britain, however, did not extend to the main political parties of the working-class. Whereas in Germany there was a strong movement in the Social Democratic Party for unity with the Communist Party, coming to fruition in the Soviet zone with the formation of the Socialist Unity Party, the application of the Communist Party of Great Britain for affiliation to the British Labour Party was met with stiff resistance on the part of the Labour leadership, although in the period leading up to the first post-war Annual Conference of the Labour Party, the first one to be held with a majority Labour government in office, the need for political unity was clearly demonstrated.

In France, the elections were fought against the background of a vicious anti-communist campaign, in which the leaders of the Socialist Party easily outdid their reactionary rivals. In spite of this, the Communist Party, though losing a few seats, actually improved its voting power.

The elections in Italy were accompanied by a referendum on the monarchy, which resulted in a defeat for the House of Savoy by 12,717,923 votes to 10,719,284. The election results proper, however, were inconclusive; but the Communists polled 4,204,000 votes and won 104 seats, assuring them at least of a share in the key positions of the new government. The Christian Democrats emerged as the largest single party with the Communists and Socialists combined holding about 40 per cent of the seats. No party had a clear majority and it was not expected that there would be a long period of stable government either in Italy or France.

In Czechoslovakia, however, as noted in the previous chapter, the elections gave the Communists and Social Democrats, a combined total of 152 seats - a majority of four over all the other parties. This was enough to give the premiership to Klement Gottwald, the leader of the Communist Party. Commenting on this in the July 1946 issue of *Labour Monthly*, William Rust wrote:

> The reasons for the Left victory in Czechoslovakia are to be traced to the strength of Socialist-Cmmunist unity ... and the deep-rooted belief of the masses that their future is closely bound up with the Soviet Union, for which they have a great love and admiration. Anti-Soviet propaganda and the contrasting of the advantages of western democracy over "eastern totalitarianism" fall on deaf ears in Czechoslovakia. Such talk cannot wipe out the memories of the Munich betrayal by the western powers, nor the knowledge

that the decisive role in the liberation of Czechoslovakia was played by the Red Army.

The results of the elections in all three countries confirmed, as William Rust put it, "the trend of the working class towards the Communist Party." The elections also showed that important sections of the peasantry were taking the same road. William Rust did not underestimate the strength of the reactionary Catholic parties in France and Italy, nor the opposition of the French Socialist Party to working-class unity. He believed continuation of divisions within the working class to be the chief obstacle to the establishment of stable governments, so essential to the fulfilment of the urgent tasks of economic and social reconstruction.

Not even in Britain, notwithstanding Churchill's notorious "iron curtain" speech at Fulton, did the man-in-the-street take readily to the anti-Soviet propaganda that was fast becoming the order of the day. On the 30th March, 1946, a considerable blow for friendship with the Soviet Union was struck when 983 delegates from all parts of Britain met in conference at the Central Hall in Westminster and decided to merge their respective organisations, British-Soviet Friendship Houses, the National Council for British-Soviet Unity, the Russia Today Society, the Women's British-Soviet Committee and the Anglo-Soviet Youth Friendship Alliance, into one body: the British Soviet Society, a name that was to be changed to the British-Soviet Friendship Society in 1950 in order to counter a slander that the object of the organisation was to set up Soviets in Britain.

There had, of course been earlier friendship societies in Britain, the first being the Society for Cultural Relations with the USSR, set up in Britain in 1924, the year the USSR was founded. The Friends of Soviet Russia had been formed in London in 1929, changing its name to the Friends of the the Soviet Union in 1931 but continuing to publish its monthly magazine under the original title of *Russia Today* for many years. In July 1938 the Friends of the Soviet Union again changed its name and became the Russia Today Society, one of the founding bodies of the subsequent British-Soviet Friendship Society.

At the founding conference of the British-Soviet Society in 1946, the Rev. Stanley Evans was elected Chairman, with Gordon Schaffer as Vice-Chairman and Sir George Young as Treasurer. A National Council of 30 members was also elected, to which it was agreed to add a further 30 members to be elected at regional conferences in the following April.

At the first meeting of the National Council, the Bishop of Chelmsford, Dr. Henry Wilson, was elected President. Other officers elected were Tom Brown, Secretary; Ernest Brown, National Organiser; Reg Bishop, General Editor of *Russia Today*; Mabel Quin, Secretary of the Women's Department; and Helen Guiterman, Secretary of the Youth Department.

On the 26th May, at a rally held in Trafalgar Square, 60 new members were enrolled. Later in the year, a delegation from the Society travelled to the Soviet Union visiting nine cities in four of the Union Republics. The delegation reported back at a number of meetings, the first being in the Central Hall, Westminster, on the 17th September.

The Society continued to play an important part in the struggle for peace and friendship with the Soviet Union up to the time of the latter's tragic demise.

The Nuremberg trial of war criminals, which had begun on the 20th November, 1945, came to an end on the 1st October, 1946. In Britain, the trial of two British traitors, who had broadcast Nazi propaganda from Germany throughout the war, had ended some ten months earlier. On the 19th December, 1945, John Amery, son of L.S. Amery, former Secretary of State for India, and brother of Julian Amery, later to become Conservative MP for the Pavilion Division of Brighton, was hanged at Wandsworth prison. He had pleaded guilty to eight counts charging him with broadcasting enemy propaganda, inducing British subjects in captivity (who were named) to fight for Germany against Britain and Russia, and with making public speeches on behalf of the enemy in Antwerp, Lyons and Paris while Belgium and France were under enemy occupation. The other traitor, William Joyce, better known to wartime radio listeners as Lord Haw Haw, was hanged in the same prison on the 3rd January, 1946.

In the early hours of the following 16th October, death sentences by hanging were carried out on ten of the twelve leading Nazis who had been condemned at the Nuremberg trial. These were Joachim von Ribbentrop, Wilhelm Keitel, Ernst Kaltenbrunner, Alfred Rosenberg, Hans Frank, Wilhelm Frick, Julius Streicher, Alfred Jodl, Fritz Sauckel, and Artur Seyss-Inquart. The other two were Martin Bormann, who had been sentenced in his absence, and Hermann Goering, who had cheated the gallows by taking cyanide in his cell shortly before the time fixed for his execution. Rudolph Hess, Walter Funk and Erich Raeder had each received life sentences; Baldur von Shirac and Albert Speer had each been sentenced to 20 years imprisonment, Constantin von Neurath to 15 years imprisonment and Karl Doenitz to 10 years imprisonment. Hjalmar Schacht, Franz von Papen and Hans Fritsche had been found not guilty.

Major-General I.T. Nikitchenko, the Soviet member of the Tribunal, had expressed disagreement with the decision to acquit von Papen, Schacht and Fritzsche, and with the sentence of life-imprisonment on Hess, whom he believed should have been given the death sentence. In the November, 1946 issue of *Labour Monthly*, Palme Dutt wrote:

> The acquittal of von Papen and Schacht by the western judges sounds the all-clear to the Junkers and trust magnates, the real architechts of Nazism, just as the evasion of Goering by the complicity or neglect of his American guards creates the flimsy basis for a new Nazi myth. American big capital prepares fusion with the chief German monopolies which created Nazism.

On the 19th October, 1946, the *Sunday Express* had quoted from the testimony given at the Nuremberg trial by Captain C.M. Gilbert, the United States psychiatrist attached to prisoners as follows:

> Schacht laughed in his cell at the suggestion that German industrialists were to be indicted for rearming Germany. "If you want to indict industrialists who helped Germany to rearm," he said, "you will have to indict your own too. The Opel works, which did nothing but war production, were owned by General Motors."

On the same day, the *New Statesman and Nation* had reported plans for the fusion of the British and American zones of occupation in Germany, which were understood to include plans for linking Anglo-American (mainly American) monopoly capital with German monopoly capital:

> The merger of the British and American zones is already taking place, and it has been stressed that one object of this merger is to

reduce our financial commitments. This can only be done on the assumption that American big business is encouraged to obtain controlling interests in German industry, and the German trusts are reconstructed on American credit.

In New York, the reactionary press was already gleefully looking forward to the coming struggle of Byrnes and Bevin against the Potsdam agreement and the whole post-war settlement of Germany, including the rebuilding of German monopolist reaction with the backing of Anglo-American capital. Commented Palme Dutt: "Roosevelt is at the present moment being given a public memorial in London, to cover up in the usual fashion the betrayal of the policies for which he fought."

Towards the end of his life, Roosevelt had seen, according to the intimate memoirs of his conversations published at the time by his son, that the way to peace lay in the conscious acceptance of the principle of the peaceful co-existence and co-operation of the two contrasting social systems of capitalism and socialism.

On the 10th November, 1946, a general election in France resulted in a polarisation of the conflicting forces in the country at the expense of the centre parties: the Socialist Party, the Popular Republican Movement (MRP) and the Radicals. The Communist vote was up from 5,203,046 in June to 5,475,955, but the vote of the extreme right-wing Republican Liberty Party was also up during the same period from 2,623,679 to 3,136,630. In addition a few seats were won by de Gaulle, whose followers were described by Derek Kartun, in the December, 1946, issue of *Labour Monthly* as "a new group of political careerists with no programme save a blind support for de Gaulle and his authoritarian views on the constitution."

On the 2nd December, the *Daily Worker* caused a stir with its exclusive disclosure of an Anglo-American military pact providing for the standardisation and co-ordination of armaments, and the co-operation of commands etc. There was a hasty denial by the War Office, but the following month the whole sinister step was officially announced. On the day of the signing of the Anglo-American military pact in New York, an "Agreement on Joining the British and American Occupation Zones in Germany" was also signed.

Chapter Three
LABOUR AND BREAD

THE 45TH ANNUAL CONFERENCE of the Labour Party opened in Bournemouth on the 10th June, 1946, with Harold Laski presiding. In his opening address, Harold Laski began by acclaiming the great Labour victory at the polls, which he rightly saw as carrying the great victory in the vast international conflict a stage further. He continued with a catalogue of the parliamentary achievements of the Labour government in its first year of office:

> The nation is today the master, for the first time in its history, of the vital mechanisms of finance and credit. It is about to own the coal mines. Within two years, it will have in operation a great system of social insurance rivalled only by that of the Socialist Dominion of New Zealand, and a great system of national health service in advance, alike in range and quality, of any other in the world. Important decisions have been taken which mean that, before the next general election, transport, iron and steel, gas and electricity will be industries owned by the nation and operated on its behalf under democratic control. At long last, the Home Secretary has promised us a great measure of prison reform. We have no doubt that the Minister of Health, whose illness we all regret, will disappoint the eager hopes of the Tory Party and call enough new houses into existence to redress the balance of the old. Nor shall we complain if, as he achieves this urgent obligation, he leaves stricken by the wayside those powerful combinations in the building trade which so mysteriously claim to increase efficiency by raising prices. Let me add only an expression of relief, in which I am sure the whole Conference will share, at the repeal of that mean and ungenerous Trade Union Law Amendment Act of 1927, which had been, for nearly twenty years, the Tory response to the heartening comradeship of this movement during the General Strike.

On the international record of the Labour government, Laski was less sure. He claimed that the decision to agree to the independence of India

LABOUR AND BREAD (1946)

would be "a noble page in the archives of freedom" and he coupled this with the decision to evacuate Egypt. But he regretted that Spain was still crushed beneath the ugly tyranny of Franco. Of Greece, he had this to say:

> The return of the King would be a sorry end to the brave struggle of a nation which first taught the world the significance of freedom; and I desire to say with blunt emphasis that we should place no confidence in a regime led by a King who has not only already broken the constitution he was pledged to observe, but behind whom, also, there crouch old and evil vested interests whose sole concern is to equate their private enrichment with the public welfare.

He congratulated Bevin, prematurely unfortunately, on "the approaching settlement of the Indonesian question;" and complained that "grievous as are the crimes committed by the Germans under Hitler's domination, no good is done either by economic folly like that of Potsdam." This was probably a reference to reparations for the destruction wrought by the German armies in the countries they had occupied - including the Soviet Union.

"We are mindful of the heroism of the common people of China in this war," he said. "There, we hope, as in Yugoslavia and Rumania, in Hungary and Poland, the evil traditions of a dying semi-feudal society will be replaced by the will to experiment with freedom and democracy." But he was not convinced that this would come about through the processes of "the one-party state."

Not surprisingly, he went on to note that "the co-operation between Russia and ourselves is far less adequate than all of us here desire." He called upon the Soviet Union, having "experimented with distrust, to experiment in friendship." He believed that the common people, both in Britain and the Soviet Union, had the right, based upon a massive experience, to say to their leaders that co-operation is the only alternative to destruction.

In this context he believed it was painfully necessary to point out that "no small part of the responsibility for Russian suspicions must be borne by those who have decided upon secrecy in relation to the atomic bomb." He could find no justification for it. He did not know that Washington had already formulated plans, within two months of the atomic bombing of Hiroshima and Nagasaki, for a "preventative" nuclear war against the

PEACE AND THE COLD WAR I

USSR and other countries that had set out along the road to socialism.

His speech ranged widely over the problems and difficulties that were emerging all over the world now that the fighting had ceased. The job of reconstruction was the main task confronting the victorious nations and everything now depended upon it. "We all know," he said, "that the age of socialist planning has arrived; the only issue that remains uncertain is whether those who fear its advent are likely to be wise enough to co-operate in its peaceful application."

The morning session of the second day of the Conference, on the 11th June, opened with a Parliamentary report delivered by the Prime Minister, Clement Attlee. "For the first time" he said, " we have a report of the work of a Labour government in power, a Labour government supported by a great majority in the House of Commons, a Labour government carrying out the policies of the socialist movement." He referred to the nationalisation of the Bank of England and of the coal mines. "Those two have already become law, but others are marching on. The Cable and Wireless Bill is in Committee, and so is the Civil Aviation Bill. Others are in preparation and the process will continue.... Seventy-three Bills have been introduced. Fifty-five have already received the Royal Assent. There are a lot of fish in the basket, and they are not just minnows.... Look at those three great measures of social reform: National Insurance, National Insurance Injuries and the National Health Services."

Turning to the problem of housing, he said: "Some people seem to think that one could build all the houses that one wants in the winter.... Houses are being built, houses are in building, houses are being completed. We shall carry out the programme set us, not to solve the problem in 12 months, but, with the resources available, to go steadily ahead on our policy of providing houses for the people." Attlee admitted that there were difficulties. "But," he said, " difficulties are made to be overcome. Our home problems are affected all the time by the world situation.... Coal shortages and transport shortages again are not just home problems. They are foreign problems."

In the debate that followed, Sidney Silverman, MP for Nelson and Colne, first congratulated the Labour government on the energy it had shown and the initial steps it had taken to grapple with the many difficult problems confronting the nation, and them went on to draw attention to an uneasiness in the minds of some people, "not so much in home affairs as in affairs abroad." He pointed to "a spirit of cynicism, of pessimism, and of apathy," outside the ranks of the Labour movement. "We in the movement do not entertain that spirit," he hastened to add.

Nevertheless, a delegate from the Orpington Labour Party (L.F. Moore) confessed that "my own local party have, on occasion, been puzzled and perhaps a little uneasy at the preoccupation of the movement with what goes on inside Parliament and its failure to use great events and occasions to rally the people to their policy." He instanced the termination of lend-lease as a case in point. "Many of us waited for a clarion call to stir the imagination of the people, and rally them to the great cause we have at heart," he said.

There was uneasiness too on the subject of the reorganisation of industry. Moving that "when industries are nationalised, direction shall not be left to those who were previously in control," Irene Marcouse of the Holborn Divisional Labour Party said: "What we ask for in this resolution is that democracy be introduced into the industries which are nationalised now and in the future" and that the government "should look among the workers themselves ... to find people suited to this task." In seconding the motion, F.W. Petit of the West Lewisham Divisional Labour Party warned that "unless the structure of the whole nationalisation plans of our government has an absolutely secure foundation, it is liable to fall." He went on to explain that the right foundation could only be laid by putting the right people in charge, and that by this he meant people with a socialist outlook. He was supported by Ian Mikardo, MP for Reading, who said: "I am deeply disturbed by the choice of some of the people chosen to administer the government's policy. Some of us just cannot believe that a socialist policy can be successfully run by anti-socialist administrators."

Anticipating that by the following year's Annual Conference the railway industry would be in the throes of transition from private to public ownership, J. Benstead of the National Union of Railwaymen pledged that the government could rely upon "the wholehearted co-operation of the transport workers of this country" but warned that the success of this operation or otherwise would rest "upon the part to be played by the workers in nationalised industry." He called for "the maximum of consultation with those who are going to do the everyday work in the industry." There is no doubt that many of the rank and file delegates to the Conference expected far more from the Labour government than it was prepared to give.

Replying to the motion, Emanuel Shinwell, Minister of Fuel and

Power, said that he did not propose "to engage in controversy on points of minor difference." He agreed with the motion and stated, a trifle ambiguously perhaps, that "we must employ the best men for the job," and that "there can be no question of square pegs in round holes, no questions of inefficiency." The motion was carried.

On the morning of Wednesday the 12th June, the section of the Parliamentary Report dealing with foreign affairs was commended to the Conference by Philip Noel-Baker MP, speaking on behalf of the National Executive Committee. His opening remarks, reflected his concern for the growing disillusionment, not only of some of the delegates but of large sections of the population:

> When they talk about foreign policy, numbers of people are content to say: "Good heavens! What an awful mess." We had eight years of appeasement and disintegration, the breaking up of the machinery of peace, the undermining of democratic institutions throughout the world. We had dictators driving us to a lunatic race in arms. Then we had six years of total war. We have seen large parts of two great continents conquered by the Axis and then reconquered. We have witnessed physical destruction on a scale never before imagined.... What did they expect, these people? Did they seriously think that we could emerge at once into prosperity, friendship and good understanding? Did they believe that after decades of fascism, parliamentary institutions would spring up ready-made on the soil which dictators had drenched with the blood of all who stood for democracy and peace?

He admitted that there were many problems with regard to Indonesia, Indo-China, Egypt, Germany, Italy, Spain, Thailand and many other countries. He assured the delegates that the Labour government supported democracy in Spain and hoped that his words would help to dispel "the fantastic notion that the government are supporting Franco or that they have lent him help in any way." He referred to the harsh things that had been said about the government's policy in Indonesia. "It was said that we were bolstering up Dutch imperialism against a people striving to be free. That was a gross injustice to ourselves," he complained. "We were equally attacked for our policy in Indo-China. There again, I believe, our action helped a French socialist Colonial Minister, our comrade Moutet, to achieve a great advance in freedom."

LABOUR AND BREAD (1946)

This so-called "great advance in freedom" was, in fact, an attack on the Provisional Government of the Democratic Republic of Vietnam, established on the 2nd September, 1945, by the Liberation Army of the Viet Minh Front after it had driven out the occupying Japanese forces. The attack was launched on the 23rd September, by French military forces with the support of British troops who were in Vietnam ostensibly to disarm the Japanese. It was the start of a war that was to last until May 1954, when French troops, assisted by US military units, were finally routed in the historic battle of Dien Bien Phu.

In the debate that followed, B. Horinsky of the South Paddington Divisional Labour Party quoted from the election manifesto of the Labour Party, *Let Us Face the Future* - wherein it had been written:

> We must consolidate in peace the great wartime association of the British Commonwealth with the USA and the USSR. Let it not be forgotten that in the years leading up to the war the Tories were so scared of Russia that they missed the chance to establish a partnership which might well have prevented the war.

Horinsky then expressed the opinion that "the position today is as fraught with danger as ever it was in 1939," and informed the delegates that "war with Russia is openly discussed in the United States," and that "reactionary circles in this country are licking their lips at the prospect of wiping out the Soviet Union."

But it was on a motion on relations with the USSR, moved a little later in the proceedings by E. Cook of the South West St. Pancras Divisional Labour Party, that the whole debate on foreign affairs came to life. The motion was moved in the following terms:

> This Conference is of the opinion that world peace can only be based on a British foreign policy directed to ensure firm friendship and co-operation with the progressive forces throughout the world, and in particular with the USSR, and that such a policy should over-ride British imperial interests.
>
> "The Conference reaffirms the pledges made by Conferences of the Labour Party in the past, to respect, co-operate and assist in every possible way the struggles of the working-class movements in all countries towards socialism, and of colonial peoples towards their liberation.

This Conference recognises that to this end every endeavour should be made to eradicate the remnants of fascism throughout the world. The Conference therefore calls upon the government:

(a) To maintain and foster an attitude of sympathy, friendship and understanding towards the Soviet Union, and to do all in its power to establish the interchange of trade and cultural relations with the USSR, including the exchange of weekly broadcasts on the lines of the BBC *American Commentary*.

(b) To repudiate Mr. Churchill's defeatist proposal to make the British Commonwealth a mere satellite of American monopoly capitalism, which will inevitably lead to our being aligned in a partnership of hostility to Russia.

In moving the motion, E. Cook cautioned the delegates that "if we make a mistake on relations with the Soviet Union, then civilisation will go down the drain." He reminded the delegates that the motion pledged the Labour Party once more "to press our government to eradicate the remnants of fascism throughout the world," which, he said, was not being done in Germany. He instanced reports from newspapers as far apart politically as the *Daily Herald* and *The Times* to the effect that "denazification has not gone forward in the Western zone anything like as fast as it has gone forward in the Eastern zone." He drew attention to the situation in Greece and to the difficult question of Franco Spain. "Fascism," he insisted, "is not being rooted out everywhere." He expressed the pleasure of all the delegates on what the government had done on the home front, but warned that the future depended "on having a sound foreign policy."

Contrasting the attitude of the Foreign Office to the USA, with its attitude to the Soviet Union, E. Cooke complained that the foreign policy of the British government was tying us too closely to America. "Our joint Chiefs of Staff meet regularly with America," he said. "We have no such meetings with Russia. Day by day and week by week we are entering new financial and economic commitments with America. With Russia trade has come almost to a standstill."

Seconding the motion, Muriel Kiewe of St. Marylebone Divisional Labour Party said: "There is some disturbance in the minds of the rank and file members of our movement.... There is the feeling that we are heading for a third world war.... I fear that all these great social reforms, which we have struggled so long to secure and which we are now

LABOUR AND BREAD (1946)

beginning to see blossom into colour, will go sour upon us if we are going to be denied the confidence of a future peace. What is creating this haunting fear is the impasse which has been reached in our relations with the Soviet Union. Let us stretch out a real and generous hand not only to the Soviet Union, but to those other countries in Europe which are struggling in their way, as we are in ours, to give their people prosperity and happiness. We must convince Russia that our actions in Greece were not the survival of the days when imperialist Britain and Russia were traditional potential foes over our interests in the Near East and in the Indian Ocean.... I feel that it is up to us to show the Soviet Union that a new spirit is now ruling Great Britain."

Striking a new, if rather naive note, F.H. Hayman of the Camborne Divisional Labour Party said: "My party is particularly concerned with the relations between the people of Britain and the people of Soviet Russia, because we believe that here we have two countries with socialist governments.... Millions of our people want to know Russia better.... These are two great socialist governments, and we want our Russian comrades to share our pride as we see the ship of state, after a long and perilous voyage, sailing quietly into the socialist harbour on a flood tide."

Koni Zilliacus, the more experienced MP for Gateshead, on the other hand, did not mince his words when he came to the rostrum:

> We are not winning the peace today. The foreign policy of the great powers ... is being based on ideological, diplomatic and military preparations for war between the Anglo-American bloc and a Russian bloc.... It is not possible for a socialist government to have national unity with capitalist parties in foreign policy. Mr. Attlee set forth the reasons for that in his book *The Labour Party in Perspective*, and explained why the Labour Party does not believe that you can separate home policy from foreign policy and, therefore, why it is impossible for a socialist party to have national unity in foreign policy with a capitalist party.... Today we are so close to the United States as to please even Mr. Churchill, who wants an alliance with the United States; and we have drifted into a position of such hostility to the Soviet Union as to please even Mr. Churchill. What is called for is the immediate application of the Anglo-Soviet Alliance. We have offered to prolong that alliance for 50 years, but so far, we have never had one single conversation with the Russians about how to do it.... The Anglo-Soviet Alliance calls for our not

concluding any separate treaties in Europe with our former enemies. If we could get a clear policy that the Labour government will in no circumstances tear up the Anglo-Soviet Alliance and conclude separate treaties with our ex-enemies, together with the United States but without the Soviet Union, then we shall have gone a long way to make the Anglo-Soviet Alliance a reality.

Entering the debate at that point, Sir Richard Acland of the Tiverton Divisional Labour Party, said: "I do not say that foreign policy must be right when a Tory party disapproves of it, but I do say that foreign policy cannot be right if every aspect of it is approved by the men who approved Munich."

Among the many other countries that had problems, besides those mentioned by Philip Noel-Baker in introducing the section of the Parliamentary Report dealing with Foreign Affairs, was Palestine, in respect of which Nathan Jackson of the Paole Zion-Jewish Socialist Labour Party moved a motion calling on the Labour government " to remove the present barriers on Jewish immigration and land acquisition," so that, in the words of a previous Labour Party Conference declaration, Jews could, if they wished, "enter this tiny land in such numbers as to become a majority." Thus did coming events cast their several shadows before them.

In the afternoon, the Foreign Secretary, Ernest Bevin, wound up the debate. With unlimited time at his disposal, he ranged freely over a number of subjects, reminiscing the while on his personal pre-war activities. Coming at last to the motion on Palestine, he admitted that it was "a terrific problem," and added: "We shall have to come to the conclusion that ... the land will have to be publicly owned.... Because if you have to raise the Arab life to a standard equal to that of the Jews you cannot do it if their land is taken away from them."

On the motion advocating "friendship and co-operation" with the Soviet Union, Bevin complained that it implied that he was not sympathetic to the idea. He reminded the delegates:

> When the Soviets did not have a friend I got dockers and other people to assist in forming the Council of Action and stop Lloyd George attacking them. I fought the Arcos raid and called it silly. I fought Churchill's interventionist policy, for which we are paying now.... I helped to form, in Transport House, Anglo-Russian

commercial relations, about which this Party does not know much.... The thanks I got for it was an attempt by the communists to break up the union that I built. I said to Maisky on one occasion: "You have built the Soviet Union and you have a right to defend it. I have built the Transport Union and if you seek to break it I will fight you."

Replying to the accusation that he was supporting the setting up of a Western Bloc, Bevin said:

> It ill behoves those who say, when there is an Eastern Bloc already in existence, that we are setting up a bloc somewhere else. But I have not pressed unduly even for an alliance with France or with the western powers, because I have been actuated all the time in this approach by the wish not to divide Europe.... I am not going to be a party, as long as I hold this office, to any design, any strategy, any alignment of forces, any arrangement of defence (which we must still have) to attack Russia.... But this division of Europe, this awful business of a line from Stettin to Albania, if that solidifies - which God forbid! - we shall have two camps in Europe by the very force of events, and that will be the road to another struggle.

Bevin did well to recognise that there was a division in Europe, but he did badly when he failed to recognise that this was a division between the emerging world socialist system and the old alliance of capitalist states, of which Britain, although described by Bevin in his speech as "partly socialist," was an integral section. He ended on a demagogic note with the words: "Let Europe live again. To let it live again will be the quickest way of obliterating the memory of Hitler. Give us a chance to eradicate the horrors of Nazism, and bring back that old cradle - which, after all, it was - the cradle of civilisation, that it may nurture into being a new and glorious civilisation."

On being put to the vote, those motions on foreign affairs that had been opposed by the platform (if they had not already been withdrawn) were lost.

Moving the section of the report dealing with applications for affiliation, Herbert Morrison said confidently: "Only three months or so ago there were ominous signs that there was a possibility this Conference might decide that the proposals for the affiliation of the Communist Party to the Labour Party should be conceded, or, at least that the vote would be a tight one ... but we know now that, as far as one can predict any decision in this great assembly, the application will be rejected." Nevertheless, he thought it desirable that a statement should be made of the reasons why the National Executive was resisting the application. He then launched himself into a vitriolic condemnation of the Communist Party that would have done credit to Dr. Goebbels at his worst. After stating that the Labour Party believed in "constitutional government" and "parliamentary democracy," he went on to assert that "the Communist Party believes neither in constitutional government nor in parliamentary democracy." Warming to his subject, he continued in the following strain:

> They do not believe in the principles of civil liberty, and we do. We believe in the right of every citizen to denounce the government, to criticise it and to agitate for its replacement by another. If we had not possessed these political liberties we should have been unable to achieve our triumph at the last General Election. The Communist Party, in the making of its own policy, is a dictatorship radiating from the General Secretary to the Political Bureau down to the rank and file. The rank and file of the Communist Party have no great rights in the making of Communist Party policy. They get their orders from above. In our view, democracy and liberty and the principles of self-government will not mix with tyranny and dictatorship. Therefore we affirm that it is inconsistent as a matter of principle and practice for the Labour Party and the Communist Party to live in the same political family.
>
> Next we affirm that the Communist Party is not only a political party, but is a conspiracy. Indeed, it is a little doubtful whether it is not more of a conspiracy than a political party. The Communists have their party members open and avowed, they have their secret members unavowed and undeclared but functioning in various Labour organisations and elsewhere, and they have their recognised "fellow travellers." They organise their factions and their nuclei in the trade union movement and the trades councils as far as they can. They issue secret instructions to their people as to what they are to do, and the considerable amount of money they get hold of is itself a matter of mystery.

LABOUR AND BREAD (1946)

All of the above, of course, were arguments that had been advanced repeatedly by the right-wing leadership of the Labour Party throughout most of its existence. Unfortunately Herbert Morrison was on surer ground with his next set of arguments, in which he criticised the leadership of the Communist Party for its line on "national unity" in the context of the 1945 General Election, as the following extensive quotation, in reply to the argument that Communist affiliation was necessary for the unity of the Labour movement, clearly shows.[6]

> We have had some of this "unity." They have treated us to opposition, both fierce and unscrupulous, in the course of their existence. They have, it is true, also, at times, insisted on giving us their support, largely to our embarrassment; and even in connection with the preparation for the last General Election, when they were seeking to give us their support, they advocated a line of policy which was inconsistent with the principles either of Karl Marx, the doctrines of class-consciousness, or the doctrines of the class struggle. For what did they urge at that time? I will tell you. Mr. Pollitt said in a booklet answering certain questions, which was published in May, 1945 (as near to the General Election as it could be), that they would fight in the General Election "to secure the ending of the Tory majority, and after that election the continuation of national unity, but national unity based upon a new government having behind it a majority of Labour and progressive Members of Parliament.... This new national government should include representatives of all parties supporting the decisions of the Crimea Conference who were anxious to solve in this spirit the grave and urgent new problems that are bound to arise, and who will back an agreed programme of economic and social progress for the people of Britain."
>
> Well, who were the parties that supported the decisions of the Crimea Conference? If we turn to the Parliamentary record we find that at the end of February and the beginning of March, 1945, there was a debate in the House of Commons on the Crimea Conference

---

[6] See Chapter IX of *War of Liberation* by Ernie Trory for an evaluation of this policy and Harry Pollitt's own reference to the political mistakes made by the Communist Party of Great Britain after the Crimea Conference.

decisions. In the division at the end of that debate 415 MPs voted for approval of the decisions and only two against, namely, the two ILP members, who had demanded a division. Behind this policy for the General Election there was, therefore, first of all, a belief that Labour could not get a clear Parliamentary majority. That was defeatism, just before the election began. Secondly, the policy was based on the belief that there should be another national government, another coalition of Tories, Labour, Liberals, Independents and others - in fact, according to that Parliamentary vote the only people who were to be specifically excluded were the mild, small, unoffending members of the ILP, which I thought was rather rough on them.

Herbert Morrison was within his rights in seizing upon this heaven-sent opportunity, created by the Communist Party itself, to score an almost unanswerable propaganda point in opposition to Communist affiliation to the Labour Party. Or he would have been if he had not been prepared, shortly afterwards, to capitulate completely to the financiers of the City of London, thus paving the way for the partial rejection of the Labour Party by the voters at the following General Election; and its complete rejection at the subsequent General Election that followed in its turn some 20 months later. Also, it would have been more honest of Herbert Morrison at least to have noted that Harry Pollitt, in his political report to the 18th Congress of the Communist Party, which had opened on the 24th November, 1945, had acknowledged that "in a complex and changing situation we did make political mistakes in the practical application of our general line of policy," and that Pollitt had gone on to say: "Now the struggle for the fulfilment of the decisions of the Crimea Conference, on which the immediate future of world peace and social progress depend, must be carried out by the Labour government." Subsequent events, however, were to show that the right-wing leadership of the Labour government had no intention of mobilising the people of Britain for the fulfilment of the decisions of the Crimea Conference.

The mistaken policy of "national unity" put forward by the Communist Party of Great Britain had followed closely upon the fiasco of the liquidation of the Communist Party of the USA that had been first mooted by Earl Browder in a speech delivered in Bridgeport on the 12th December, 1943. Taking the Crimea Conference as his point of departure, he had declared: " capitalism and socialism have begun to find the means of peaceful co-existence and collaboration in the framework of one and the same world."

In a speech to the extraordinary session of the National Committee of the Communist Party of the USA, held on the 8th February, 1944, to discuss Earl Browder's proposals for the liquidation of the CPUSA, William Z. Foster, President of the CPUSA, had criticised these proposals and accused Browder of losing sight of the fundamental principles of Marxism-Leninism. Without diminishing the importance of the Crimea Conference, Foster considered that it had not in any way changed the class nature of capitalism. "Trailing after the big bourgeoisie is the historic error of social democracy," he added. Nevertheless, at a Congress of the CPUSA, held on the 20th May, 1944, the Communist Party of the USA did dissolve itself and set up the Communist Political Association of the United States, describing itself as "a non-party organisation of Americans which, basing itself on the working class, carries forward the traditions of Washington, Jefferson, Paine, Jackson and Lincoln, under the changed conditions of modern industrial society."

At the heart of the matter had been the question of national unity. While the United States was in alliance with the Soviet Union in a just war for the liberation of Europe from the yoke of fascism, and for the liberation of Asia from the excesses of Japanese militarism, national unity was in the interests both of the workers and capitalists of the United States. The question was whether or not this could be carried forward into a post-war situation, when the decisive sections of big business would have no further interest in co-operating with the working class. That it could not, had been recognised on the 26th July, 1945, when the National Board of the Communist Political Association of America acknowledged its mistakes and set about the task of correcting them.[7]

Naturally, Herbert Morrison was not going to lose the opportunity of using this disastrous catalogue of political deviations in the USA to cast doubts upon the advisability of taking the Communist Party of Great Britain into the Labour Party as an affiliated body, especially as some of the leaders of the Communist Party of Great Britain had shown varying degrees of support for the arguments advanced by Earl Browder.

---

[7] For a detailed analysis of this series of events, see Chapter IX of *War of Liberation* by Ernie Trory.

PEACE AND THE COLD WAR I

"In the United States in 1944," explained Herbert Morrison, "the leader of the American Communist Party, its Secretary, Mr. Earl Browder, advocated a policy of full co-operation with capitalism and complete desertion of socialist principles. He was supported, for the time being at any rate ... by the Communist Party [of Great Britain], for Mr. Rust, as editor of the *Daily Worker*, came out in wholehearted support of the Browder policy.... But what happened to Browder? He has since been expelled from the reconstituted United States Communist Party for gross violation of Party discipline."

Towards the end of his long speech, Morrison generously informed the Conference that he was not going to ask the Communist Party to liquidate themselves. "I did that a few years ago," he confided, "but they have not seen their way to comply with my polite request. It would really be their greatest service to the cause of unity if they would liquidate themselves, but I am afraid they will not." For good measure, he threw in a few gratuitous, though groundless insults, saying: "They like their servile state; they like their iron discipline; they enjoy their inferiority complex."

Notwithstanding Morrison's long tirade of abuse, Jack Tanner, of the Amalgamated Engineering Union, then moved the acceptance of the application of the Communist Party for affiliation, "on the understanding that the Communist Party will give an undertaking to observe and conform to the Constitution of the Labour Party." He pointed out that the road to socialism would be a long and difficult one. "As we travel along that road," he warned the delegates, "the capitalist class will make bitter and sustained attacks upon us whenever and wherever they can. They will try every diversion, deception amd sabotage, and it is not beyond the bounds of possibility that they will attempt some more serious attacks. We shall need all out strength to defeat such attacks and win new victories in the future. We shall need every support we can get." He reminded them that the Communist Party was "a very virile, active and energetic party, a tireless section of the working class."

Turning to the situation on the Continent, he reminded delegates that "where support from the Left had been refused there had been a swing to the Right. The support, which reaction is winning in the recent elections on the Continent, should be a warning." Then, replying directly to one of the points raised by Morrison, he continued:

It is said that the Communist Party would be an embarrassment

LABOUR AND BREAD (1946)

to the government in the work that the government is pursuing. Quite frankly, I think that the government, and particularly the Minister of Fuel and Power, would have been very much more embarrassed in regard to coal production if it had not been for the efforts of the communists in the coalfields. I believe it is safe to say that the position would have been very much worse if it had not been for the efforts of men like Arthur Horner. Increased production is needed in every section of industry. As I think most of you are aware, during the war the shop stewards in the engineering industry played a very important part in increasing production through the Joint Production Committees, and it is, I think, generally known that a very large proportion of the leading shop stewards in the engineering industry are communists. We urgently need a similar enthusiasm and a similar movement to that which we had during the war, so that we can get the increased production in the whole of the industries in this country. I sincerely believe that the efforts to increase production by the communists in the trade unions would be very much more effective if they were also part of the mainstream of the movement.

He ended his speech on a warning note: "If ... the decision is against acceptance of the affiliation of the Communist Party, do not imagine that the question of unity is going to be finished. The question of the unity of the working class is still going to be a very urgent one indeed, and until we can achieve that unity ... then socialism is going to be longer out of our grasp than it would be if we could only achieve that unity."

Seconding the motion, S.J. Merrells, representing the Fire Brigades Union, said that during the war the majority of the members of his Executive Council were members of the Communist Party. "In spite of that," he said, "we gave 95 per cent of our political fund to the Labour Party; we gave £1,000 to the fighting fund; we supported six candidates for Parliament and our organisation gave the officials a week's liberty to speak on Labour platforms.... In the next few years, when our party is trying to put over its policy, we shall need all the allies in the working class we can possibly get."

On a card vote the motion was overwhelmingly defeated. There was a total of 468,000 for Communist affiliation with 2,678,000 against. In the July 1946 issue of *Labour Monthly*, Harry Pollitt described it as "a blow against the best interests of the workers, now and in the future."

He pointed out that the whole of the capitalist press and the most reactionary elements in America and Europe had campaigned against affiliation of the Communist Party to the Labour Party. Summing up, he wrote:

> The Bournemouth Conference has taken a serious decision against the unity of the working class, but the issue of unity still remains on the agenda. Time, events, experience, all alike will combine to bring it forward again and again, until the conviction and determination for its realisation will have triumphed over those reactionary leaders of the Labour Party who are more anxious to secure the preservation of capitalism than the achievemnt of socialism.

On the debate on foreign policy, and Bevin's speech in reply to the discussion, Harry Pollitt wrote:

> If after one year of Tory government the international position had deteriorated as it has done since July, 1945, and especially if relations between Britain and the Soviet Union had reached the critical stage they have, one could easily imagine how the mass pressure of the movement would have made itself felt.... Short shrift would have been given to any attempt to place the responsibility on the Soviet government or its people.... From the moment the Labour government came to power its main orientation in foreign policy has been for an alliance with aggressive American imperialism as opposed to any honest or sincere efforts to secure an understanding with the Soviet Union.

Pollitt then asked how it was that from the moment the war had ended such a change could have taken place in the relations of the three major powers. In answering this question, he pointed out that the British and American capitalists had not expected the Soviet Union to emerge from the war as the strong, virile power it had become. They had hoped that the price of victory over fascism would be a weakening of communism but such had not been the case as the votes cast for the Communists in Czechoslovakia, France and Italy had testified. These were the reasons why capitalism, through the governments of Britain and America, had renewed their traditional hostility towards the Soviet Union

LABOUR AND BREAD (1946)

and communism. Said Pollitt:

> The unholy alliance of social democracy and aggressive American imperialism, against the Soviet Union and the new world, represents the last stages of the struggle between a dying capitalist form of society and the new advancing socialist order of society.... The Labour government cannot continue to damn the Soviet Union with faint praise at one moment and in the very next breath launch a full-blooded, vicious attack against communism, meaning the Soviet Union, without causing international irritation and suspicion, not only in the Soviet Union, but in the many European countries where the Communist Party is playing a key role in the governments of these nations.

The extent to which the wartime alliance of the three big powers had deteriorated can be judged by information, given by Pollitt in his article, that "certain sections of American imperialism are boasting of new rockets that can fly from America to the Urals," and that reactionary elements in the USA are unashamedly stating their belief that "the wiping out of thirty million Russians would be a small price to pay for the abolition of communism." Pollitt thought that honest Labour supporters would find increasing difficulty in justifying the Labour government's policy of alliance with American imperialism against the Soviet Union.

The concern and anxiety at Bournemouth was well founded," wrote Pollitt. "When all the clapping and the applause that the leaders of the Labour Party received there has died away, and sober reflections begin to mature, as the international situation unfolds, it will not be long before we see a mass movement beginning to develop to secure a reversal of the present, reactionary policy. It is this fight for unity of the Big Three, which alone can make the United Nations Organisation a success and which can guarantee the future peace of the world, which is the supreme issue before mankind at this moment"

At the morning session on the following day, Thursday, the 13th June, the Rt. Hon. Herbert Morrison, Lord President of the Council and a member of the National Executive Committee of the Labour Party, moved the section of the Parliamentary Report dealing with economic affairs. Looking back, he reminded delegates that in the early part of 1945, a little over a year ago, rockets were still falling on London. "A large part of our youngest and most vigorous people were scattered world-wide," he said, "unable to produce anything." Now, in 1946, demobilisation was already under way and expected to be completed by the end of the year. "By then," he pointed out, "the number employed on manning and equipping the armed forces will be down to about the June 1939 level." Turning to production, he noted that 1946 had started well and that there had been "remarkably little loss of time from trades disputes" despite the repeal of the Trades Disputes Act. At the end of the First World War, in 1920, 27 million working days had been lost through disputes. In the nine months from July 1945, which was the month of the General Election, till March 1946, only three million working days had been lost through disputes.

The reconversion of industry from a war basis to a peace basis was proceeding, claimed Herbert Morrison, "with order, with plan, and according to systematic principles as compared with the muddle, the inflation, and the smash [sic] that was characteristic of industrial reconversion under capitalist anarchy at the end of the previous war." There was, however, one disturbing feature in this industrial reconversion. Increases in production were coming largely from industries that were built up during the war. "Those industries which were cut back during the war," warned Morrison, "have been having much more of a struggle and, unfortunately, they include the industries concerned with housing (that is, making bricks and house fittings and the actual building of houses), and also the textile and clothing industries."

Referring to the recent election manifesto of the Labour Party, Morrison said that it was implicit in *Let Us Face the Future* that we should develop a strong organisation under the government for economic planning. "This means a break with the past," he insisted. "It means a socialist breaking of new ground in the relationship between the state and industrial affairs. It means that we are determined to embark in the sphere of the economics of industry with constructive planned organisation as against the Tory anarchy of past governments and administrations."

Brave words, but already Morrison was hinting that it would not be possible to avoid all repercussions in this country if, for instance, "there should be a large depression in the United States of America - which heaven forbid!" In Morrison's view, "the whole socialist argument for marrying production with consumption, for the maintenance of correspondence between production and consumption, this basic economic truth applied to the life of our own country is really an economic truth that requires to be applied to the whole world and its problems." Later in his speech, he spoke of the situation in the United States where "huge quantities of exports of coal, food and industrial products have been lost on account of strikes, which have set back, not only American but world recovery." He thought the world "very sick, very shattered" and warned that for many months to come "food and fuel and goods which are badly needed will be lost through the unreasonableness of people."

Not for Herbert Morrison the prospect of building socialism in one country, particularly not in co-operation with the land of existing socialism that had already proved that it could be done. From the very beginning it was only too clear that the wagon of the British Labour government was to be firmly hitched to the United States star.

Gordon Walker, MP for Smethwick, also appealed to the delegates not to underrate the dangers of an American slump. "A free capitalist country," he said, "inevitably gets into a slump. The next time it may not be so disastrous for the world as it was in 1929, and I think the American government, if and when a slump comes, will take action on a large scale to stop it. Nevertheless, it will do us and the world great harm." But here again there was no mention of developing trade with the Soviet Union and with the developing socialist countries as an antidote to an American slump. Gordon Walker thought that Herbert Morrison's speech was "one of the most important we have heard in this Conference, because it shows that our Labour government is tackling the fundamental problems of a democratic socialist state." George Brown, MP for Belper, agreed with him, though he thought that success in "carrying out the planning that Mr. Morrison has outlined will be governed most largely by the degree to which we can make the workers behind us really feel an almost religious fervour for their part in this thing."

Later in the day, Harold Laski introduced Leon Blum as a fraternal delegate from the liberated countries. Said Harold Laski: "I have explained to our comrade, Leon Blum, that all of us remember with vivid emotion his visit to our conference in 1940, and that when we were planning this conference it seemed to us right and fitting that one who typified in himself the spirit of democracy and libertarian socialism should represent all the countries freed from the yoke of Hitlerism."

It will be recalled that during his speech to the 39th Annual Conference of the Labour Party, at Bournemouth in 1940, Leon Blum had taken advantage of his position as a fraternal delegate to try and justify the law, then recently passed by the French government, imposing the death penalty for communist propaganda. "It is not the death penalty for propaganda," he had insisted, "it is the death penalty for treason to the French state.... In France we can find no difference between the propaganda of the Nazis and the Communists."

In the interim, Leon Blum had been incarcerated by the Nazis in the infamous concentration camp at Buchenwald; but he had still not learned the need for working-class unity. Indeed, he came to the microphone prepared to continue his crusade against communism where he had left off in 1940. "The only possible homogeneous government in a country like France, or in the rest of Europe, and the only government which could get a clear majority in the country or in Parliament," he conceded, "would be a government of proletarian unity as a result of fusion by the Socialist and Communist parties." He believed, however, such a fusion to be impossible "so long as any doubt exists about the sincerity of the professions of democratic faith made by the communists about the dependence on their attitude towards the policy of the Soviet government."

Later in his speech he posed the problem that confronted both the Socialist Party of France and the Labour Party of Britain, i.e., how to exercise socialist power in a capitalist country:

> I know how easily there can be confusion of thought between the legal exercise of power within the framework of capitalist society and the conquest of power in a revolutionary sense as the prelude to, and the condition of, a social transformation. I know that this confusion, which is almost inevitable, leads by an iron logic to disappointment, and indeed as long as the capitalist structure remains, any socialist government is condemned to disappoint some hopes."

And so it was to prove, both in France and in Britain, where the respective leaders of the Socialist and Labour parties could not bring themselves to believe in a "proletarian unity" that involved the communists; nor yet in policies based upon peace and friendship with the Soviet Union. But the absence of these prerequisites for the successful "social transformation" of a capitalist society into a socialist society did not prevent the delegates to the 1946 Labour Party Conference from greeting the end of Leon Blum's speech with "loud and continued applause."

LABOUR AND BREAD (1946)

On the 16th June, 1946, the Communist Party issued a statement, under the heading *Unity in Action*, commenting on the decisions of the Bournemouth Labour Party Conference in general and on its rejection of the application of the Communist Party for affiliation in particular. "The decision can encourage only the enemies of Labour, who now feel themselves stronger to prevent the working class from achieving its demands," it said. "It is for this reason that the rejection of affiliation has been hailed by Churchill, the Tory press and the bitterest enemies of the common people all over the world.... The widespread uneasiness of the Labour movement over the composition of the Nationalisation Boards, over the appeal for the 'best brains' from the capitalists instead of working-class representation and control, over the excessive compensation contemplated, is equalled only by the alarm of the workers over rising prices, fares and rents and the continued delay in providing houses, combined with the inactivity of the government in ending luxury feeding and the Black Market in the midst of the food crisis."

Ever since the end of the war it had been apparent that shortages of food and fuel would continue for some time. World food stocks, which had been built up during the early part of the war, has already begun to drop as early as 1944. The situation had been discussed at the Hot Springs Conference of the United Nations in July of that year but none of the food importing countries, including Britain, had been prepared to look ahead and face the possibility that the terrible effects of the war might bring about a world famine. The governments of the western world had gambled that there would be good harvests and that droughts would not occur in the first year after the war.

In the autumn of 1944 and in the early months of 1945, before the General Election, the then Minister for Agriculture and Fisheries in the Coalition government, Robert Hudson, had decided to reduce the wheat acreage in Britain. This folly was defended by Clement Attlee in the House of Commons as late as the 4th April, 1946, when he said: "It was quite reasonable for the Coalition government to decide that we could allow our own wheat production to fall from its peak." Only the Communist Party had been opposed to this policy.

According to the 1946 Cabinet records, however, released to the public under the 30-years rule on the 1st January, 1977, there was scarcely a Cabinet meeting on the first half of 1946 when the shortage of cereals was not discussed. Fearful that "widespread industrial disturbances" might threaten essential services, the Cabinet discussed a plan to set up a secret organisation in the event of such an emergency. Troops were used by the Labour government against an unofficial strike of warehouse staff at Smithfield market on the 15th April, 1946; and were used again against the dockers at Southampton on the following 8th July, when 2,000 men came out on an unofficial strike after the port authorities had tried to cut manning levels.

The Cabinet also discussed the squatters' movement. Nearly a thousand army camps had been occupied by people desperate for homes and the movement was spreading to include the occupation of unoccupied properties in the towns and cities. But it was the fear of a breakdown in public order and possibly even bread riots due to shortages that gave the Labour government most cause for concern. The gamble on the good harvests had failed and the droughts had come. To make matters worse, the United States could no longer be relied upon to send the supplies that Britain needed.

At a conference on the 4th June, 1946, representatives of the Food Ministry met and consulted with master bakers on ways and means of implementing a scheme to ration bread. The master bakers stated that they were opposed to the whole idea and that the scheme put forward by the Food Minister was unworkable. A hurriedly-formed British Housewives' League, consisting largely of middle-class Tory ladies, began to harass the government with petitions and demonstrations. The press gave wide publicity to their activities, which later drew from John Strachey, the Food Minister, the remark that "the Beaverbrook, Rothermere and Kemsley Press is undertaking a raging campaign in favour of agitation to gamble with the bread of the people."

On the 27th June, Lord Moran, Churchill's personal physician, recorded in his diary that Churchill had said to him of the Labour government: "They've made an awful mess of this bread business. By August or September there may be no bread in the shops." And such might well have been the case had the government not decided to introduce bread rationing.

At about that time, I wrote a letter to the editor of the Brighton *Evening Argus*, which was published on the 4th July. I reproduce it here by way of acquainting the reader with some of the facts that were not given the same publicity in the press as those released by the British Housewives' League and other organisations opposed to bread rationing:

LABOUR AND BREAD (1946)

Let us face the facts about bread rationing. When the Labour government decided to continue the Tory policy of decreasing the wheat acreage, it did so in the belief that the United States of America would meet its international obligations. This she failed to do. American exports of grain up to the end of May fell short of the promised amount by over a million tons, despite the fact that Americans are now eating 14 per cent more food than they did before the war, and in the face of reports from Kansas, Oklahoma and Texas that the elevators are choked up and wheat is being dumped on the ground. By keeping their wheat off the world markets, American speculators are making a bid to break price controls, and American financiers are taking advantage of the consequent food shortages to impose their reactionary policies on the peoples of those European countries that have dared to elect socialist governments. Bread rationing is now a necessity and it is useless to try and blame the situation on the Labour government. We must greatly extend the wheat acreage for next year and we must once more dig for victory.

With hindsight, I am not so sure that I ought to have been so adamant about the uselessness of trying to blame the situation on the Labour government. Certainly Attlee ought to have been blamed for not opposing the reduction of the wheat acreage in Britain when he was in the Coalition government before the 1945 General Election. And equally certainly he ought to have been blamed for relying too much on imported food from the United States when he became Prime Minister after the General Election. But, of course, the Tory-led Coalition government had been the real culprit in 1944.

On the day that my letter appeared in the Brighton *Evening Argus*, reports of the government decision to ration bread were also given press coverage. In the House of Commons on the previous evening, John Strachey had declared: "on the facts and figures, it has become absolutely necessary to ration bread." He went on to point out that by the end of August there would be eight week's supply of wheat or flour in Britain. That was based on the assumption that both the United States and Canada would continue to supply Britain with the usual quantities of wheat during the months of July and August. Delay in the arrival of wheat, Strachey explained, would be disastrous if the government did not take the precautionary measure of rationing bread.

PEACE AND THE COLD WAR I

Since November, 1945, Britain had sent large quantities of cereals and other foodstuffs to India, Italy, Poland, Greece, Yugoslavia, South Africa and Belgium, where there were large populations of people who were actually starving. This food was supposed to be replaced by the government of the United States. In addition, 400,000 tons of wheat, flour, barley and potatoes had been sent by Britain to the British zone of Germany as a direct contribution. "The government was fully justified in sending these amounts," said Strachey, "and I for one am proud to be a citizen of a country that has made a contribution of this kind." He warned that if the "thousand calory ration" in the British zone broke down there would be incalculable political and social consequences for western Europe.

Turning to the wider picture of the world stock position, Strachey pointed out that during the past cropping year the wheat exporting countries had had a surplus for export of 24 million tons but that the importing countries needed 32 million tons, leaving a deficit of eight million tons. "How can we expect Britain, by far the greatest importer of wheat in the world, to avoid the consequences of a situation like that?" he asked. "We shall remove bread rationing on the very day that it becomes possible to do so compatible with the safety of the British people."

Meanwhile the antics of the British Housewives' League continued. On the evening of Friday, the 12th July, 1946, the Brighton branch organised a big meeting in the Dome, which was addressed by a Mrs. Irene Lovelock, described in the press as "the wife of a minister of religion." She had flown from Kettering to be present. She was introduced as the founder of the League, which she claimed had been started by several women in a queue. "We are sick of the queues," she said. "Last year 22 women committed suicide through standing in queues." She thought that stories of starvation in Europe and India were much exaggerated.

According to the *Sussex Daily News* of the 13th July, the meeting was "by no means a smooth one, there being interruptions throughout." At times the speakers could not be heard at all, the hecklers claiming that it was a Tory meeting and not a non-political one. Another of the speakers, a Mrs. Ward Bateson of Yorkshire, replied to this accusation by stating that on joining the British Housewives' League, she and her friends had resigned from their various political parties. "We are determined to have a Housewives' Party in Parliament," she said. "We are going to have the balance of power." A challenge from local members of the Communist Party for the sponsors of the meeting to hold a public debate on bread rationing was turned down.

On the 21st July, in spite of the protests of the master bakers, the grocers, and leading members of the British Housewives' League, bread rationing became a fact of life. There was a strike of bread vansmen in Northern Ireland but elsewhere the opposition collapsed. In Sheffield and Rotherham the Master Bakers rescinded a resolution not to operate the scheme; and the Isle of Thanet Master Bakers decided to do their best to operate it. Speaking in Newmarket, Tom Driberg, MP for Maldon, Essex, described the situation that had arisen on the previous Saturday, when the women of some familes had bought so much bread that other families had been left short, as "the best illustration of the necessity for bread rationing."

In general, bread rationing was accepted as a necessity arising from the devastation of the Second World War. Increased rations were negotiated for workers in heavy industry and for the miners. There were grumbles and the Tories tried to make political capital out of the problem. But most people thought that rationing was fairer than allowing a free-for-all and a black market.

Chapter Four
THE 1946 TU CONGRESS

THE 78TH ANNUAL TRADES UNION CONGRESS opened in Brighton on the 21st October, 1946. Like the Labour Party Conference that had been held earlier in the year, the Trades Union Congress reflected the trials and tribulations of the working people of Britain. A future historian, picking up the official report of this gathering, would find in its 600 pages details of all the problems that had troubled the people of Britain in the year that had gone before.

The Congress was formally opened by the President, Charles Dukes of the National Union of General and Municipal Workers; and a civic welcome was conveyed by the Tory Mayor of Brighton, Councillor Walter Clout. The latter took advantage of the opportunity afforded to express his concern over what he described as "the unauthorised strike," which he thought would be "a very serious thing for the TUC to consider."

The Mayor's civic welcome was followed by a more down-to-earth welcome by Labour Councillor A. H. Wood, President of the Brighton and Hove Trades Council. After apologising for the high cost of accommodation in the town, he went on the speak of the low wages in the hotel industry and informed the delegates that "we are organising a meeting of the workers in the week that follows Congress, and we are going to distribute handbills in the establishments where you are staying." Referring to the representation of the Labour Party on the Brighton Town Council, he noted: "We have 23 seats out of 76 . . . and we look forward during the next few years to obtaining a majority." In the event it was to take another 40 years.

There followed the usual votes of thanks, and the presentation of a bound copy of *Seventy Years of Trade Unionism* to the Mayor, who expressed his thanks. Charles Dukes, then delivered his Presidential address, in the course of which he made the following remarks:

> During the last twelve months we began the writing of a new chapter in the social and political history of our country, a new chapter indeed in the history of the peoples of the world. A year ago when our Congress met at Blackpool, we were rejoicing at the advent

of a Labour government with an ample majority. Today we can offer to the Labour Prime Minister and his colleagues, in all sincerity, our cordial congratulations and our thanks for their hard work and splendid achievements in their first year of office. No government ever strove more wholeheartedly, or with equal success, to cope with the social, economic and financial problems which confronted them.

A little strong, one might think, in the context of world history, but in the euphoria of the moment, forgivable. Referring to the programme of the Labour government, he said: "Step by step and stage by stage the government is taking hold of basic industries like mining, and iron and steel production: it is integrating with these great social enterprises essential social services connected with fuel and power, gas and electricity, and all forms of inland transport." He also spoke, with equal emphasis, of the government's social security programme, of "its vast plans to provide, by collective insurance, against the destruction of family life, and the breaking up of people's homes." Continuing, he went on to say:

> These measures are measures of social safety. They are the embodiment of a humane and far-sighted policy, which aims at ridding our country of the grim fears of want, of hunger, of misery and destitution, which beset every wage earner as the possible fate of his family if he falls out of work or is injured, or falls sick, or grows old. Insurance against these contingencies and hazards of everyday lives as working people is now an accomplished fact.

Nevertheless, he conceded that there were difficult problems in the production of food, of raw materials, and of manufactured goods. "This country's economic needs," he insisted, "can only be met by a steady and large expansion of our production. The goal of full employment depends upon it."

And upon full employment, although he did not make this point, depended his hopes of a workable system of social security. As long ago as 1942, in his much publicised report on *Social Insurance and Allied Services*, Sir William Beveridge had listed three "assumptions" upon which his welfare scheme depended. The first of these had been "comprehensive health and rehabilitation services for prevention and cure of disease and restoration of capacity for work, available to all members of the community." The second had been allowances for every child after the first. And the third "assumption" had been: "Maintenance of employment, that is to say, avoidance of mass unemployment." William Gallacher, Communist MP for West Fife, had said at the time that he thought the third "assumption" would determine all the rest.

In his Presidential address, Charles Dukes had paid tribute to the Labour government "for its bold and swift decision to repeal outright the infamous Act of 1927, which imposed restrictions and deprivations of elementary human rights upon trade unionists." But here too, there were problems. "In the transitional stages of the change that is taking place in our economic life today, we as trade unionists will be called upon to exercise much patience in negotiations and to make real sacrifices, even where legitimate claims are in question, for the common good," Charles Dukes had added. This was to become a recurring theme in the years that followed.

In moving a vote of thanks to the President, Jimmy Young of the Association of Engineering and Shipbuilding Draughtsmen, said he thought the crux of the address had been "in pointing out that we are in a period of change" and that there are problems to be faced in adjusting to changes. The seconder, J. Crawford of the Boots and Shoe Operatives, thought that the outstanding factor in the President's address was responsibility: "responsibility to the community which we seek to serve in this great movement; responsibility to the changed circumstances created by the advent of a workers' government; responsibility to the international organisations of the working class."

The question of international solidarity was another theme that constantly recurred in the speeches made by delegates to the Trades Union Congress of 1946. Reading these speeches again at a distance of some 50 years, one wonders what became of the high principles proclaimed and advocated at this great gathering of working people. According to the report of the General Council, there were present 793 delegates appointed by 192 unions representing 6,671,120 members. In the course of time, the affiliated membership almost doubled, but never were the principles of international working-class unity more earnestly enjoined.

In the International Section of the Report, it was noted that in furtherance of the decisions of the World Conference of Trade Unions, held in Paris in September and October, 1945, the World Federation of Trade Unions had been formed, comprising more than 66 million organised workers in 56 countries spanning both the capitalist and

TRADES UNION CONGRESS (1946)

socialist worlds. As a consequence of this, the International Federation of Trade Unions, which had not included the trade unions of the socialist countries and of the people's democracies, had dissolved itself. At the first meeting of of the executive committee of the World Federation of Trade Unions, Sir Walter Citrine had been elected President, with Louis Saillant of France as General Secretary. These appointments had been endorsed at a subsequent session of the World Conference but Sir Walter Citrine had resigned his presidency in June 1946 to take up a position on the National Coal Board. His place had been taken by Arthur Deakin of the Transport and General Workers' Union.

It was also noted in the International Section of the Report that the re-establishment of German trade unionism was being closely watched and that delegations from the World Federation of Trade Unions (WFTU), from the National Council of Labour and the General Council of the TUC had visited Germany - the two latter bodies, however, restricting their investigations to the British control zone. On the other hand, a delegation of six from the WFTU, which had included Sir Walter Citrine, had visited all four zones of occupation in Germany in February 1946. This delegation had noted that "in some areas, denazification has by no means been completed in the sphere of public administration" and that in industry, directives calling for denazification had "far too often been ignored by the military government charged with their implementation."

The report, that is to say the report to the TUC, does not state in which areas directives calling for nenazification were being ignored, but there was plenty of evidence to show that they were being vigorously implemented in the Soviet zone.

The delegation had urged "the absolute necessity for a speedy and complete denazification of industry at all levels from top management to supervisory employees," and had called for trade union representation on "commissions charged with denazification of administrative and public services" as well as of industry. "It is the trade unionists who have the most intimate knowledge of Nazis and Nazi supporters ... it is they who should be charged with primary responsibility for denazification." The delegation had also called for "the most careful scrutiny of the composition of the police, and the building of a police force imbued with true democratic principles." Other recommendations included that "trade union newspapers be authorised" and that "buildings formerly belonging to ... the so-called German Labour Front, set up by the Nazis" and now confiscated by the military "be made available as trade union offices."

In the report of the General Council of the TUC on the subject of the WFTU delegation, it was stated that "the visit was of great value, since the Allied control authorities were able to apply the WFTU recommendations." To what extent this optimistic evaluation of the situation was justified by future events will be seen in the chapters that follow.

The report also noted that the Executive Bureau of the WFTU had discussed the continued existence of the Franco government in Spain and had adopted a resolution calling upon its affiliated members to approach their respective governments with a view to securing the breaking-off of diplomatic relations. The General Council of the TUC had endorsed this resolution and had drawn the attention of the British Foreign Office to the depth of feeling in the trade union movement over the continued existence of the fascist regime in Spain.

At the Moscow meeting of the Executive Bureau of the WFTU, in June, 1946, the matter was carried further when recommendations to the national centres were agreed. These included the organisation of demonstrations in support of the Spanish people's fight for liberty; and the sending of resolutions to the General Assembly of the United Nations demanding decisions favouring the restoration of democracy in Spain.

The General Council of the TUC had endorsed these recommendations and conveyed them to the Prime Minister with a request for an interview. On the 18th July, it had issued a manifesto in which it had expressed pride in the support of the British trade unions for republican Spain during the previous ten years and reminded the Labour government that we had just fought a war against fascism. In spite of this, the manifesto continued: "Franco Spain now affords a refuge to the fascist remnant in Europe. It described "the arrogant hostility displayed by General Franco and his accomplices towards the United Nations Organisation" as a threat to peace and security, and called upon the government to deal with this threat "promptly and decisively." It affirmed "its fullest solidarity with the people of Spain" and called upon the United Nations to "give expression to the feelings of the civilised world that diplomatic relations with the present Spanish government must be broken off." In further support of the recommendations of the WFTU, the TUC, in association with the London Trades Council, had organised and held a mass demonstration in Trafalgar Square on the 25th August.

The fate of the trade union movement in Greece and, of democracy in general in that country, was also in the balance. The International Section of the Report of the General Council to the TUC noted that, as a result of a visit of representatives of the WFTU to Greece, a Congress of the Greek General Confederation had been held in March, attended by 1,736 delegates representing 1,350 organisations. The proceedings had taken place in accordance with the laws and regulations laid down by the WFTU, and it had been recommended subsequently by the Executive Bureau of the WFTU that the Greek Confederation of Labour be accepted as an affiliated body. However, a serious position had arisen as a result of a decision of the Greek Supreme Court that the regulations upon which the election of representatives and officers of the Greek trade unions had been based were unconstitutional and not in accordance with Law 281 of the Greek Constitution. At the time of the 1946 Trades Union Congress, the matter had not been resolved. In an appendix to the report, it was pointed out that "the ruling of the Supreme Court of Greece was founded in the existence of laws and ministerial decrees enacted under conditions of dictatorship and political reaction."

Then there was the problem, as reported by the General Council of the TUC, of the resettlement of Polish forces in Europe and in the Middle East. The numbers involved exceeded 160,000, of whom more than half were in Italy, with about 50,000 in Britain and smaller numbers in Germany and the Middle East. Subject to some safeguards, the British government had agreed to create a special resettlement corps, under military control, in which the Poles would be enrolled on the disbandments of their own units, pending arrangements to train them for absorption into employment in Britain or their emigration to other countries. Concerning the criticism that some of the Poles were fascists and had fought against the Allies, the War Office had informed the General Council of the TUC that 22,000 had been conscripted by the Germans for forced labour and that they had escaped to Allied lines at the earliest opportunity.

In the discussion that followed, it soon became clear that after the problems of manpower and production the most controversial subjects on the agenda of the TUC were those relating to Spain and Greece and to the conduct of the Polish forces in Britain and elswehere who were refusing to return to their own country now that the war was over. In all these issues, the leadership of the TUC took up a defensive position.

Most of the morning session of the second day of the Congress was taken up with internal matters, and with inter-union and organisational affairs. But mid-way through the morning, the President welcomed and introduced the fraternal delegate from the All-Union Central Council of Trade Unions of the USSR, M. P. Tarazov. During the course of his speech, he said:

> Now, as never before, the development of relations and unity of action of the trade unions of all the democratic countries is of the utmost importance in the fight for peace ... We are proud of the fact that in the hard days of war the Soviet trade unions, in co-operation with the British, American and French trade unions, took an active part in the setting up of the World Federation of Trade Unions. The WFTU was set up in response to the demands of the great and small democratic nations. A little more than a year has passed since the day of its establishment, and it has achieved a great deal in serving the interests of the workers and the cause of peace and security, and in the fight against war-mongers and the remnants of fascism. . . .
> Our workers closely observe what is happening in the international sphere. They see clearly, and rightly estimate every intrigue of the reactionaries. Our working people cannot react calmly and without indignation to the toleration by the governments of some countries of the Franco regime in Spain and to the establishment of a fascist regime in Greece. The working people of our country voice their indignation against Franco who shoots and tortures in prisons the fighters for democracy. They voice their indignation against the monarchist regime in Greece, which breaks up the trade unions and throws their leaders into prison. We are sure that the workers of Great Britain make common cause with the workers of the Soviet Union in the fight against these nests of fascism.
> Not a few resounding speeches have been made in some countries; not a few resolutions have been passed in defence of democratic Spain, the working people of Greece, the miners of South Africa, the people of Indonesia, and so on. Till now, however, little practical action has been taken to bring about effective results.
> I have no doubt that all these questions, as I see from the agenda of your Congress, will find their proper reflection in your resolutions and activities, directed to the advantage of the working class of the

whole world. Allow me, in conclusion, to wish you the fullest success in all your deliberations for the benefit of the working people of Great Britain and for the benefit of securing a stable and lasting peace and universal security.

In presenting M.P. Tarasov with the Gold Badge of Congress, and with it the usual gold watch, the President, Charles Dukes, said of the recipient:

> We have all listened with marked interest to what he had to say regarding the necessity for the building of world peace, for the development of economic betterment and the fight to establish freedom in every country throughout the world. If there is one thing above all else in which the British trade union movement would wish to co-operate, it is in making the world a more peaceful place to live in, and to see that our social ties, our trading possibilities and the fraternity of our respective countries, and our culture, are developed along a continuous line. I should like to say to Comrade Tarasov that he will take back from this meeting the accord of the delegates of this British Trades Union Congress in all those sentiments which make for a strengthening of the ties between our respective countries.

Speaking to paragraphs 283-285 of the Report of the General Council (on problems of production), George Gibson drew the attention of delegates to the fact that, of the last 30 years, ten had been spent in waging war. "Those ten years," he went on, "have turned this country from a position in which it was the greatest creditor nation in the world into a position of being a debtor nation." Then, turning to the immensity of the problem that now confronted the Labour government, he said:

> It not only had to deal with the destruction and dislocation of war, but was confronted with the fact that vast tracts of our cities were laid waste. It had to deal with the situation which had arisen through the most effective and wholesale organisation of man and woman power that had ever been accomplished and turn that to the purpose of peace. I think we might remember also, and it might be set out for the world to see, that this country in pursuing the war made a measurable sacrifice not only in wealth and treasure, but

nearly one in every three dwellings in this country were either damaged or destroyed by enemy action. We lost nearly half of our merchant fleet, plus the lives of 30,000 British seamen. We exhausted all our industrial equipment. We sold practically all our former investment to pay for the essential raw materials of industry and after that we secured credit in countries abroad and pledged ourselves to debts that amount to over three thousand million sterling.

Our Russian fraternal delegate has told you of the immense problem that confronts the USSR in re-building. Our problem is less immense in physical dimensions but we have the added complication that most of our raw materials have to be imported from abroad.

This immense task has to be faced at a time when nearly three-quarters of the world is suffering from the effects of the war and when many of the essential materials of rebuilding are in short supply.... To those who suggest that the way out is a complete freedom of industry, I would point out the example we see in the United States. The United States is blessed with raw materials in abundant supply, blessed with an industrial machine which was increased by war, and yet that country finds itself in immense difficulties because private enterprise, given free rule in an economy where there are limited opportunities for production, finds its profits by selling in the highest market regardless of the well-being of the mass of the people....

It is suggested that £150 millions is required to re-equip the coal industry, £120 millions for the re-equipment of the cotton industry ... and there is also our task of rebuilding, which must be faced if our people are to enjoy the high standards we all desire. I know, of course, that there are difficulties and shortages ... one shortage impinges upon another and brings new problems. If we could send coal to Sweden, she would send us the timber which she is now burning because of her shortage of coal, and more cellulose for newspapers, if we decide that newspapers are a desirable thing. If we could send more coal to Denmark, we should get more food from there....

The problem which confronts us is to pay our debts and pay for our imports upon which so much depends. The whole of our textile industry depends upon imported materials. To the extent of about 70 per cent, our wool industry depends upon imported materials and our iron and steel trade depends to the extent of 60 per cent to 70 per cent upon imported ore, and so I might go on. The rubber trade, the copper trade and other things that we need for various industries must be brought in from abroad and must be paid for. They must be paid for by exports....

I do not know whether any American delegates are here, but one of the catastrophes of the war was that America became a creditor nation over-night, and still appears to think that she can lend money abroad and refuse to take the payment in goods; that cannot be done. This much can be said for Great Britain, that when we were a creditor nation, the markets of Great Britain were open to accept food and raw materials in payment of interest. Now our struggle has the addition that we must export goods to pay for the things we eat, and we can only get them by working and producing....

We were threatened with a hold-up in the north-west recently because of a shortage of linseed oil for the electrical industry. Well, that shortage is there because the monsoon failed in India last year and they are too short of rice to be able to export the linseed. We use enormous quantities of linseed in paint manufacture, in linoleums and the electrical industries.... We owe India one thousand million sterling, and if she could be supplied with the goods she wants from this country, the Indian standard could very soon be raised. So all these production problems impinge upon the problems of the world.

We are short of structural steel; and many new factories the government proposes to build, and which have been licensed and for which plans are available and which are intended to be built in the development areas to absorb regional unemployment, are being held up because of the shortage of structural steel, although steel production has been at a higher level in this country than ever before.

This was a fair description of some of the problems that the Labour government faced in tackling the reconstruction of Britain. They were problems that called for socialist solutions. Indeed, George Gibson acknowledged as much in the concluding passages of his speech when he said:

> The new Britain will not just happen; it has got to be built and it

has got to be built for all practical purposes on the ruins of the old. So there are new consequences: the peaceful development of our country, the prosperity of our people, the opportunity of our children and the chance to create a new British Socialist Commonwealth.

Unfortunately, although in those early days of parliamentary power the Labour government and the leaders of the TUC could still pay lip-service to socialism, neither body fully realised the role of the state and the need to curb the power of the financiers and industrialists by breaking up the existing organs of capitalist state power and replacing them with organs of state power loyal to the working class, as the governments of the emerging socialist countries were doing in central and eastern Europe. Nor did they see the importance of developing the closest possible trade relations with the Soviet Union and other socialist countries as a safeguard against the economic attacks that were to cause them to retreat from their socialist principles when the opposition hardened.

Yet warning voices were raised, even in the Trade Union Congress of 1946. In the discussion that followed the speech delivered by George Gibson, A.G. Tomkins of the Furnishing Trades Association took up the question of the importation of timber and plywood:

> Mr. Gibson has referred to the fact that Sweden could export timber to this country if we had the coal. I do not expect him to know the timber trade as well as those who are in it, but in our experience missions have gone from Timber Control to nearly every country under the sun except the one that really has the timber and plywood. So far as I am aware Russia has a quarter of the world's supply of oak, and oak is our main raw material. It has enormous production resources for plywood.... I suggest to Mr. Gibson that he should bring his influence to bear upon the President of the Board of Trade to obtain independent information about world timber resources instead of relying upon the merchants and brokers who have been [the] functioning Timber Control since 1938.

On the question of the shortage of manpower in industry, which George Gibson scarcely mentioned in his catalogue of shortages, G.B. Hunter of the Distributive and Allied Workers said:

This question of production is the most vital and important question facing this country today. The country and the Labour government will stand or fall by production.... Congress has to face up to this situation. It has to face up to the fact that there is not the manpower in this country to carry out the whole operation which the Labour government has put before us. The manpower in 1939 was in the neighbourhood of 21 millions, but the commitments which this government has entered into in the field of foreign policy are going to drain from that manpower something like two million men. We have to face up to the real conditions. Are we going to increase our exports, to increase production, or are we going to increase our commitments, and so have more compulsory service in the forces and drain away the best of our manpower? Youths of 18 are not being accepted for jobs today. Their training in skilled occupations is being sabotaged. A big section of manpower is being wasted there.... Can we afford to maintain troops all over the world - in Palestine, in Greece, and other places - and so sacrifice our own well-being in this country and sabotage production here?

Speaking to Congress on behalf of the mineworkers, Arthur Horner referred to the speech made by Lord Citrine on the previous day, in which he had stated that "it should be well within the capacity of the existing personnel to bridge the gap between shortages and the extra 100,000 tons Mr. Shinwell was asking for." Arthur Horner did not agree with Lord Citrine on this issue and called for an increase in the manpower available for coalmining. "The manpower situation at the present time is the worst in living memory," he said. He estimated that there were no more than 693,000 men in coalmining and compared this with the situation as it had existed in the past:

> In 1920 we had 1,200,000 men in mining; in 1939 we had 770,000 men, and in 1946 this country cannot get the coal with less than 700,000 men. I think Lord Citrine was meaning that if we could hold the 700,000 we should bring about the result he described. But we are not doing so. Our manpower is disappearing at the rate of 66,000 a year, and only 10,000 are coming in to replace them.

Arthur Horner made it clear that the mining community was not to blame for this situation. "We do not accept any special responsibility for the supply of our children for the pits.... In the end this industry will secure its manpower ... by producing conditions and rewards which will attract not only the sons of the miners but those of the educated people in the towns and cities.... The existing manpower cannot do the job. They will do their best and we ask this Congress to understand ... and to support measures to enable them to maintain their effort ..."

In his reply to the debate, George Gibson said of the situation in coalmining that it was not his intention to apportion blame. On the subject of buying timber from the Soviet Union he said that there was already a working party dealing with the problem. To some extent this problem was "mixed up with that of the availability of foreign exchange."

Later in the afternoon of the same day, the Right Honourable George Isaacs, MP, Minister of Labour and National Service, addressed the Congress and gave the delegates a series of statistics relevant to the discussion on manpower and production. In the past 14 months, some four million men and women had been demobilised and a further three-and-a-quarter million had been released from employment in war industries. There had been an intake into the armed forces but a net figure of seven million had been transferred to normal peacetime production. The demobilisation had been carried through with remarkable smoothness. There had been some resultant unemployment. Since the end of the war it had risen at one time to 380,000 (mainly short-term unemployed in transition from the armed forces) but this compared favourably with the situation shortly after the first world war, when unemployment had risen to one and a half million. Since the end of the second world war, three million days had been lost through disputes. This sounds a lot but it has to be compared with thirty million days lost through disputes in the same length of time after the first world war. No doubt the improved situation was due to the fact that the majority of workers in industry still regarded the Labour government as their own - as one that would solve the problems it faced in the interests of the working class.

Other factors that had to be taken into account when estimating the future size of the labour force in Britain were the drop in the birth rate during the 1930s and the proposal to raise the school-leaving age. The latter would in itself reduce the potential workforce by three-quarters of a million. Of those still available for work, many of those recently demobilised had been in the armed forces almost since they had left school and had not had time to learn a trade. Concentrating on the building trade, the government had set up courses for men leaving the armed forces. It had also given financial grants to those whose apprenticeships had been interrupted by the war, enabling them to carry on where they had left off. At the time of the Congress, 20,000 apprentices had already come under that scheme. There was also a scheme for training supervisors and foremen and 50,000 craftsmen had already taken the appropriate course. Even disabled persons had been pressed into service as a result of the government's appeal to industry to see that they comprised at least three per cent of all workforces.

George Isaacs then turned his attention to the vexed question of the Polish refugees who did not want to return to their native lands for one reason or another:

> Polish servicemen are here in our country and we have to face the question of either finding them employment or driving them back to God knows what conditions. It has always been our policy to be an asylum for those in trouble, and I am happy to tell you that we have the active co-operation of the Trades Union Congress General Council on this question of the employment of Poles and we wish to work through that organisation to carry this thing through. I have no time to read you the principles governing this question, but they have been agreed by a joint body and we shall adhere to those principles. The Polish Corps, which has been established, has already started and up to the 11th October has registered 18,500 Poles.

These included men in the Polish Army formed in the Soviet Union under the command of General Anders as a result of an agreement signed on the 30th July, 1941, between the Soviet Union and the Polish government-in-exile in London. The Soviet government had financed the formation of this Polish Army and had supplied it with the same equipment as it had supplied to the new Soviet Army units then also in the process of formation. But when the time had come to go into action, General Anders had refused point-blank to deploy his army on the Soviet-German front. In order to break the deadlock, the Soviet government had agreed to a proposal from Churchill that the Polish Army under General Anders should leave the Soviet Union via Iran to fight on another front. It so happened that this Polish Army had left on the eve of the Battle of Stalingrad, which did nothing to enhance its popularity in the eyes of the people of the Soviet Union - nor indeed in the eyes of most of the peoples of the rest of the countries in the anti-fascist coalition.[8]

In the discussion that followed the contribution to the subject made by George Isaacs, it soon became clear that the question of the resettlement of the Polish forces still in this country was indeed an urgent one, but one that the majority of delegates to the TUC did not see in the same light as George Isaacs. After accusing the Minister of Labour and National Service of leading Congress "to believe that we have got 160,000 anti-fascists who have not got a country of their own," L. McGree of the Amalgamated Society of Woodworkers went on to say:

> When this question was first debated in the House of Commons, we were given to understand that the strength of General Anders's army was 80,000, and as soon as it was discovered that there was a possibility of hospitality in this country, the figures rose from 80,000 to 200,000. It was a magnificent piece of recruitment, if I may say so! The overwhelming majority of the so-called refugees have never fired a bullet or handled a rifle in this battle against Hitler fascism. We have had applications that they shall join the ranks of industry in this country. Unless they are to become non-unionists, they will make application to join their appropriate union. The fascist officers have done their job superbly. The first qualification of the applicants is that they are to be 100 per cent Jew-baiters. They have done their job well. Their second qualification for hospitality in this country is their hatred of the present Polish government, and the third excuse is that they do not think they will be here so very long as they will be mobilised for war against the Bolshevists. There is no room in this country for these people. Furthermore, what is going to be the action of the Transport and General Workers' Union? Are we in the building trade, or in the furnishing industry, to give them membership? This problem has to be answered by the General Council. I say, frankly, that this matter is going to be a very great obstacle to production. How do the people of Liverpool feel when they see these Poles with their new uniforms, very well be-medalled,

---

[8] For the complete story, see *Poland in the Second World War* by Ernie Trory.

strutting about the streets, when our own boys from Burma, heroes from Arnhem, pilots from the Battle of Britain, have to take their wives and go squatting? How do they feel when accommodation can be found for these people?

There is another far more important issue at stake. What is going to be the international reaction to the depositing in this country of these avowed fascists? There are some governments and some countries which are bewildered by the present foreign policy of our government. This is one of the "babies" we are carrying for British foreign policy. We say frankly that there is sufficient work in Poland in the rebuilding of the devastated areas there, and if any of these Poles are worth their salt, they will return to their country, redeem themselves, and work out their own salvation among there own people. In conclusion, I say that to have this well-organised, well-disciplined military force in this country is going to be a constant cause of internal friction. For these reasons, we ask the General Council, very seriously to reconsider their position, and to bring pressure to bear on the government to reverse its policy and send these people back to their own country.

This was strong stuff. It revealed the gulf on this issue between the Labour government and the rank and file of the trade union movement. But if the contribution of L. McGree was startling in its opposition to the policy put forward from the platform, it was nothing compared with the facts placed before the delegates by C. McKerrow of the Transport and General Workers' Union who spoke next:

The Poles were not the only foreign forces in this country during the war period. The others - the vast majority of them - have gone back home. They have gone home because they were anxious to go home, just as our lads in the forces were anxious to get back here. Not so the Poles, or at least a large majority of them. Why is that? Is it because, as the previous speaker said, this army intends to march into Poland to free the country? It is stated in the paragraph that the War Office informed the General Council that 22,000 are not fascists because they were forced into the German army, and took the first opportunity of escaping to the allied lines. But it has been stated in the House of Commons that over 50,000 of them fought in the Nazi army in Germany.

This problem is of particular interest to Scotland. To the Scottish people it means more, perhaps, than to the people of England because thousands of Poles have been in Scotland for years now - but you are going to see a lot of them soon. During those years of occupation in Scotland, these Poles have made themselves the most unpopular visitors that we have ever had. They strut about, like the arrogant fascists that they are, well fed, well clothed; better clothed, indeed, than our British lads. In Scotland at the present time there are more brief cases among those Poles than there are in Brighton this week. They swank around wearing their Hitler decorations as if they owned the place, and had fought for it instead of fighting against it. That in itself is bad enough. It might be tolerated, but they go further than that. They have broken up or attempted to break up, in Scotland, working-class meetings, Labour Party meetings, election meetings. That is what they are doing in Scotland at the present time. They spoil advertisements of working-class meetings, they pull down posters, and that sort of thing. The feeling against the Poles in Scotland at the present time is very bitter indeed. At a conference of my union, there were 51 resolutions on the agenda, of which 17 (exactly one third), dealt with this very important question. When the debate took place it was the most heated debate, I think, I have heard in a union conference for a long time. Ordinary trade unionists, Labour councillors some of them, were on their feet. One said: "If the government does not put these people out of Scotland, the people of Scotland will have to do so." Only two days later the people of Scotland, in my particular part of Irvine, started to do it. A fight broke out in the town where I work, and in a very short time the whole town was in it. The Poles marched to their camp and brought out bayonets. Many people were taken to hospital. The British troops, our lads, returned to their camp and brought out machine guns, and if it had not been for the police, drawn from a wide area, there would have been a massacre in that area that night.

Replying for the General Council, Sir Joseph Hallsworth said: "It is obvious from the reception given to the remarks of the two preceding speakers that there is a considerable amount of feeling on this question in Congress." This was borne out when his declaration that he was "not concerned with the political aspect of the matter" was greeted with cries of "Why?" His answer to this was that the General Council had not been concerned with the political aspects of the matter. When this was greeted with further cries of "Why?" he replied: "The General Council has been concerned with this matter from the standpoint of the interests which this General Council is delegated to guard on behalf of its affiliated organisations."

At that a delegate shouted: "What about the appointment of fascists?" Apparently taking this personally, Sir Joseph Hallsworth retorted: "No one is going to charge me in this Congress with being pro-fascist." On the question of the employment of Polish forces in Britain, he suggested that delegates should regard this "from exactly the same standpoint as that from which we have regarded the appointment of Italians and Germans," adding: "You cannot deny this fact, that we have had to look at this question very largely from the standpoint of aiding our own people to repair the ravages of war by employing people whose countries were the cause of the troubles to which they were subjected."

Sir Joseph Hallsworth drew the attention of delegates to paragraph 238 of the General Council's Report, which laid down four principles: 1. that there should be appropriate consultations with the trade unioins directly concerned before the introduction of Poles into any particular industry; 2. that no Poles should be employed in any grade of industry where suitable British labour was available; 3. that where Poles required further training for filling posts in industry, the conditions of their training should be comparable to those applying to British ex-servicemen; and 4. that any Pole placed in a suitable occupation who for any reason left it, should only secure subsequent employment through the local office of the Ministry of Labour. In the concluding passages of his speech, he remarked:

> If there is any organisation here, affiliated to the Trades Union Congress, that resents the employment of this foreign labour, then, through its own machinery, it can make its views felt and the General Council will be satisfied with whatever action it takes.... If you ask the General Council to go beyond that, it is difficult to see within the powers given to them in the Standing Orders of Congress, that we can do so.

It was not, of course, "foreign labour" as such that the delegates were objecting to, it was the openly-proclaimed fascist views of the Poles in question. A delegate from the body of the Congress asked: "What about the reference back?" To this the Chairman replied: "The people who came first on the platform ought to have done that. If all this feeling that we have heard really exists they might have thought it important enough to put a resolution down." Nevertheless, he permitted W.J. Ellerby of the Civil Service Clerical Association to move the reference back of the offending paragraphs. During the course of his speech, E.J. Ellerby said:

> What I feel is that since the General Council has some doubts as to whether it can move further than it has done in this matter, Congress should make it clear what it wants the General Council to do. I want to move the reference back to provide, in addition to the four paragraphs already given, which allow the unions great power of protection, that in no circumstances shall the General Council countenance the employment of any known fascist.... The Council, through Sir Joseph Hallsworth, said that some of the information given by the first two speakers was new. That may be true, but he did not particularise which information it was. I thought it was well known that thousands of these Poles were ex-enemy agents, and that they had fought against our lads, and I should have thought that that was a sufficiently forceful consideration for the Council to have decided that it was undesirable, at any rate, for those elements to remain in the country. We do not want them in the country ... and we want the General Council to say so on our behalf.
>
> So far as my union is concerned, we had a considerable staff at Nottingham, and the War Office stated that the buildings in which the staff were accommodated were to be vacated. We pointed out that there were suitable camps around Nottingham which our people could occupy, and we were informed that those camps were required for Polish forces, so the Poles were placed in a priority category and the workers of the Civil Service had to suffer accordingly.
>
> Those of you who are familiar with civil liberty in this country ... will remember that there was quoted yesterday, from the top table, the preamble to the United Nations Charter. People concerned with that will notice that the Council for Civil Liberties is trying to draw attention, from time to time, to cases of Poles in the Polish forces who are not reactionary, and who have been subjected

to bad treatment ... because of actions of enemy agents in the Polish forces. For these reasons we want the Council to understand our position; and we move the reference back accordingly, so as to ensure that any members of the Polish forces who are known fascists ... shall not be allowed to remain in this country and no attempt shall be made to meet the manpower situation in this way.

The reference back was seconded by A. Torode of the Sign and Display Trade Union who thought there was no doubt that Congress was seriously perturbed about the matter. He felt that many delegates held the viewpoint that "this Polish Army is a great potential fascist force that will be working in every way that is open to it not only against our own democratic institutions but also to complicate further the extremely difficult and dangerous situation which our government has to deal with on the continent of Europe." He appealed to Congress to support this reference back unanimously, adding that "there are already signs in our own country that our native-born fascists are not yet defeated.... We do not want to add to our difficulties by having a force of a quarter of a million Jew baiters and fascists in our own ranks. Let them go back. They will have plenty to do in their own country."

Opposing the reference back, G. Gardner of the Amalgamated Weavers' Association said: "If you will remember, in 1939, Poland was attacked by German Nazis on its front and by communist Russia on its back." This brought loud cries of "No" from a number of delegates. Unperturbed, G. Gardner then declared: "These Poles who escaped and came to Britain have been the front line men in the fight against Nazi tyranny." In view of the remarks made by previous speakers, it was not surprising that another outburst of cries of "No" surged through the Congress. Such was the uproar that the Chairman was forced to intervene. "Just let him make his case," he said. "It will not alter your vote." This produced a round of applause from the delegates.

G. Gardner then completed his speech, which consisted of a rehash of all the smears against the then Polish government that had appeared in the press since the end of the war. His main plea was that those Poles who had stayed in Britain would be imprisoned or worse if they were now returned to Poland. He made no attempt to answer or refute the charges that had been laid against them regarding their conduct in Scotland and in other parts of the country.

The Chairman then called upon Sir Joseph Hallsworth to reply to the reference back. He began by saying: "There are many thousands of Poles here. They cannot all be got back to Poland at once." Once again there were cries of "Why?" To these, Sir Joseph Hallsowrth replied: "There are transpoprt difficulties for a start. Really, you must be practical." Rising on a point of order, a delegate shouted: "Were not these Poles brought to Britain in a few weeks....?" The Chairman once more called for an end to the repeated interjections.

When order had been restored, Sir Joseph Hallsworth made his case against the reference back of the relevant paragraphs of the report. "If you carry the reference back you will leave the position entirely chaotic and not subject to control, and I am sure that is not what Congress wants." He then pledged that the General Council would be prepared "to examine, and examine without prejudice, some of the evidence that has been given in the speeches."

The mover of the reference back, W.J. Ellerby, was invited to accept this assurance but he insisted that the question be put because he did not accept the view that the General Council would have no powers if the reference back were carried. On a card vote, the reference back was lost by 3,300,000 votes to 2,416,000.

The Chairman declared the reference back lost but there was no disguising the fact that the majority of the delegates present were very worried about the position of the pro-fascist refugees in Britain who had fled from the newly-formed democratic republics in central and eastern Europe rather than face retribution for their part in the war on the side of the Nazis. We did not know it at the time, but it later transpired that it was not only the Polish fascists in Britain that had eluded the net that had been spread for them. Sanctuary had been given in the United States to leading German scientists who had worked for Hitler; and a number of the political leaders of the Third Reich had escaped to South America with valuables they had looted from the peoples of the countries they had occupied.

During the afternoon session, the delegates heard a fraternal address from Louis Saillant, General Secretary of the World Federation of Trade Unions. In his address, besides giving a brief history of the WFTU, he painted a picture of the then current situation on the trade union movement worldwide:

> A year ago, in October 1945, the World Federation of Trade Unions was first established. Our Federation has the peculiarity of

being a new organisation of an old trade union movement. When this organisation was born last year, its affiliated organisations had a declared membership of 66.5 million ... and at the meeting of the Executive Bureau in Washington, the affiliated organisations, as well as those in process of affiliation, had a declared membership of 71 million.

The reason for this increase is twofold. In the organisations new national centres have been formed since last year, and have affiliated to the World Federation of Trade Unions - the national centres of the Belgian Congo, Korea and Japan. We have two other national centres in the process of affiliation - the Philippines and Malaya. But it is also due to the growth in membership of existing organisations.

Thus, the British TUC has had an increase in membership, so has the French CGT, while the Polish organisation has this year had the greatest increase it has ever had, from 800,000 members to 1,600,000. Also, in Rumania, Finland, Czechoslovakia and Latin America, our organisations have grown and increased their membership. All this proves that the World Federation of Trade Unions is a force of attraction. Why? Because the World Federation of Trade Unions represents the international unity of the workers.... Organised unity has been realised ... with the trade unions of Soviet Russia. Our experience shows, and history proves, that there can be no constructive international trade union action without unity, and there can be no unity without the Soviet trade unions.... Our unity is made greater by the presence within the Federation of 6 million members of the Congress of Industrial Organisations of America. That unity is indispensable.... Those who do not understand this are lagging a century behind the historic progress of the social forces leading the labour world towards its emancipation and inevitable liberation from the capitalist yoke....

We are a democratic organisation. We have to implement the decisions and resolutions adopted by the World Trade Union Conferences in February, 1945, in London and in October, 1945, in Paris, originally convened by the British TUC. How far have we gone in the implementation of those decisions? We decided to intervene in favour of the restoration of democratic trade unionism in Germany. There are at present three million organised workers in Germany. The co-operation of the World Federation of Trade

Unions with the Allied Control Council in Berlin for the improvement of trade union facilities and labour legislation has not been spectacular, but without our action German trade unions would be floundering in the greatest difficulties. My experience in this field of action leads me to believe that there will be no democratic Germany if the German trade union movement does not give birth to new principles and mentality among the Germans. The German workers must learn that they have, like others, duties towards the international community, and that the conception they have had so far of their rights and superiority over other nations is a thing of the past. It is on this basis that the World Federation of Trade Unions carried on its work of reorganisation of the German trade union movement.

We also decided to act for the re-establishment of the General Confederation of Labour and trade union freedom in Greece. You all know the moving and troubled story of the Greek Confederation of Labour in the past year. The Executive Bureau of the World Federation of Trade Unions made some decisions in Washington. These decisions were taken unanimously. The first decision is that we recognise ... only one trade union executive, the one elected by the Greeks on the 1st March, 1946. It is not right to say, or think, or believe that there is trade union freedom in Greece. The World Federation of Trade Unions proposes a new Congress under its own control as soon as the government has restored trade union freedom in Greece. If we are not understood and if we do not obtain satisfaction, the World Federation of Trade Unions, in accordance with the Charter of the United Nations, will appeal to the United Nations Organisation. The coming weeks will show whether the World Federation of Trade Unions will be able to obtain satisfaction.

The other decision taken by the Conference in London and the Congress in Paris was the struggle against the dictatorship of Franco and the restoration of a free and democratic trade union movement in Spain. I know that this point is a delicate one to raise. Nevertheless I do not hesitate to say that after the end of the Second World War, which has been called the war of democrats against tyranny, the darkest spot on the light of victory was the Franco regime which, with the regimes of Hitler and Mussolini, was responsible for plunging Europe into a sea of blood. The General Assembly of the United Nations, which is opening today, must put an end ... to this regime. Otherwise the peoples of the world will begin to doubt the sincerity of the democratic principles on which is based the Charter of the United Nations.

Louis Saillant then went on to inform the delegates that the World Federation of Trade Unions had asked for representation on the United Nations Organisation. Some progress had been made in this field. There was also the question of a permanent relationship with the International Labour Organisation and other international bodies. The World Federation of Trade Unions had played its part in the implementation of new labour legislation in Iran and the protection of child labour in that country. And it was engaged in a survey of the rights of workers in South Africa. Finally there was the attitude of the World Federation of Trade Unions to peace. It had noted the unsettled atmosphere that had existed in the diplomatic world throughout the whole of the past summer. Louis Saillant could not understand why the big three powers were able to agree on the conduct of the war but could not yet agree on the establishment of the resultant peace. "If it is necessary," he said, "then let Attlee, Stalin and Truman meet and send a message of peace to the world which will give confidence to the people and enable labour and the creative effort of man to become the sole standard of strength and the only value guiding the light of mankind."

On the fourth day of the Congress, the Prime Minister, Clement Attlee, came to the platform amid loud applause and the singing of *For He's a Jolly Good Fellow*. After paying tribute to George Isaacs, Minister of Labour and National Service, who had addressed the Congress on the subject of manpower on the previous Tuesday, he reminded delegates that although the changeover from a war economy to a peace economy had been a remarkable achievement, there were still great problems to solve - particularly in housing and in the production of consumer goods. "We are living in a period when there is a pronounced shortage of labour," he said. "Full employment is a policy not only socially desirable, but economically necessary.... To match the economics of full employment we need the ethics of full employment.... The provision of houses, coal, capital and consumer goods to the extent which the nation requires depends on the earnest efforts of all those engaged in production and distribution." He then turned to the achievements of the Labour government during its first year of office:

PEACE AND THE COLD WAR I

When I addressed you last we had just had the King's Speech setting out Labour's programme. You know how the promise of that speech has been implemented. Great social reform measures have been passed. Labour's policy of nationalisation has been applied to the coal industry, to the Bank of England, to cables and wireless. The Trades Disputes Act has been repealed. The session now coming to an end will be memorable in history for the extent of its achievements and for its having seen the first great acts of socialisation passed into law. We have in this been faithful to the pledges which we gave at the General Election though for some reason... our opponents seem to think ... that we ought to have carried out a Conservative policy.

He then turned to the international situation, where many believed that he had indeed continued to carry out a Conservative policy. After proclaiming that "our object is to establish peace on sure foundations," he warned that his government could not ignore "disturbing features in the world today." From this platform he launched himself into a vitriolic attack upon the world communist movement in general and upon the Soviet Union in particular:

Let me say that democracy is becoming a much abused word. It is often used, by those who have never understood or practised democratic principles, to mean the achievement of power, by hook or more often by crook, by the Communist Party - while freedom means the denial of liberty to all those who refuse to accept the communist philosophy. Everyone who does not take his orders from the communists is described as a fascist. The criterion by which these people seem to judge their actions is that if in any part of the world the Communist Party, by no matter what means, is in power, that is democracy. If anywhere the communists fail, then, however fair the conditions, it is regarded as fascism. Thus, an election in Greece, supervised internationally, which results in an anti-communist majority is at once denounced. On the other hand, a plebiscite taken where the Communist Party is in power is regarded as the sacred voice of the people....

I see on your agenda that the only resolution on foreign affairs is one which, I must say, is filled with the kind of misrepresentation to which we have become accustomed from the members of the

Communist Party, their dupes and fellow travellers....

We are not following selfish and imperialist aims, but that does not mean necessarily that we concede at every point the claims of others. You may be sure that the government will do its utmost to try to promote harmony in the world, but the task of building on secure foundations the fabric of peace cannot be accomplished by the actions of governments alone. There must also be a union of hearts between peoples. It is one of the tragedies of the world that the Soviet government appears deliberately to prevent intercourse between the Russian people and the rest of the world. They are not allowed to know what is being done and thought by their fellows in other parts of the world. The growth of personal friendship between individuals is frowned upon. The Russian newspapers give fantastic misrepresentations of the world outside Soviet Russia.

Attlee stopped short of repeating the "iron curtain" phrase invented by Dr. Joseph Goebbels and so eagerly taken into his repertoire by Winston Churchill, but he came very near to it when he said: "A wall of ignorance and suspicion is being built up between the nations." He deeply regretted that policy and hoped for a change.

Speaking on the Supplementary Report on Greece, during the afternoon session, A.F. Papworth, for the General Council, referred to Attlee's use of the phrase "by hook or by crook" and questioned his interpretation of the events in Greece. Following him, F. Foulkes of the Electrical Trades Union, took exception to Attlee's attack on the good name of his organisation "as sponsors of the foreign policy motion, part of which deals with Greece." At that the President intervened to say that he could not allow the contents of a fraternal delegate's speech to be made the subject of discussion. To which F. Foulkes replied that he was sorry that the fraternal delegate in question, the Prime Minister, had been allowed "to deal with motions on the agenda which are not before Congress."

Referring to the Supplementary Report on Greece, F. Foulkes said he was disappointed. "We say that this government's action ... in taking British troops to Greece has decided not only the restoration of the monarchy but the extermination of those people who are opposed to the monarchy under the present regime in Greece."

J.R. Scott, representing the Amalgamated Engineering Union, then moved the reference back of the report. He pointed out that the Greek

Federation of Labour had held a Congress on the 1st March under the supervision of three representatives of the WFTU, including one member of the General Council of the British TUC. The Congress, which had been attended by 1,736 delegates representing 1,350 organisations, had elected its officers and an administrative committee by ballot in accordance with the existing laws and regulations of the WFTU. "Those elections," said J.R. Scott, "were annulled by an illegal government decree on the 28th July this year." The elected executive had been dismissed and replaced by government nominees, of whom seventeen (out of a total of twenty-one) were supporters of the monarchist regime. "I understand," continued J.R. Scott, "that members of this dismissed executive have been arrested and sent to prison for refusing to hand over the documents of the Greek Federation of Labour and there is at the moment wholesale suppression of trade unions, trades councils, trade union branches and trade union apparatus.... I want to say that the conditions do not exist in Greece to provide for democratic rights. I implore the General Council to take this report back and replace its conclusions with a demand that the attack of the Greek government will not be supported for a moment. All decrees must be cancelled forthwith."

The reference back was supported by P. Belcher of the Tobacco Workers' Union, who told how a meeting of the Greek Tobacco Workers' Union, held in its own premises, had been invaded by the police who had arrested all 78 of the members present. Thirty-four of them had been held in prison for three weeks, and twelve of their number were subsequently given prison sentences of from six to fifteen months.

"British troops are in Greece," said R. McLennan of the Electrical Trades Union, "and we have been told that these troops are there in order to maintain law and order. Whose law, and whose order, is being maintained in Greece at the present time? It is fascist law and fascist order against the working class and the democratic people of Greece.... In the final paragraph of the supplementary report it says that 'constitutional methods and principles have been followed in deciding the question of the monarchy.' I ask anyone in the Congress if they believe that that was followed in the conduct of the plebiscite which resulted in the restoration of the Greek monarchy."

J. Crawford of the Boot and Shoe Operatives, however, suggested that "this Congress would be well advised to make no declaration in opposition to such a constructive policy as has been put forward." He asked, "Do you not trust Mr. Papworth and Sir Joseph Hallsworth as delegates informed upon this question, representing this Council, to put your policy to Mr. Bevin?"

The President then called upon Sir Joseph Hallsworth, a member of the General Council who had represented the British workers at the 29th Session of the International Labour Conference in Montreal earlier in the year, where he had opposed recognition of the credentials given by the Greek government to a delegation not truly representative of free workers' organisations. "The stand we took at Montreal on behalf of the workers was not questioned by the British government - it was too narrow an issue," he said. "The British government thought they should vote to accept the validity of the Greek delegates' credentials because the government in power was the only government that could appoint any delegate whatever. I disagree with this view, but on that they took their stand. But this is the important point. The British government, neither then nor at any other time, has ever challenged the rightness of the view we took for the freedom of the workers' trade union movement in any country to be unfettered in its choice of representation.... I believe that the assurance we have got will be along the lines that this General Council has authorised today, and its declaration is in line with Congress decisions up to now and in line with the pronouncement of the World Federation, upon whom now the main responsibility for seeing this through rests. We are backing up what the World Federation of Trade Unions is trying to do. You will do no good by referring back this Report."

Replying to the discussion, A.F. Papworth first drew attention to the fact that the delegates were discussing not only the Supplementary Report but the whole of the Report, and then to the fact that the document of the WFTU, which with its six clauses had been accepted by the General Council, was also part of this Report. The WFTU was looking for unanimity among the delegates in the interests of all concerned. In the end the reference back was withdrawn.

The motion on foreign affairs, to which Attlee had taken exception during his fraternal speech, was moved on the following morning by F. Foulkes of the Electrical Trades Union. It condemned the policy pursued in Greece by the British Labour government, as well as the continuation of economic and diplomatic relations with General Franco's Spain. It condemned the failure of the denazification programme in Germany and the deterioration of relations with the Soviet Union along with "the tying of the economy of Britain with that of capitalist America." The motion was opposed by the General Council and was lost.

On the 28th November, D.N. Pritt, KC, MP, shocked by Attlee's attack on the Soviet government at the Trades Union Congress, wrote him an open letter, which was published in the press. Here is an extract:

> You asserted that it [the Soviet government] prevents intercourse between its people and the rest of the world and does not allow them to know what the world in doing and thinking.... I have just been in the USSR for the first time since you and I were there in 1936 ... and I saw and heard enough to convince me that your assertions were completely wrong.... I talked with writers, scientists, doctors, lawyers, actors, architects, sportsmen, trade unionists, factory directors, collective farmers. They displayed not just a general knowledge of our life and politics, but a detailed and intelligent acquaintance with our housing and town-planning, our music and theatre and literature, our law and wartime legislation, and much more. I wish *our* press would tell us as much about *them*.
>
> You talk of building a wall of ignorance and suspicion. There certainly is one, but *they* did not build it, and the ignorance is not *theirs*. It was built in part by the string of anti-Soviet journalists and others who abused the opportunities afforded by personal friendships.... It was buit by those who decided that the "secret" of the atom bomb was safe with Du Pont but not with our Soviet ally; and it was cemented by those Labour MPs who clamoured, unrebuked by their leader, for repudiation of Potsdam - the policy carefully designed to prevent the rebuilding of Germany as an anti-Soviet weapon. There is not yet much material available to convince the Soviet Union that this game will not be tried again.

Writing in the December, 1946, issue of *Labour Monthly*, Harry Pollitt noted the contrast between the Bournemouth Labour Party Conference "with its victory and illusory atmosphere accompanied by the complete domination of the platform," and the Brighton Trades Union Congress "with its sober and serious facing up to acute and urgent political and economic problems and the positive and constructive role of leadership played by the delegates from the floor." He believed this to be "because of the part played by so many speakers who are members of the Communist Party as well as active workers in their trade unions." Later, in the same article, he wrote: "One of the reasons, of course, why a Trades Union Congress essentially takes on a more serious character than the Labour Party Conference, is that the delegates are representing organisations which are daily and actively engaged in the class struggle, delegates who come up every day against problems arising from issues concerning wages, hours and compensation."

At the beginning of 1946, I had been working as an enumerator on the Family Census, which the Royal Commission on Population was conducting throughout the country. The commission, set up under the chairmanship of Lord Simon by the Churchill government, had only just been put into operation under supervisors at the local Food Offices. In Brighton, forms had been sent to a sample of 8,000 women (about one in ten of all married women in the area) with the object of ascertaining statistics regarding the increase in the population, probably as a guide to future social legislation. Some of the questions were quite personal, asking whether the recipient was still married, how many children she had and what kind of work her husband was engaged in.

I was one of some 60 enumerators working in Brighton and Hove. The work was interesting and I found the women I called upon anxious to give the government the information it required. My area was in Moulsecoomb, a large council estate on the outskirts of Brighton, once a model for the whole country but then run down through lack of repairs during the war. We were paid 1s.4d. for every completed form collected. I was later interviewed on my experiences in this work by a reporter from the *Brighton Gazette* and an article on the subject appeared in that newspaper on the 26th January.

The job was only of a few weeks duration but the income was welcome as I was, at the time, struggling to establish a small publishing company. Known at first as Acorn Press, I was forced to change its name when it was discovered that a company of that name already existed. What to call it? My in-laws were then living in Crabtree Arcade, Lancing, where my two sons, Michael and Robert, had been born. My memory went back to the time when I had been living, as a small child, on the Crabtree Estate in Fulham, London. So, in the first year of its existence, Acorn Press became Crabtree Press. Founded in 1945, it was incorporated on the 16th September, 1946.

The first three books to be published by the company were all from my own pen. It seemed as good a way of starting as any. After all, who was going to entrust their work to an entirely unknown publisher in the smallest way of business that it was possible to conceive.

Mainly about Books, a collection of articles on bookish subjects that I had written for a variety of magazines, was published by Acorn Press in October, 1945, and was well reviewed, especially by the magazines in which the articles had originally appeared. Thus, *Russia Today* opened its review by reminding its readers of an article published in its columns the previous November, and went on to remark: "That article forms one of some 30 articles by the same author that go to make up this attractive book." It also noted that "more than half the items are of Russian interest and others deal with Marxist literature." With this in mind, the *Railway Review*, organ of the National Union of Railwaymen, thought the title incomplete and suggested it should have been called *Mainly about Books from, and on, Russia*. But it noted that two of the essays that were included, on Marx and Engels, had appeared originally in the *Railway Review*. Although the reviewer thought the book "a doubtful venture" he admitted that it was "stoutly bound and well printed." He concluded by wishing the author "all success," the equivalent, in those days, of the American: "Have a nice day!"

Browsing through these reviews some 50 years later is a nostalgic experience. The *Mid-Sussex Times*, for instance, drew the attention of its readers to the fact that "Mr. Trory, who now lives at Brighton, is well known in Burgess Hill and Haywards Heath" and was kind enough to declare that he "writes with authority, showing a particularly extensive knowledge of Russian literature, and has a concise and very readable style." I hope the latter is still true, even if my "knowledge of Russian literature" can no more be regarded truthfully as "extensive" now than it could have been then.

Finding its own interests catered for, *The Librarian* reviewer wrote: "From our point of view, this is more interesting than many other books because it contains articles which have previously appeared in our own pages. They are all short pithy articles on topics of the day as represented in books and libraries and range in their subjects from China to Peru." Whatever happened to the article on Peru?

There was a particularly satisfying review in the *Irish Democrat*, which naturally centred around my article *Engels on Irish Affairs*, originally published in the March, 1945, issue of *The Bell*, an Irish magazine edited by Sean O'Faolain. I was pleased to note that the reviewer thought I had "a freshness and a forthrightness of style that should appeal particularly to workers," and that "no flounces or erudition are allowed to clutter up the honest desire to convey information about his pet topics." The review ended with a passage that I had quoted in my article in *The Bell*. It was taken from papers left by Engels after his death and rescued by his friends:

> The English have attempted to reconcile to their dominion people of very different races. The Welsh set great store by their nationality and speech, but they have been assimilated by the British Empire. The Scottish Celts, although they were rebellious until 1845, and since have been almost exterminated, first by the government and then by their own aristocracy, have now no thought of rebellion. The French of the Channel Islands fought hard against France during the Great Revolution. Only the Irish are too much for English imperialism.

The review in the *Monthly Journal* of the Amalgamated Engineering Union was more of a history of my political activities than a review of my writings. I reproduce the first part of it here as a brief way of letting my readers know what I was about at the time:

> Books should justify themselves by their titles, and titles in a perfect world will conform to the contents of books. This somewhat sententious [I had to look this word up in the dictionary] [9] observation is excited by the collection of papers published by Ernie Trory, who is an active member of the AEU. He has served on the Brighton, Hove and District Trades Council, and was a foundation member and first President of the Haywards Heath branch of the Union. As the son of a former [Conservative] member of the Brighton Town Council, he has done most of his trade union work in the Sussex area, although he was actually born in London. He has taken a prominent part in the work of the labour and trade union movement, and for a period represented the Sussex District Council of the Shop Assistants' Union on the Sussex Federation of Trades Councils. He holds a TUC bronze medal for organising services to the movement.

---

[9] "Full of meaning: aphoristic, abounding (often super-abounding) in maxims" - *Chambers's Twentieth Century Dictionary* (1971 edition).

He is now a committee member of the Brighton 1st Branch of the AEU and its representative on the Brighton and Hove Labour Party.

There was no mention of the fact that I had been a member of the Communist Party for eleven years, and that for the last two of these I had been a full-time Communist Party organiser - prior to my call up into the army and my subsequent expulsion from the CPGB. Nor was this fact mentioned in the more dramatic review published in the *Railway Service Journal*, which also devoted three-quarters of its over-enthusiastic text to a review of my political life:

> The ideas of Ernie Trory drove him forth from his father's well-known Brighton hotel without the paternal blessing. Added odium invested him for revolting against life as apprentice to a gent's outfitter. That was ten years ago. Standing on his own two feet ever since, he sought a living from a food factory, then bread roundsman, then twelve month's unemployment, living as may be. Then two years as a political organiser. Called up on outbreak of war to the Army, discharged in 1941. Motor fitter with Southern Railway, left for health reasons. Then drove builder's lorry and after that a laundry van. Motor fitting again and organised a private firm solid. Formed new branch of AEU. Travelled and wrote in between. 1936 [the chronology is confusing], Moscow and Leningrad, saved up and spent last penny on trip. 1935, walked across Spain from Santander to Oviedo, with special attention to Asturias. Travelled several continental countries, all with frugally saved earnings.[10] Contested Tory ward in November elections and shook it.[11] Now saved enough to found publishing business that will grow.

In the short paragraph that followed, the reviewer, J.H. Davis, managed to find enough space to report that the book "is not light reading, but the information is tremendous.... It may even, presently, be quoted as a textbook." Fortunately I decided not to hold my breath

---

[10] See *Between the Wars* by Ernie Trory, for a more coherent description of these events.
[11] See Chapter IX of *War of Liberation* by Ernie Trory.

whilst waiting for this to happen.

My second book, *New Foundations* was a collection comprising two series of articles previously published in the *Railway Review* and a third series that was to have been published in the same journal but which, in the event, had fallen a victim of drastic cuts in the paper supply then available. This book was published by Crabtree Press in March, 1946, being described on the dust jacket as "A New Book about Nationalism, Race Hatred and the Jewish Problem." It was not well reviewed in the trade journals and most of the Jewish press condemned it for its attacks on Zionism. I am not sure that it was even reviewed in the *Railway Review* where two-thirds of the articles had been published originally.

Shortly after this, Crabtree Press began publishing a series of *Labour Directories* with the names and addresses of local trade union and Co-operative and Labour Party branch and ward secretaries. In 1946, five were published: for Brighton and Hove, Lewes, Croydon, Horsham and East Grinstead. The directories carried advertising, which was the main source of revenue, and were sold at ninepence each. Crabtree Press also published, during 1946, a slim volume of poetry, under the title *Dawn Music*, by Philip Chadwick, and *Near the Sun: Impressions of a Medical Officer of Bomber Command*, by Victor Tempest. This had a Foreword by Sir Archibald Sinclair, former Secretary of State for Air. None of these books became best sellers.

Towards the end of 1946, an event of great importance to the local trade union movement was celebrated. It was the centenary of the Brighton 1st Branch of the Amalgamated Engineering Union, which had a continuous history from its foundation on the 24th October, 1846. In connection with this event, a Centenary Celebrations Committee was set up and I was commissioned to write the history of the branch. This I did, in the context of the history of the development of metal-working in Sussex from the year 2000 BC.

There is evidence of metal-working in Sussex during the bronze age, and of iron being worked in Sussex by the Britons before the Roman occupation. Here is a paragraph from the book dealing with a period much later but still before the discovery of coal:

> From the days of Elizabeth the mining and working of iron had made Sussex the foremost industrial county of England. Throughout the Weald iron ore lay in great quantities, and the vast tracts of forest land covering Sussex provided the fuel, either burnt in its

natural state or converted into charcoal, for the smelting furnaces. In those days Sussex was known as the Black Country. It provided the whole of England with bells for its churches, firebacks and irons for its hearths, gates and railings for its parks, and monuments and tombstones for its graves.

The book was published in October, 1946, to coincide with the centenary celebrations organised by the AEU. I called it *The Sacred Band*, a quotation from an article on trade unions written by Dr. William King and published in the *Co-operator* in 1829: "Hail sacred band - the workman's friend! the workman's hope!" Dr. King was an Owenite, an idealist, and was deeply concerned with the conditions of the poor in Brighton, especially of those who were "industrious, sober, steady and quiet."

In my book I traced the history of the Brighton 1st Branch of the AEU from its foundation as a branch of the Old Mechanics in 1846, through the amalgamation of 1851 that gave birth to the Amalgamated Society of Engineers, and on through the subsequent amalgamation of 1920 that brought into being the Amalgamated Engineering Union. It covered the history of two world wars and the General Strike of 1926, ending with the completion of a hundred years of continuously recorded history, through its minute books, in 1946.

The documents contributed by old members, which were invaluable to me in writing the book, formed the basis of a Centenary Exhibition. Here is a report of the exhibition as it appeared in both the *Sussex Daily News* and the Brighton *Evening Argus* on the 21st October, 1946:

> An armchair and table, presented to the Brighton Trades Council by Prince Kropotkin on his return to Russia after 40 years's exile, take pride of place at an exhibition opened on Saturday in celebration of the centenary of the first Brighton Branch of the Amalgamated Engineering Union.[12] These two items of furniture, formerly the

---

[12] The armchair and table referred to were kept in Room One of the Brighton Labour Club in London Road, where the Brighton 1st Branch of the AEU held its meetings. Hence their significance in the exhibition. As Minutes Secretary, I sat at the table with the President during branch meetings.

property of Richard Cobden, formed part of the furnishing of the study in which Richard Cobden wrote his attacks on the Corn Laws.

The exhibition, which is staged at the premises of Messrs. Roslings, London Road, Brighton, and will remain open for a week, has for its basis, material collected by Ernie Trory for his book, *The Sacred Band*, written for the centenary. There is a display of photographs, drawings, letters etc., accumulated by the Union, throughout the years, including a photograph of the Labour group on the Brighton Town Council in 1924; and one of the Brighton Trades Council in June, 1896.

It was on the 24th October, 1846, that a group of engineering workers from the North of England, who had settled in Brighton to work in the railway shops, formed a branch of the Friendly Society of Steam Engine and Machine Makers and Millwrights. In 1851, the Old Mechanics [a name by which the aforementioned union was more familiarly known] became a part of the Amagamated Society of Engineers, Machinists, Millwrights, Smiths and Pattern Makers [the ASE for short], which in 1920 became a part of the AEU [Amalgamated Engineering Union]. The exhibition was opend by the Mayor of Brighton, Councillor Walter Clout.

My book, *The Sacred Band*, was well received on publication. Reviewing it in the *Daily Worker*, Allen Hutt described it as "an interesting job which should encourage others to tackle the working-class history of their own locality." The *Brighton and Hove Gazette* said: "The book makes fascinating reading, for besides being a record of the local trade union and labour movement, it sheds new light on the history of Brighton, telling the story of the common people, a story too often obscured by the Regency era."

The *Sussex Daily News* gave ten and a half column inches of space to a review by Hamilton Fyfe, one-time editor of the *Daily Herald*, who concluded that it was "a contribution well worth while, though some of his [the author's] political asides may cause eyebrows to go up and set foreheads frowning."

It was reviewed in the *Monthly Journal* of the AEU by Wally Hannington, who remarked that "if one imagines that local trade union history makes dull reading except for the workers of that area, such ideas are positively disproved by this book, which makes most interesting reading from beginning to end." In the closing sentences of his review,

PEACE AND THE COLD WAR I

Wally Hannington drew attention to the fact that the book was dedicated "to those members of the movement who regularly attend their branch meetings."

It may come as a surprise to readers of my more recent publications that Crabtree Press is now more than 50 years old. It was originally intended to be a commercial undertaking but it lost money from the start. Some people have the knack of making money; others have not. When it became apparent to me that I was in the latter category, my first thoughts were to wind the business up. On second thoughts, however, I decided to keep it alive in case I wanted to bring out anything of my own.

In 1974 I published *Between the Wars*; and since then another 17 titles, including this one. Crabtree Press is still losing money but is now well known in a small but growing circle of socialist activists. I like to think that it would be missed if it suddenly ceased to exist. There is no doubt that it played, and continues to play, a small but significant part in the struggle against the anti-Soviet and anti-communist propaganda that was, and still is, the basic feature of a cold war that, despite the collapse of socialism in Europe, is still very much with us.

Chapter Five
THE COMMUNIST VIEW

AT THE OPENING of 1947, four wars were still raging in various parts of the world: in China, in Indo-China, in Greece and in Palestine. There was a truce in Indonesia, under cover of which Dutch troops were being trained and equipped in Britain. Writing in the February, 1947 issue of *Labour Monthly*, Palme Dutt commented:

> The wars might be thought of concern to the United Nations. In practice, the United Nations is powerless to act, since four of the five leading powers of the United Nations are engaged in these wars. All the Permanent Powers of the Security Council except the Soviet Union are engaged in one or other of these wars. The United States and Chiang Kai Shek are jointly engaged in the war on Chinese democracy. France under its present leadership, despite the protest of the [French] Communist Party, is engaged in Indo-China in warfare against Viet-Nam. Britain is engaged in Greece and in Palestine.

In the same article, and not entirely unconnected with the above, Dutt noted that there would be two important conferences during February, 1947. Both would be discussing "the new problems of Britain and the post-war world." The first would be the Congress of the Communist Party of Great Britain. The second would be the British Empire Conference of Communist Parties - "a new venture bringing together for the first time accredited delegates from the growing Communist movement in all parts of the British Empire."

Previously there had been Commonwealth Labour Conferences but these had represented, in the main, only the privileged sections of the white workers. The Empire Conference of Communist Parties would represent the vanguard of the working masses of the five hundred millions of the Empire, without distinction of race or colour.

The views of its delegates on the shortage of man-power in Britain would be particularly interesting. Government solutions to the problem were being sought in proposals for the settlement of Polish fascists in

Britain and for the retention in Britain of German prisoners of war, both vigorously opposed by rank and file delegates at the 1946 TU Congress. *The Times* had a third proposal. In an editorial on the 17th January, 1947, it called for "a selective immigration of up to 500,000 foreign workers during the next few years." But, as Dutt pointed out:

> The latest return for November [1946], shows 1,510,000 in the armed forces, and 474,000 engaged in making equipment and supplies for the armed forces: a total of close on two millions or one-tenth of the available man-power, and a multiplication of the armed forces more than threefold on the pre-war figure of 480,000. Yet, when the question is raised why demobilisation has been slowed down, and why these enormous numbers are necessary, Mr. Attlee in reply points, not merely to the needs of defence or obligations under the United Nations and in ex-enemy countries, but to imperialist commitments in the Near East or the Far East. If all armed forces were brought home, except for [those in] ex-enemy countries, and the level of armed forces brought down, it should be possible to release one million men.

Dutt also drew attention to "the key dilemma of Britain's present economic situation - the deficit on the balance of payments." This was in the region of £400 million, of which £300 million was for "overseas military expenditure." This deficit was being met by American and Canadian loans that were expected to be exhausted by the end of 1948.

It was said that Britain must line up with America and support American policy in Spain and Greece and in Germany and in the Near and Far East because Britain was dependent upon America; but the main reason for Britain's economic dependence upon America lay in the crushing weight of it's imperialist commitments. Dutt's proposal was to "cut the losses of an outworn, criminal and bankrupt system of Empire, and build instead a new Britain as a free and equal partner of the free peoples of the world."

The 19th Congress of the Communist Party of Great Britain opened on the 22nd February, 1947. In introducing the *Report of the Executive Committee*, which had been published in December, 1946, Harry Pollitt said:

THE COMMUNIST VIEW (1947)

Our Congress meets at one of the most critical periods in the history of Britain. It is not a case of speculating on when an economic crisis will develop in America; we have to face the fact that there is a crisis in Britain now.

Two years of compromising with big business at home and imperialist policy abroad, has at last compelled the government itself to declare officially "the position of the country is extremely serious." The Labour movement, solid to the core against Tory attacks and intrigues for a new coalition government, is profoundly disturbed.

The Communist Party, while defending the government against the unscrupulous and hypocritical attacks of the Tories who have the main responsibility for Britain's economic position, demands an immediate reorganisation of the government to face the position. Those minister's deeply compromised in placating big business and pursuing an imperialist foreign policy must be dropped. The government must be strengthened with men prepared to smash the imperialist monopoly and vested interests once and for all, men prepared to organise a real economic plan to save this country from disaster.

Pollitt believed that Britain's problems had to be seen against the background of the world position following victory in the anti-fascist war. On the one hand, the collapse of the Axis powers and the strengthening of the Soviet Union and the new democracies in Europe had politically weakened the hold of imperialism. But on the other hand, the emergence of the USA as the dominant imperialist power, with its vast accumulated capital controlling three-fifths of the world's capitalist production, acted as a rallying point for all the remaining reactionary forces in Europe. In this situation, Britain held a key position. Said Pollitt:

> Upon its policy depends, not only the solution of the home problems that confront the people but also the peace of the world. The present policy of the government, combining with American imperialism in a bloc against the USSR and the new democracies in Europe, lending armed and diplomatic support to reaction in Greece and Spain, concerting a common plan for rebuilding German capitalism, using imperilaist force in the Middle East, India and Indonesia, not only endangers the success of the United Nations and

the stability of world peace, but intensifies every problem of home reconstruction. The Labour government's policy of maintaining the old imperialist commitments beyond the economic strength and manpower of the country, and relying on cheap imported foreign labour, and trying to solve the crisis without any real and drastic encroachments on the system of capitalist profit and privilege is leading to disaster.

Later in his report, Pollitt introduced the Communist Party's solution to the fuel crisis: its plan for coal, which was considered by the Party to be the crux of the production problem. "What Britain needs," he said, "is an overall economic plan... But no plan will work without coal:"

> The reasons for the present crisis are clear and unchallengeable. They are: first, the delay in the nationalisation of the mines; second, the unsatisfactory composition of the coal board; third, the gamble on the weather during January and February, despite knowledge of the five million tons deficit and the urgent warnings of the miners' leaders and the Communist Party; fourth, the compromise policy towards big business and in particular Britain's foreign policy; and fifth, a complete lack of faith in the creative powers and political understanding of the working class....
> What is immediately necessary? 1. Firmer control of the industry in the hands of the workers and Labour movement; 2. Measures to attract manpower and to keep production enthusiasm at the highest possible point; 3. The speediest mechanisation and modernisation of the pits; 4. Efficient transport; 5. Allocation to priority users in industry and home, drastic economies and the maintenance of fuel economies for the next nine months in particular.

On the subject of controls, the Communist Party advocated the appointment of "an Emergency Committee with plenary powers" comprising miners' representatives, representatives of the government, and managers' and deputies' organisations. Its chairman should be a leading miner.

Pit consultative councils should be established, meeting weekly and reporting direct to Regional Emergency Committees. The production target should be 220 million tons annually. Drastic measures should be taken to ensure the necessary machinery and manpower be found to make it possible to reach such a target.

Pollitt pointed out that the country needed another 100,000 miners but that men were not coming forward because of the poor wages and conditions in the industry. In 1947 a miner on haulage earned a weekly wage of £5 and a craftsman working underground earned £5.6s. compared with £5.10s. for a building craftsman and £6.3s. for an engineer on minimum piecework. Pollitt called for a system of bonus payments to be worked out giving the miner at least 25 per cent above time rates as well as special reductions in income tax. On the question of cost Pollitt said:

> It would cost a fraction of what the general crisis has cost already, or the amount we are spending on keeping British lads in Greece, Palestine, India and other places, where they are not wanted, and where they ought not to be.

More cutting and loading machines were urgently needed. An article in the *Financial Times* on the 20th January, 1947, had revealed that only one per cent of the coal cut in 1945 had been mechanically loaded. By using machines, production could be raised by 70 per cent or even more. According to the *Financial Times*: "An order for 50 machines was placed over two years ago: and it may surprise many to learn that only 18 are actually at work today producing some 36,000 tons of coal a week, although 56 projects have been approved.... We therefore demand the most drastic measures to organise the engineering industry for the rapid output of mining machinery."

As for transport, Pollitt deplored the concept of ministerial circles that nothing could be done until the railways had been nationalised. "The railways," he said, " should be requisitioned now. Luxury travel, the Pullman trains and the Golden Arrows, should be cut out. Priority for coal trains should be the order of the day." In the meantime, road transport should be fully used.

Dealing with the economy as a whole, Pollitt noted that although every other progressive country in Europe had a National Economic Plan, "a practical, binding plan for production over the next two, three or four years, a plan known and understood by the whole people," here there was no such thing:

We are fully aware that in Britain, where capitalism is still the basis of its economy, there cannot be the same kind of planning on a one hundred per cent scale as there is in the Socialist Soviet Union; but the decisive question is, are we taking over the key points in industry on the basis of a plan and at the same time compelling the rest of industry to adjust itself to the main purpose of such a plan? The position is, in fact, that isolated industries are being nationalised without being related to any national plan....

What kind of plan do we need? First, while in the existing political conditions we cannot achieve complete planning in every industry, we can and must make sure of meeting key needs. The nationalised state sector of our economy can play a great part in this and must be immediately extended.

Second, we need much firmer controls to make sure that the private capitalists are compelled to work within the framework of the national plan and are not allowed to throw it out of gear.

Third, the plan depends upon the political conviction of the working people that it can be carried through in spite of the resistance or sabotage by the capitalists. It will succeed only if it is made clear to the workers from the outset that as the plan advances it will strengthen and improve their position and weaken that of the employers - that its fruits are higher wages and increased living standards and not increased profits.

Later in his report, Pollitt explained why it was necessary to support nationalisation as part of the fight for planned production for the people as a whole:

We know that nationalisation under present conditions is not yet socialism. It does not yet end class divisions and the drawing of rent, interest and profit by the exploiting class. This basic change has still to be achieved. The value of nationalisation of a series of key industries in the present reconstruction programme lies in the extent to which it serves as a lever to carry through economic planning in the interests of the people, to weaken monopoly capitalism and to strengthen the working-class movement.

To achieve effective economic planning and control, we believe nationalisation should be extended, not only to the basic auxiliary industries of coal, power and transport serving the interests of capitalist industry as a whole by the more efficient service that nationalisation can provide, but should reach into the sphere of basic productive heavy industry by the nationalisation of steel.

Turning to the fight for peace, Pollitt regretted that the Labour government had so far completely failed to pursue a socialist peace policy:

> We have only to look at its record in relation to Greece, Spain, Indonesia, Palestine and the Middle East as a whole to appreciate this fact. The Labour Government has, moreover, maintained its armed forces in the Empire, refused real independence to India and Burma, failed to operate the Potsdam decisions, shown hostility to the new democracies in Europe, allowed its relations with the Soviet Union to deteriorate, and actively built an Anglo-American alliance.

In explaining "the meaning and aim of American imperialist policy," Pollitt quoted from a statement, published in the August, 1946 issue of *Political Affairs*, made by William Z. Foster, Chairman of the Communist Party of the USA:

> The major objectives of American imperialism are to reduce the British Empire to a subordinate position; to cow or smash the USSR; to subjugate China to the status of a satellite country; to reduce Latin America to a semi-colonial system of the United States; to take charge of the internal economics of Germany, Japan and various other countries; to dominate the Atlantic and Pacific oceans with its big navy and air force - in short, to establish American imperialist hegemony over the other peoples and areas of the world.

"Those who have followed the discussions at various Peace Conferences, in the Security Council and General Assembly of the United Nations," continued Pollitt, "see that American policy is simply designed to achieve the aim of world imperialist domination. That is what lies behind Anglo-American policy in relation to the Danubian states, or the Trieste question, or Greece, and the hostility of the British and American governments to the Soviet Union and the new European democracies."

Pollitt recognised that there were "many points of difference between British and American interests, which can become sources of major conflicts." He instanced as examples the need for markets and the struggle for oil in the Near and Middle East. "Why then," he asked, "is Britain's policy so completely subservient to America?" He thought that the answer to this question lay in the fact that since the British Empire was no longer strong enough by itself to wage a struggle for its former position of world supremacy, it had to accept the role of junior partner to the more powerful United States of America.

The idea of a United States of Europe, excluding the Soviet Union and the democratic peoples' republics of course, was actively canvassed by the more aggressive powers in western Europe; and wholeheartedly supported by the USA. The aims behind the idea were set out in a speech made in America by John Foster Dulles. Pollitt considered the comments upon this speech, made by the *Observer* on the 19th January, 1947, worth quoting in his report to the 19th Congress of the CPGB:

> He [Dulles] was frank in basing his arguments on the need for providing a check to Russian expansion and in particular the advance of communism. Despite the triumph of American diplomacy under Mr. Byrnes in the past year, he [Dulles] said: "in most of the world, effective popular leadership is in the hands of persons who are sympathetic to Soviet communist doctrines, and who turn to Moscow for moral support." To counter communism, Mr. Foster Dulles called for American "spiritual and intellectual vigour - and the leadership which that bestows."

Pollitt pointed out that although the Labour government denied "identification with any particular bloc or grouping" there was, nevertheless, the Anglo-American military alliance, the unity of purpose of the British and American policies in Austria and their co-operation in the building up of German monopoly capitalism by merging the British and American zones of occupation in that country. "But," continued Pollitt, "the peoples of the world are determined that the wheels of history are not going to be turned back." He found encouragement in the fact that the world forces fighting for peace were then much stronger, more united and better organised than they were in the aftermath of the First World War:

> Think of the strength of the Soviet Union. Think of the Balkan lands, no longer puppets in the game of imperialist power politics;

the influence of France with its Communist Party of over a million members.... In Germany, instead of fascism, we see a Socialist Unity Party of 1.6 million members and a growing Communist Party in the Rhineland. In Italy [there is] a Communist Party with a membership of over two millions and a firm united front agreement with the Italian Socialist Party.

In Japan, too, the Communist Party is developing. Large areas of China are under communist leadership, the National Liberation movements are playing their part in the fight for peace, and we can take great pride in the work of the Communist Parties of India and South Africa....

All these are the new world forces fighting for peace, world forces that can be relied upon to resist every attempt to undermine the unity of the United Nations and to see that its important decisions and those of all conferences of Foreign Ministers are translated into action.

On the negative side, however, Pollitt was compelled to draw attention to the sabotage, by Britain and America, of the decisions of the Yalta and Potsdam conferences, in support of which he proposed a ten-point programme that included the ending of British financial, military and political support for reaction in Greece; an end to British diplomatic and trade relations with Franco-Spain; and an end to Britain's imperialist policy in India and in all colonial and mandated territories.

Membership of the Communist Party of Great Britain at the end of March, 1946, the latest figure available before the 19th National Congress of February, 1947, was 42,143. Figures for the circulation of the *Daily Worker* were not given but the withdrawal of recent newsprint restrictions in September, 1946, had enabled its management to increase the size of the paper to six pages daily and to launch a circulation drive "aimed at winning 50,000 new readers by the end of the year." In the Political Resolution passed by the Congress, it was agreed to call for a campaign to raise the circulation of the *Daily Worker* to 150,000 copies a day. If this were to be achieved by the addition of 50,000 new readers, as called for in the *Report of the Executive Committee*, it meant that the circulation was already standing at 100,000.

In a book published in August, 1947,[13] Harry Pollitt included a chapter headed *The British Road to Socialism*. In it he said: "Marxists have never maintained that the road to socialism in any country is neatly mapped-out and time-tabled, that each country will pass to socialism in the same way and at the same speed, with similar forms of state organisation, with similar methods of overcoming opposition. Communists have never said that the Russian Revolution of October, 1917, is a model which has to be exactly copied." He rightly stated:

> The progress of democratic and socialist forces thoughout the world has opened out new possibilities of transition to socialism by other paths than those followed by the Russian Revolution.

These "new possibilities," of course, could not be denied. The danger lay in coming to regard them as "probabilities" and relying upon them as such; in planning exclusively for a parliamentary road to socialism. The first edition of *The British Road to Socialism*, however, as a programme, was not to appear until 1951. In the meantime, Pollitt seemed to have no illusions about the way in which the people's democracies in Europe were advancing towards their goals.

"If the people of eastern Europe have found new roads," he wrote, "it is because in the course of the war they fought with such heroism and with such success, not only against the aggressive forces of fascism, but also against their own landowners, bankers, industrialists and quislings. It is because, also, the strength of the Soviet Union protected them from the intervention of foreign reaction, and allowed the people in these countries to develop freely along the path they had freely chosen." To which he added, significantly: "The strength of the progressive forces in the world makes the advance to socialism easier in every country, but in the last analysis the character of transition is determined by the unity and strength of the working-class and democratic movements within each country. Socialism is not an article of export, and each people must move to socialism in its own way."

In the light of the foregoing facts, Pollitt then proceeded to analyse the situation in Britain after two years of a Labour government, elected for the first time with an overwhelming majority of seats in the House of Commons.

He recognised that, as yet, capitalist control of the state was, in fact,

---

[13]*Looking Ahead* by Harry Pollitt.

substantially untouched. The economy was still overwhelmingly capitalist. The secret police, military intelligence and the heads of the Civil Service remained virtually unchanged. "Our ambassadors," he wrote, "are still from Eton and Oxford, with even Harrow and Cambridge a small minority."

He pointed out that the full economic programme of the Labour government only envisaged the nationalisation of 20 per cent of British industry, and even that was a long way off. "The wealth of the nation and the power of the state," he said, "are still, in spite of two years of Labour government, for the most part in the hands of the old ruling class." Later, in the chapter on *The British Road to Socialism*, he added the following:

> We should have no illusions that the capitalists will gracefully accept such changes. We know from experience in this and all countries that no ruling class ever allows power to slip from its influence without furious and prolonged resistance. Socialism will never be given on a plate. But in the measure to which the Labour movement is united, in the measure to which it presses forward energetically for the fulfilment of its programme, the development of a general economic plan, extended nationalisation, reduction of rent, interest and profit, democratisation of the armed forces, the courts and the state, increased working-class and popular control of industry, new recruitment of personnel from the Labour movement for every part of the state machine - to that measure it will succeed in changing Britain. In that measure it will reduce the power of the capitalist class, increase the power and control of the workers and the people, and carry Britain along a new road to socialism in which British democratic institutions will be preserved and strengthened, and which will not necessarily be the road the Russian workers and peasants were compelled to take in 1917.
>
> It would be stupid to think that it is possible to map out at this time every stage of this road, but the key is the unity and determination of the Labour movement, the refusal at any stage to withdraw before counter-attacks of the capitalists, the steadfast resistance to the colonisation of Britain by the American trusts.

In a section headed *Marxism and Reformism*, Pollitt indicated that whereas the reformists in the Labour Party saw the state as a neutral organ above politics and above classes, the Communist Party saw the state as "a weapon of class power." Pollitt saw that in the Britain of 1947 the state was still operating in favour of the old ruling class.

He called for new personnel to be found at all levels and for the removal of all obstacles to the expression of the popular will by obsolete state organs. But he stopped short of calling for the arming of the working class and of the people as a safeguard against the possible resistance of the capitalist class, although he recognised that "a Labour government only means progress towards socialism to the extent that it carries on the struggle for removing power from the hands of the capitalist class."

On the question of foreign policy, the weakest part of the programme of the Labour government, Pollitt correctly stated:

> The reformists see foreign policy as a form of diplomatic negotiation between states; Marxists understand that states can only be judged and understood on the basis of the class that holds power in them, and that foreign policy, like home policy, is a class battle.

Chapter Six
THE MANPOWER CRISIS

ON MONDAY, the 26th May, 1947, the 46th Annual Conference of the Labour Party opened in the Winter Gardens, Margate. Altogether, 1,020 full delegates had been accredited, representing 3,631,000 members. Of these, 2,670,000 were affiliated via their trade unions and 895,000 through their individual membership of the Labour Party.

After the preliminary speeches of welcome, the Chairman of the Conference, Philip Noel-Baker MP, delivered his address, pointing out that the Labour government then in office was the first government since 1832 "not to lose a by-election for two whole years."

There is no doubt that the Labour government and the Labour Party, at that stage, still had the confidence of the people of Britain. "By every test," declared Philip Noel-Baker, "the Party is stronger than it was two years ago." The individual membership had, in fact, trebled during that period.

Since the end of the war, five million men and women had been demobilised and industry had been switched from war to peace; a million and a quarter people had been rehoused. On the subject of food, Philip Noel-Baker claimed that the ration was well above "what millions of our people could afford to buy before the war." They were rationed then, in times of plenty, by their poverty.

Referring to coal, he quoted the words of a Liberal economist who, six months earlier, had said: "A hundred thousand extra workers in the coal mines might make the difference between our continued existence as a great power, with reasonable prospects of economic progress, and a lapse into impotence and economic chaos." In reply, Philip Noel-Baker pointed out that "in eighteen weeks from Vesting Day we got 20,000 more. And the coal is coming." Nevertheless, that still left the coal mines 80,000 men short.

But peace, as the speaker well knew, was uppermost in the minds of the whole nation. "If we could end the fear of war! That's the crux on which, for our generation and for our children, all else turns.... As the Prime Minister has said, we must make the United Nations the over-riding factor in international affairs. We must make its institutions work."

One of the earliest items to be discussed during the morning session of the first day was a reference to the British Soviet Society in the National Executive Committee report, which declared membership of that society to be incompatible with membership of the Labour Party. A motion to remove the British Soviet Society from the list of proscribed organisations, moved by E.J. Squibb of the Southampton Divisional Labour Party, appeared to many to be in keeping with the appeal of the Chairman of Conference for peace. He was supported by several speakers but others opposed the motion on the grounds that membership of the British Soviet Society was open to communists. Speaking for the National Executive, Harold Clay hoped that the report would be approved. "We cannot accept the position," he said, "that when we close one door and thereby limit the possibility of providing new platforms for the Communist Party, they open another and find people in our movement who are prepared to give them assistance." The report was adopted.

F.M. Miller of St. Pancras Borough Labour Party then moved the reference back of Appendix IV, dealing with a recent visit of a delegation representing the National Executive Committee of the Labour Party to the Soviet Union as a "Goodwill Mission" during July-August, 1946. Members of the delegation had pointed out to the Chairman of the Moscow Soviet that the Labour Party in Britain had won the General Election with a tremendous majority and that the resulting government "was not only charged with the task of transferring a war economy into a peace economy but into a socialist economy." The report noted that the delegation had been received by Stalin in the Kremlin and that members of the delegation had "talked with the leader of the Russian people in an easy and conversational manner on the tasks that confronted Britain and Russia." Morgan Phillips, then Secretary of the Labour Party, had stressed "the desire of the British Labour movement and the whole of the British people for real and enduring friendship with Russia." After a general discussion, Stalin had said that he was gratified to know that our "two great countries were travelling in the socialist direction." Stalin also said that he was glad to receive the assurance of the delegation that the British people desired friendship and understanding with Russia but that he felt it would have been amazing if this had not been the case "now that we both had the same aim, the achievement of socialism."

Stalin had said that he agreed that the Labour government had

THE MANPOWER CRISIS (1947)

adopted the right line "in dealing with the public ownership of basic industries first," but that he would like to know "what were the dangers of reaction from the enemies of the Labour movement, and from the industrialists who were dispossessed as a result of the government's actions."

The reason given by F.M. Miller for moving the reference back of this stimulating, if somewhat naive, report was that it gave a false impression, i.e, "that the Soviet government represents the peoples of the Russian Empire." F.M. Miller claimed that the mass of the Russian people were against their government and that no mention was made in the report of the "slaves." He believed that "as long as there is a slave in Russia, we ourselves are not free."

F.M. Miller was followed by Harold Davies MP, who declared: "Never before in my recollection have I heard a speech like the last one coming from the rostrum of the Labour Conference. A moment ago we took a resolution on the British Soviet Society. The Conference agreed to turn down affiliation with that body. Very well, but Russia may completely misinterpret the trend of this Conference when that resolution is followed two minutes later by a speech such as we have just heard.... I appeal to you to support your executive who, I know, are as anxious for friendship with the USSR as any member of the Communist Party or anybody in the world."

Replying for the National Executive, Harold Clay said: "I think it was unfortunate that we had Mr. Miller's speech and that it came in the place that it did. With regard to the report for which my colleagues and I were responsible, we tried in a very brief compass to think about the things we saw and the things we ourselves could find out and to give some impression of the interviews we had. We went on a goodwill mission, limited to a certain extent by the time, and by the fact that there were certain people it was desirable to see if the purpose of the mission was to be achieved. We found very great friendliness, not only from those whom we met in high quarters, but in the factories we were privileged to visit.... We found a nation which had been engaged in a gigantic task in the period between the two wars, whose country over very wide areas had been devastated during the war, and which was now setting about the task of rebuilding, which will be difficult and will take a long time. We believe that Russia will be assisted in that task, and we shall be assisted in ours, to the extent to which we can create goodwill and understanding between the peoples."

The motion for the reference back was not seconded and Appendix IV was approved.

Ernest Millington MP, representing the Chelmsford Divisional Labour Party, then moved the reference back of the paragraph on the United Europe Committee in the Report of the International Department. The report officially discouraged members of the Labour Party from associating themselves with the United States of Europe Committee, whose chairman was Winston Churchill. "We heard this morning that if members of our Party associate themselves with the British-Soviet Society they impair their membership of the Labour Party," said Ernest Millington, "I believe that association with this Tory inspired anti-Soviet organisation established by Winston Churchill should even more invalidate membership of any socialist organisation.... I ask you to support a motion to refer this paragraph back to the Executive for a definite statement of policy on the question."

The motion was seconded by K. Zilliacus MP, representing Gateshead Labour Party and Trades Council, in order to draw attention to one of the publications of the International Department, *Cards on the Table*. He said that this document threw overboard "the foreign policy on which this Party was returned to power, set out in *International Postwar Settlement* and summarised in *Let Us Face The Future*...."

R.H.S. Crossman, representing Coventry East Divisional Labour Party, asked whether *Cards on the Table* had been approved by the National Executive; whether it was, in fact, an official statement of policy or merely a discussion pamphlet.

Intervening in the discussion on behalf of the National Executive, Hugh Dalton MP said that *Cards on the Table* was issued "in the ordinary course, as many other documents have been issued, seeking to put in an accurate and interesting fashion, for as wide a public as it can reach, certain accepted principles, as we think and as those who drew it up think, of Labour policy."

With regard to Churchill's "United Europe" Committee, Hugh Dalton drew attention to a statement issued to the *Daily Herald* following a meeting of the National Executive Committee held on the 22nd January, 1947. The statement, signed by Morgan Phillips, had read as follows:

> The National Executive Committee at its meeting today gave consideration to the fact that members of the Labour Party were

sponsoring a new organisation under the leadership of Winston Churchill, the "United Europe" Committee. The National Executive Committee came to the conclusion that while it is desirable to encourage the maximum co-operation between the nations of Europe, it should be clear that an organisation led by Mr. Churchill is not likely to stimulate such co-operation at the present time. The Labour Party is firmly committed to the belief that the future of Europe depends on the success of the United Nations and on the strengthening of friendly collaboration between Russia, America and Britain. Mr. Churchill's Committee explicity excludes Russia from Europe, and in view of his personal record and his known opinions it is likely to be interpreted, rightly or wrongly, as aiming essentially at the elimination of Russian influence in Europe. In these circumstances, I was directed to advise members of the Labour Party to withhold their support from the "United Europe" Committee and to concentrate such of their energy as is not absorbed in direct work for the Party on organisations such as the United Nations Association, whose aims and inspiration are above suspicion,"

The policy of the Labour Party on the issues raised by Messrs. Millington and Zilliacus having been clearly stated, the reference back was defeated. It was obvious, nevertheless, that there were some members of the Labour Party prepared to tag along behind Churchill whose anti-Soviet policy, not yet full-blown, was already beginning to take shape.

Another issue that caused some of the delegates concern was the proposal to extend the operation of the National Service Act from 1949, when it was scheduled to end, until 1954. This was discussed on a motion moved by V.F. Yates MP, representing the Ladywood Divisional Labour Party, which expressed the strongest disapproval of military conscription and urged the Labour government to abandon it.

The main arguments against conscription appeared to be: a. that the Labour Party had always been against it, and b. that "no mandate for conscription was obtained from the country, the trade union movement or the Labour Party." This from the speech of the seconder of the motion, John S. Worrall of the Attercliffe Divisional Labour Party. The same points were made over and over with little or no reference to the foreign policy that had made conscription necessary, though Sidney Silverman MP, came near to the point when he said:

I do not believe, in spite of the new-fashioned socialism of London University, that you can really divide questions of defence policy from questions of international policy, nor do I believe that the question of whether you can raise your forces by conscription or by voluntary means has any relation to the number of men you require. . . .

Tomorrow we shall have a debate on economic affairs. We have debated them in the House of Commons. We gave three days to the economic White Paper, another day to the Army estimates, another to the Service estimates. And what was the burden of it all? That in this great creative revolution through which the world is passing . . . our country is on the verge of collapse for want of 600,000 men. What serice will these conscripts render during these years to justify our adding this burden to the burden that industry already carries.

Speaking in support of the motion, Miss Edna Falkingham, representing the Union of Shop, Distributive and Allied Workers said: "I should like to recall Mr. Morrison's speech in November on economic hurdles and bottlenecks. He said that bottleneck number one was manpower, and bottleneck number two was coal; and that our voice in the world's councils would be more powerful if we had thirty million tons of coal in reserve than if we had a whole cluster of atom bombs." Replying for the National Executive, Harold Laski said:

The alternatives are simple and direct ones: either to recruit the Army in the old way, the way of poverty and hunger and unemployment, or to recruit the Army by giving to its members privileges so outstanding that it becomes a special caste in the community as a whole. There is no historic ground for the argument that where democracy and conscription are united there must develop tyranny on the one hand and militarism on the other. . . . Referring to a previous speech, he asked: "Does Mr. Silverman really think that the Prime Minister and the Chancellor of the Exchequer and the Lord President of the Council and their colleagues are going to jeopardise the experiment upon which the whole future of this movement depends, that in fixing the necessary number of men required to safeguard our commitment to the United Nations . . . they are deliberately building up a great armed force in order to wreck the experiment of which they are the architects and in a very special

THE MANPOWER CRISIS (1947)

sense the guardians? I may be forgiven for saying that into the minds of many of those who spoke in favour of this resolution there are lurking shadows of a past that history has made obsolete.

But as a previous speaker, Miss Falkingham of USDAW, had said: "We are told of our commitments, but we have never yet been told what our commitments are." It also has to be said that some of the replies given by Harold Laski to those who were supporting the motion were also affected by the shadows of past history. On a card vote the motion was lost by 2,332,000 votes to 571,000.

The question of manpower came up again on the morning of Wednesday, the 28th May, during the discussion on the report of the National Executive entitled *Labour for Higher Production*. Moving the adoption of the report, Herbert Morrison confined himself almost entirely to generalisations, with no specifics and only one statistic. "My main point," he said, "is that we, like the Russians, are pursuing a deliberate policy of 'less today for more tomorrow.' If we don't, tomorrow will be a more miserable affair than today. And none of us want that." He prepared the delegates for a further tightening of working-class belts by explaining why it was not possible to tax the wealthy any further:

> There are some sections of the community which are being pretty severely tested at this moment. It won't do us any harm to remember that, and to show a little understanding.... Of the employing class we are asking and indeed insisting that they should do more than bow to the inevitability of controls and planning.... We are asking them to run their businesses within much narrower limits of discretion than those which they have been used to and for a net reward which, in real spendable terms, is less than they have been accustomed to.... Of the managers and technicians in industry we are asking something else, also very difficult in its way. We are asking not so much a change of loyalties but a development and a deepening of their allegiance, so that they think of themselves first and foremost as servants of the community.... They too are being asked to devote their brains and skill and experience to the common task for rewards which, after taxation and in terms of what they can buy, are, for the time being, worth a good bit less than formerly. And that brings me to the position of the whole of the so-called middle class which has, for some time past, been experiencing a painful and difficult

reduction in their living standards, I know very well that their incomes are often (though not always) higher than those of workpeople. But after all it isn't any easier for anyone to do without all sorts of comforts. Many of this great middle class voted for us two years ago.

Did this sound more like an apology for letting the business community and the "great middle class" down than a simple statement of fact? On the subject of class generally, Morrison had this to say:

> Only forty years ago this was a completely class-ridden country, and everyone, including the bulk of the working class, accepted this as a law of nature. Today we have got a widespread national acceptance of the goal of social equality and economic democracy as the right and proper goal for our country to set before itself. This is so big an achievement that we are apt to miss it altogether....
> I know very well that there are still great inequalities and some bad examples of luxury spending even in our austere community today. But the fact remains that 90 per cent of our people who have the lower incomes command 67 per cent of our total national purchasing power today as compared with 55 per cent before the war.

This, of course, was the solitary statistic in Herbert Morrison's speech to which I referred earlier. Granted that it was an improvement on the pre-war situation, a step in the right direction, it still meant that 10 per cent of "our people," those who had the higher incomes, were still commanding 33 per cent of "our total national purchasing power."

But if Morrison's speech was short on specifics, the shortage was more than made up in the long debate on the relevant motions that followed. Calling for "more, not less, socialist planning and control of industry," Tom Sargeant, representing the Hampstead Divisional Labour Party and moving a composite motion in their name, said: "Socialist economics mean seeing and dealing with our problems as a whole in real physical terms, with all the money-juggling, all the manoeuvres for private profit, all the waste of duplicated effort, cut down to a minimum." Said Fred Lee, MP for Hulme:

> So far as the future is concerned, can we really expect the workers of the country to believe such slogans as "We work or want"

THE MANPOWER CRISIS (1947)

when we see so many people who are neither working nor wanting....

We are in a position in which we have only two productive workers to every five people in industry.... At the end of hostilities, very many women who were doing a most important job of work went out of engineering. We find many of them now are working in the football pools, getting far greater remuneration than the engineering industry can offer. Having regard to this disparity so far as the miners, engineers and other people upon whom we have to depend are concerned, the government must pass some measure, either to stop further people getting into those unproductive jobs or giving better incentives in the way of reduced taxation, and so on, to those who agree to remain in heavy industries which are so vital to us all.

Moving "that this Conference believes it imperative, in view of our manpower and production problems, that we review our military commitments and the distribution and organisation of the Armed Forces, in order that they may be reduced considerably...." Harold Davies MP, representing the Leek Divisional Labour Party, said: "This issue is not the issue of conscription. I am one of the people who voted for National Service. We are concerned with the proposed size of our peace-time Forces and their relation to our economy and to our defence."

The motion was seconded by Ian Mikardo MP, representing the Reading Trades Council and Labour Party, who referred to the speech made by Harold Davies MP, and said:

> He mentioned our balance of trade. I think he is quite right in saying that at some time between now and our next Annual Conference we shall have to take another American loan - and this time it will be on their terms - we shall have to tighten our belts furiously, or we shall have to cut down on our military expenditure. Where does this deficit in our balance of trade come from? Not from importing food, or raw materials, or machinery. In 1946 our expenditure on overseas commitments - military commitments - on soldiers, troops and their administration overseas, was almost exactly the same as the amount by which we overspent on our import-export balance....
>
> A few days ago Ernest Bevin said in the House of Commons that

if we cut down our military commitments in the Middle East, it would lower the pay packet of every British worker. That is not only not true; it is the very opposite of the truth. For one thing, nobody is suggesting that we should cut right out of the Middle East, and nobody is suggesting that we should do without Middle East imports. But nobody is going to convince me that we cannot buy oil from Iraq, cotton from Egypt and oranges from Palestine without having 200,000 soldiers standing by to watch the deal being done. We did it before the war with less than one-tenth of that number. I say to the Foreign Secretary, and I say it with respect, that he ought to take some of his own advice and go down to his working-class housewife constituents in Wandsworth and tell them that they cannot get cups and saucers because they have gone abroad to pay for hundreds of new barracks in the deserts on both sides of the Suez Canal.

The essence of this speech was underlined by Richard Crossman MP, representing the Coventry East Divisional Labour Party. "The question of the eighteen months' service does not affect the economic crisis at all," he said, "as the Act comes into force in 1949. What we are concerned with is the 1.1 million men still in the forces next month, and we are asking you to tell the Cabinet that that is too many. We are not saying that there are not risks involved. But this country is faced with two sorts of risks today - with strategic and economic risks; and the economic risks this next eighteen months, the period with which we are now concerned, are greater that the strategic risks...." Continuing, he went on to say:

I listened to Morrison with great interest and enthusiasm, and then I began to think that he should have told us what we are going to do to face the crisis when the dollars run out. There are only two sorts of dollar expenditure of a really large sort. One is on food, the other is on foreign commitments. You can either cut down the number of your troops abroad or the amount of food you can import.

Speaker after speaker called upon the government to get its priorities right and to release men from the armed forces. Or as it was put in a motion moved by G.P. Wilson, representing the Cannock Divisional Labour Party: "so to reorientate its foreign policy as to enable a substantial reduction to be made in the numbers of the armed forces, thereby making a substantial increase in the available manpower for industry."

THE MANPOWER CRISIS (1947)

The debate continued in the afternoon with a number of thoughtful contributions but it was left to A. Naesmith of the United Textile Factory Workers Association to bring home the full significance of the need for increased coal production. He said:

> The shortage of coal made itself evident in the national textile industry in the latter part of December and it gradually intensified the difficulties of the industry during January and February. There are mills in Lancashire where the textile operatives have drawn only five week's pay out of fourteen weeks during the period when the coal crisis was upon us. The supply of yarn, which is the life blood of the manufacturing industry, fell from 13.5 million pounds per week to something like 4 million pounds per week.... Our economic survival is dependent entirely upon our mining friends.

Replying to the discussion on behalf of the National Executive, Hugh Dalton MP admitted that "there are too many people in some industries and too few in others." He asked: "How could it be otherwise, in view of the fact that we are only gradually crawling out of capitalist chaos into socialist order?"

On the morning of Thursday, the 29th May, Koni Zilliacus opened the debate on International Policy. It centred around a long composite motion, reproduced here in full simply because it is both a statement of what Labour policy ought to have been and an irrefutable argument for its implementation:

> This Conference congratulates the government on its decision to base British foreign policy on the United Nations Organisation, and recalls that the Charter of UNO is based on the fundamental principal that the permanent Security Council members, and particularly Britain, the USA and the USSR must co-operate as equal partners and must trust each other to keep the peace.
> It urges the government to give a lead in applying this principal by instructing the Service Departments to frame their estimates and make their strategic dispositions on the assumption that Britain need not prepare for self-defence against either the USA or the USSR.
> This Conference recognises the importance of the closest relations with the USA but regrets the emergence of rival groups, and feels that it is equally vital to secure the closest co-operation with the

USSR and thus enable the Twenty Years Treaty to become a reality.

It believes that subservience to capitalist America will inevitably draw us into an anticipated slump, and that the only way to avoid this is to co-operate with all the countries with socialist planned economies.

In pursuance of these aims, This Conference pledges its wholehearted support to a foreign policy based on the Labour Party's report on International Postwar Settlement, framed by the National Executive Committee, adopted by the Annual Conference in December, 1944, and summarised in *Let Us Face the Future*, on which the Party won the General Election.

Said Zilliacus, in moving the above motion:

Yesterday the Chancellor of the Exchequer made an extraordinarily serious statement to this Conference and to the country. He told us that the American loan is running out, and that in order to make ends meet we shall have to cut our imports, which means lowering our standard of living, except in so far as we can increase production so as to pay our way in the world ... and that means, in homely language, a cut in our food rations or a cut in our Forces, because in order to increase our production and do more trade with the rest of the world we must have more manpower, and the only place where we can get our manpower is in the Forces....

On the 18th November of last year, the Prime Minister said in the House that nobody in the government was foolish enough to entertain the idea that we could measure up armaments with either the USA or the USSR. If that is true, and if we base our policy on the Charter, there is no reason why we should not cut our Forces drastically....

This country does not love experts, and quite rightly I think. Therefore, when people want to put you off listening to what I have to say, they accuse me of being an expert in foreign affairs. I am not an expert in foreign affairs. I am someone who has lived in the fight for peace through most of my life. There is one thing that I have carried away from that, and that is that peace will never be saved by the experts. It will not come from the brass hats, from the diplomats, from the governments. It will come only from the workers, and from the unity and the brotherhood of the workers.

THE MANPOWER CRISIS (1947)

A motion from the Orpington Divisional Labour Party regretted "the policy in Greece, which has resulted in putting and maintaining in power a reactionary government" and expressed the hope "that the government will withdraw our troops from their untenable situation, and thus take a very necessary step in the reduction of our military commitments...."

In moving this motion, S.H. Hassell explained: "What this resolution really says is that we followed the Tory policy in Greece and we have come unstuck. Having done so, let us go to the country and say 'we make mistakes sometimes and particularly when we follow Tory policy, but we are prepared to say so and to face the consequences....' The resolution says that there is a reactionary government in Greece. There is no doubt about that. It also says that we must withdraw our troops from their untenable situation, and by that we mean withdraw them and not wait until America is ready to step in. We mean *withdraw* and not replace."

Seconding the motion, Margaret Shuffeldt, representing the Chelsea Divisional Labour Party, said that she had been in Greece during January and February, and that food was not getting through to whole areas of the country. "We found," she said, "in the north of Greece alone that 100,000 people who were eligible under the school feeding programme had not had anything since May, 1946, just because they were in areas that were thought to be 'left-wing' areas. There are still thousands of detainees in the prisons in Greece and they are there without any trial.... All we ask is that we should carry out the recommendations of the All-Party Parliamentary Delegation that went there in August. They want everybody to come out and Greece to be free."

Other motions moved in conjunction with the Report on International Policy included one calling for the abolition of zone control in Germany and the development of a united Germany, administered by a democratically elected government. During the discussion, R.H.S. Crossman MP, revealed that the cost of control in the British Zone alone came to £150 million.

Another motion urged "the speedy replacement of Foreign Office officials and representatives of His Majesty's government at home and abroad by people more in touch with the aspirations of the common people." Moving the motion, on behalf of the National Union of Vehicle Builders, R.H. Edwards said: "If we are going to operate a new socialist machine of diplomacy, then we must have people operating foreign affairs at our Consulates and Embassies who have a sympathetic attitude towards us as a socialist movement."

Seconding the motion, Fred Ward, representing the Waterloo Trades Council and Labour Party, asked: "How can you expect a Tory to carry out even a piece of socialist policy with enthusiasm?" Elaborating, he proceeded to give a few examples: "We have Duff Cooper in Paris. He was a flop even when he was put there by his own people. We have Mr. Leeper in Greece. From what I gather, he is one of the pillars of the Carlton Club. Can we expect him to carry out work for the Labour Party in an enthusiastic manner? On the other side we have Cavendish-Bentinck who was recently sent from Poland. Are they the types of people fit to represent us abroad?"

On the whole, the discussion throughout the debate showed that the rank and file delegates had a good knowledge of what was going on in the world and a better understanding of what was required of a socialist government than the right-wing leadership.

Replying to the discussion, the Rt. Hon. Ernest Bevin, Foreign Secretary, immediately reduced the issue to one of confidence in his handling of Britain's foreign policy. "All that I ask this Conference to do," he pleaded, "is to be quite straight with me and either support the policy or reject it." Obviously he did not believe that the Labour Party Conference had any part to play in shaping it.

After noting that the discussion to which he was replying had centred, in the main, "around Europe, Palestine, the Dardenelles, and very slightly around the Middle East," he extended the terms of reference for his reply by raising the question of peace in the Far East and immediately announced that "the methods adopted at Potsdam ... will not be satisfactory in dealing with the Peace Treaty for Japan."

Coming at last to the Gateshead motion moved by Koni Zillliacus, Bevin said of the mover: "He told us he was not an expert. I thought that his resolution, however, must have been drafted by an expert in deception. He put in it, in the first few words, what everybody would accept, and he put everything else further on - which the government cannot accept." Bevin invited delegates to look at the second paragraph. "It urges the government to give a lead in applying this principal by instructing the Services Departnment to frame their estimates and make their strategic dispositions on the assumption that Britain need not prepare for self-defence against either the USA or the USSR. If that is accepted, what is the assumption? The assumption is that that is what we have been doing.... We are doing nothing of the kind, and I cannot accept what is implied...." Then, turning to criticisms of the policy of the Labour government on Greece, he said:

> Three members of the party were in the Coalition War Cabinet. They accepted the agreement of going into Greece. I do not apologise for it. It was the right thing to do. A civil war broke out. As to who promoted that war - well, you will know, the evidence has been so clear. Our troops got involved....[14]

On the question of diplomatic personnel, Bevin claimed he was "reorganising the whole business." There were now four trade unionists on the Committee of the Civil Service Commission that was selecting them:

> I have looked through the list of the young men who have been admitted since I have been in office.... There is not one entry from Harrow and only one from Eton.... Reference has been made to Rex Leeper, who was in Greece. He was doing there what he was told. Then he went to Argentina, where he did another job and helped to co-ordinate all the negotiations with the Argentines which brought off that very good agreement.... Then our friend Bentinck in Poland was referred to. He had a very difficult time with the Poles. They had promised to do certain things at Potsdam, and these were not done. They were helped on, however, and the next day we were denounced as being the Western Bloc and as doing everything else the critics could lay their tongues to.

Referring to the fact that a good deal of time had been taken up with Germany, he tried to explain the difficulties involved in making Germany a united homgeneous entity. "When we found we could not get economic unity, we carried out the fusion of the two [British and American] zones," he said. "Our one aim and object has been not to divide Europe. I went to Moscow believing that on this matter it ought to be possible to carry through full economic unity."[15]

Bevin then read out a long statement that had been issued in Berlin

---

[14] See pages 289 *et seq* of *War of Liberation* by Ernie Trory, for the full story of these unhappy events.

that very afternoon:

> As is well known, we unfortunately failed at Moscow to agree on the economic unity of Germany. We do not regard this disagreement as final and shall continue to work for economic unity as laid down in the Potsdam Agreement but our temporary failure to reach agreement has naturally made it imperative that we should overhaul the machinery for treating the British and American zones as an economic unit so as to make it function as efficiently as possible and so as to reduce the burdens falling on the British and American taxpayers and to bring nearer the day when imports of food and raw materials into Germany can be paid for by German exports. I am glad to be able to announce that agreement has just been reached between the British and American representatives in Germany to set up new machinery for this purpose. This is not the time to go into details of the plan, but it may interest you to have a general outline.
>
> There is to be an Economic Council selected by the provincial parliaments. Operating under the policies of this council is a full-time co-ordinating and executive body known as the Executive Committee. Under the Executive Committee are several bi-zonal departments headed by Executive Directors and dealing with special economic functions such as finance, food, and agriculture, transport, etc. Decisions of the Economic Council and of the Executive Committee are to be taken by a majority. The functions of the Economic Council will be to direct the permissable economic reconstruction of the two zones and for this purpose to promulgate ordinances subject to joint UK-US Military Government approval. The sphere within which these organisations will operate is exactly the same as that of the existing bi-zonal agencies. In accordance with the principal of decentralisation in administration, to which we attach the greatest importance, the maximum use will be made of the *Land* or province governments for the implementation of the ordinances.
>
> We hope by this machinery to achieve the central direction necessary for greater economic efficiency without infringing the

---

[15] For the full story of this and subsequent events see *Socialism in Germany* by Ernie Trory.

THE MANPOWER CRISIS (1947)

independence of local governments, which are an essential part of the democratic structure which we are trying to build in Germany.

The British and American military governments will delegate the greatest possible responsibility to the German agencies which are to be set up, but it will of course be necessary for powers of control to be retained and these will be carried out by bi-partite Anglo-American boards at the different levels.

We cannot guarantee that this new machinery will produce immediate results, but we are satisfied that it forms the best possible framework in which the Germans may really get down to the urgent tasks of reconstruction which are essential both for improvement of their own conditions, and for the restoration of more normal economic conditions in Europe.

And so, despite assurances to the contrary, another important step towards the division of Germany was taken by the western powers. "I repeat once more," insisted Bevin, "that the establishment of this machinery does not in any way constitute a final division of Germany into two halves but is a temporary expedient forced on us by the refusal of other powers to agree to the genuine economic unity of the whole country." History was to decree otherwise, but only the more far-seeing delegates to the Margate Conference of the Labour Party could see this in 1947.

On the question of dismissing Nazis from key positions in the Anglo-American zone of Germany, a policy that had already been put into operation in the Soviet zone, Bevin had this to say:

> It is true that the Germans are a very efficient people, but I would impress upon you that many of the most efficient were the Nazis, whereas the people we have had to bring back from the concentration camps and to put into certain positions, are very good men, but a man does not feel quite as good after he has been in a concentration camp for three or four years. That does interfere to a very large extent with the efficiency of Germany, and therefore it is necessary to exercise some patience in that field.

Did Bevin mean to exercise patience while the men from the concentration camps were mastering their new jobs, or to exercise patience while the Nazis remained in their responsible positions. Even as late as 1959, twelve years after Bevin's appeal for patience, there were no less than 800 of Hitler's Special Court Judges and Military Judges in positions of responsibility in the west German judicial system, although it had been proven that they had been found guilty of terrible crimes during the Nazi period, including the passing of death sentences on both Germans and non-Germans for their democratic and anti-fascist activities.

At the end of the debate on international policy votes were taken on the various motions. The Gateshead motion, on cutting the defence forces in order to provide more manpower for industry was defeated, as was the Orpington motion on Greece. The Guildford motion, calling, among other things, for "a politically and economically united Germany, administered by a democratically elected government, was carried. But whether this was in the face of Bevin's announcement of the economic merging of the British and American zones, or through lack of understanding of the significance of the move so skilfully disguised by Bevin, was uncertain.

The Conference ended with debates on Housing, the National Health Service and Education. Some good points were made but it all came back in the end to a question of economics. Unless cuts were made both in the manpower requirements of the armed forces and its consquent financial requirements, no progress could be made in raising the standard of living of male and female workers in industry, on the land and in the public sector. Thus, although a motion demanding the immediate operation of equal pay for men and women in public employment was carried against the advice of the National Executive by a four-fifths majority, its implementation was immediately rejected by the Labour Cabinet on the grounds that it would cost £24 million with the consequent danger of inflation - an argument which, as Palme Dutt pointed out in his *Notes of the Month* in the July issue of *Labour Monthly* only had weight on the basis of the assumption that £900 million, more than three times the pre-war figure, had to be spent on the armed forces. Summing up, Dutt wrote:

> It is true that the Margate Labour Party Conference was no longer as light-hearted as Bournemouth a year earlier in blandly ignoring the crisis confronting Britain amid a sunshine atmosphere of rosy illusions and self-congratulation. On the contrary, the ministerial speeches at Margate were full of grim and gloomy prognostications of the desperate economic situation, the necessity to

THE MANPOWER CRISIS (1947)

prepare for more shortages and postpone demands for improved conditions, and appeals to their followers to avoid divisions and maintain confidence in the Government.

But Margate failed to offer any solution for the problems of the crisis. Margate completely failed to tackle the causes of the crisis. Apart from two positive decisions on wages policy, and a creditable minority vote on manpower, Margate failed even to attempt to evolve any comprehensive economic programme to replace the present chaos by planned development. Above all, Margate failed to deal with the tap-root of all Britain's present problems, the subordination of every issue of policy to the strategic demands of a Tory reactionary foreign policy, which is squandering Britain's resources and manpower, piling up a gigantic deficit in the balance of payments, crippling home reconstruction and home standards, alienating Britain's friends among the progressive peoples, and making Britain the catspaw of American aggresive reaction. Failure to change this policy cancelled and made ineffective any other progressive decisions.

In a speech made on the 6th June, just one week after the close of the Margate Conference, Anthony Eden said: "Mr. Bevin's foreign policy differs little, if at all, from the policy which the Conservative Party would have pursued." It included an Anglo-Spanish monetary agreement, anti-Soviet propaganda over Hungary and Bulgaria, and support with Britain-trained troops and British equipment for a full-scale military offensive by the Dutch against the Indonesian Republic.

No wonder progressive opinion in America and Europe was alarmed and concerned over the weakness of the Left in Britain, while, to quote once more from Palme Dutt's *Notes of the Month* for July, 1947:

> American anti-democratic strategy, previously disconcerted at the opposition of world opinion to the Truman Doctrine, now judges the moment ripe, after Margate, to launch the Marshall Plan, nominally for European economic reconstruction, but which the reactionary advocates of the Truman Doctrine plainly hope to use for promoting a dollar-dominated western European bloc against democracy in Europe, with western Germany as it main base, and Britain as the American agent to put it through.... At home, the Cabinet, encouraged by Morrison's speech that the rich must not be taxed any more heavily ... and that further burdens must fall on the

workers, proceeds to discuss cuts in food imports and subsidies - not as a weapon to end dependence on the dollar (this talk was bluff for the Conference), but alongside further dependence on the dollar, and as the necessary counterpart of a reactionary foreign policy, requiring cuts in the workers standards.

Chapter Seven
THE ROLE OF SOCIAL DEMOCRACY

IN AN ARTICLE in the February, 1947, issue of *Labour Monthly*, E. Varga, Director of the Institute of World Economy and Politics in Moscow, wrote:

> In the European countries, an intensive struggle to win the social-democratic movement is developing between the progressive and reactionary forces.... This struggle can best be followed from the example of Germany. A considerable part of social democracy has broken with the former policy of its party and called for unity with the communists. On the 21st-22nd April, 1946, a unity congress of the Social-Democratic and Communist Parties of Germany took place, at which a united party of the working class was formed - the Socialist Unity Party of Germany.... Despite the counter efforts of the British and American occupation authorities, the union of the social democrats and communists in the Soviet-occupied zone met with a warm response also in western Germany.
>
> Ruling circles in Britain and the USA immediately came out against the unification of communists and social democrats and are now giving decisive support to the group of reactionary social-democrat leaders headed by Schumacher, who are trying to revive the old reformist social democracy in the western zones of Germany for defence of the capitalist system of society.... Undoubtedly, the further internal political development of the capitalist countries to a considerable degree depends on the outcome of this struggle to win over social democracy and on the struggle within social democracy.

In a later article, published in the December, 1947 issue of *Labour Monthly*, James Klugmann referred to a similar struggle that had been waged against working-class unity by the right-wing leaders of the social-democratic movement prior to the war:

By their constant struggle against the unity of the working class, by their unbroken hostility to the Soviet Union, by their hatred of communism and the Communist Parties, which was greater than their hatred of capitalism or reaction, the leaders of European social-democracy, between the wars, played no small role in paving the way for Hitler, the Munich capitulation and the Second World War.

But during the war, as Klugmann pointed out in his article, "tens of thousands of members of these Social-Democratic Parties, whose countries had been attacked or occupied by Hitler, watched from afar the amazing advance of the Red Army, which they had been told by their leaders to fear or despise; in many cases (in eastern Europe for instance) they were liberated by the Red Army; they saw, too, the communists leading the movements of national liberation and resistance against the Axis, and often fought side by side with them or under their leadership. Thus socialist workers, peasants and intellectuals, vowed that never again would they return to the old theory and practice of right-wing social democracy, and that liberation would see them continuing the struggle for socialism alongside the Communist Parties."

At the end of the war, in some countries, notably in Bulgaria, Czechoslovakia, Hungary, Italy, Poland and Rumania, the Socialist Parties discarded their old leaders and elected new ones more suited to the then prevailing climate. But in other countries, especially in Belgium, Denmark, France, Holland, Sweden and western Germany, the old leaders, "who had spent the war in immigration," returned to their respective countries after the war and resumed their anti-communist activities.

Later, under pressure from Britain and the United States, and following the example of Schumacher in Germany as reported by Klugmann in the article already referred to, "small splinter groups of reactionary socialists split off from those parties that had opted for unity with the communists: Giuseppe Saragat in Italy, Titel Petrescu in Rumania, Lulcheu in Bulgaria, Karolyi Peyer in Hungary. In greater or lesser degree, on issues both practical and theoretical, the struggle of these two wings, those for and those against the unity of the working class, continues and is deepening in every European Social Democratic Party."

THE ROLE OF SOCIAL DEMOCRACY (1947)

It is on the key political issues of the present day: attitude to unity of the working class; attitude to the Soviet Union and the new democracies of eastern Europe; attitude to the expansionist policy of American imperialism; to socialist theory and to Marxism that the deep differences, in theory and in practice, between the two wings of social-democracy are most clearly expressed.

In Italy and in eastern Europe, where unity of action had been developed between the Socialist and Communist Parties, the influence of the working class was strengthened in the general political field. In his article, Klugmann instanced the Pact of Unity of Action of the 27th October, 1946, between the Italian Socialist Party and the Italian Communist Party; and the Unity Pact of the 28th November, 1946, between the Polish Socialist Party and the Polish Workers' Party, both of which laid down the basis for co-operation at all levels. Similar pacts were signed in Bulgaria, Czechoslovakia, Hungary and Rumania, which carried the movement forward.

Overtures were made to all these Socialist Parties by the British Labour Party and the American Federation of Labour with a view to coaxing them back into the arms of bourgeois democracy. But they were unable to convince them at that stage that such a course would be in their interests. Wrote Cyrankiewicz, Prime Minister of Poland and General Secretary of the Polish Socialist Party:

> Nor do we forget those who today profess a deep love for the Polish Socialist Party; but they love us, not because we are socialists. They flirt with us because, flattered by imaginary hopes, they desire that we will, in the interests of Polish reaction, start a fight, say with the Polish Workers' Party. The reactionaries hope that first we will dispose of the communists, and then, when we stand alone, reaction will be able to dispose of us.

Writing in a similar vein, Pietro Nenni, the Italian socialist leader, stated:

> The unity of the working class attracts and does not repel the middle classes; the whole nation and especially the middle classes will soon convince themselves that a strong Socialist Party working jointly with the Communist Party is the best guarantee against civil war and

totalitarianism.

That statement came from the leader of a country that had languished under the jackboots of Mussolini and his Blackshirts for some twenty years until almost the end of the Second World War.

Contrast it with the actions of Leon Blum and Guy Mollet in France, where, in the first elections after liberation the French Socialist Party and the French Communist Party had together secured an absolute majority in the new Constituent Assembly but where Blum had refused the offer of the French Communists for a Pact of Unity of Action and, under orders from America, had ejected the Communist Party, the largest political party in France, from the government in favour of a tripartite alliance with the French Catholic Party and the MRP.

In mid-August, 1947, Leon Blum called for the adoption of the Marshall Plan, initiated by the United States, and loudly proclaimed "the pure, unselfish motives of the American trusts."

There may be doubts in the minds of many as to when the so-called cold war was actually declared. Did it begin with the accession of Truman to the Presidency of the United States after the death of Roosevelt on the 12th April, 1945; or did it begin with Churchill's notorious "iron curtain" speech at Fulton, Missouri, on the 5th March, 1946? Or did it begin much earlier?

Whatever the doubts as to its origins, however, there can be no doubt that the cold war as such was finally institutionalised in Britain, albeit secretly, by the Labour government during 1947, when it set up a secret Foreign Office department, known as the Information Research Department, or IRD, "to distribute anti-communist propaganda in Britain and abroad."

Details of this operation, successfully concealed from the public for 30 years, were not officially released until 1978, when they were pursued, first by *Guardian* and *Observer* reporters, but later more relentlessly by Lyn Smith, then a tutor at the Centre for Continuing Education at the University of Sussex and a research student with the Open University.[16]

The idea was the brain-child of Christopher Mayhew, a Foreign Office Junior Minister in 1947. In a confidential paper to Ernest Bevin, dated the 17th October of that year, he proposed a covert "propaganda counter-offensive" against the Russians by means of a Foreign Office department to be formed specifically for that purpose.

Foreign Secretary Bevin did not require much convincing and nor, for that matter, did Prime Minister Attlee, who, having also received a copy of the paper, invited Mayhew down to Chequers for discussions. According to Lyn Smith:

> A meeting was held on the 18th November, 1947, to discuss Mayhew's ideas in greater detail. This was attended by Sir Orme Sargent, the Permanent Under Secretary of State, FO; Ivone Kirkpatrick, Assistant Under Secretary in charge of FO Information; and Christopher Warner, an Under Secretary in the FO.
>
> Mayhew put forward his ideas: the campaign should be as positive as possible laying stress on the merits of social democracy but, he pointed out, "we shouldn't appear as defenders of the *status quo* but should attack capitalism and imperialism along with Russian communism." In fact, at this early stage, the idea was more of a "Third Force" propaganda attacking capitalism as well as communism. This, however, was not to last for, as later documents reveal, anti-communism soon came to the fore.
>
> Mayhew also explained that stress should be laid on the weaknesses of communism rather than on its strengths. In particular Russia should be portrayed as a backward country, a land of poverty for the masses and privilege for the few. He was doubtful about making civil liberty the main platform of the counter-propaganda since this appealed largely to those already converted, namely the intelligentsia. Rather the aim should be to win the confidence of the workers and peasants and the best way of doing this was to show that there was more social justice and better living conditions for ordinary people under social democracy than under communism.

There is hardly any need for comment here. In the mid-term of a Labour government elected on a manifesto professing peace and friendship with the Soviet Union, the Labour Prime Minister and his Foreign Secretary were secretly engaged in setting up an anti-Soviet propaganda machine designed to win over the "workers and peasants" of

---

[16] Her definitive paper on IRD was published in *Millenium: Journal of International Studies*, Volume 9, No. 1, dated Spring, 1980.

the Soviet Union and those countries in central and eastern Europe that had taken the path to socialism.

Yvone Kirkpatrick was entrusted with the task of setting up IRD and recruiting the right personnel, many of whom, as Lyn Smith points out "were emigrants from 'Iron Curtain' countries, often journalists and writers." The staff of the Soviet section numbered 20 at the start but steadily rose reaching more than 60 in the 1950s after Churchill had once more become Prime Minister.

Throughout the period of the Labour government, IRD gathered information from secret service sources as well as from diplomats in overseas missions. This information, after processing, was distributed to British Ministers, MPs, trade union leaders, UN delegates and, of course, the British media - including the BBC World Service. On the 22nd January, 1948, during a debate on foreign affairs in the House of Commons, so we are informed by Lyn Smith, "Bevin made a long speech decidedly more aggressive than anything hitherto and incorporating all the main IRD themes." Bevin was not the only MP to use the "notes" provided by IRD. As Mayhew admitted in an interview with Lyn Smith: "If some anti-Stalinist MP wanted information or briefing on some subject, then we were only too happy to send him the facts."

IRD had close links with an anti-communist organisation called "Freedom First," which was run by a man called Herbert Tracey but directed by a group of influential members of the Trades Union Congress. IRD publicity material was used in a newsletter that it published and distributed to several hundred key trade union organisers. There was also an international edition of this newsletter. Lyn Smith tells us that "indirect financial aid was given by an arrangement whereby IRD purchased newsletters at a price and on a scale sufficient to guarantee its financial soundness." The "Freedom First" operation, however, came to an end when accusations were made that some of the money had been used dishonestly and a junior minister was forced to resign.

Thereafter IRD decided to concentrate on international affairs, being responsible in October, 1948, for the initiation of an attack on the "Stalinist tyranny and labour-camps." That and similar "information" was supplied to journalists and broadcasters in **OHMS** envelopes, so there was no doubt as to its source. The recipients, however, were told that the documents were not statements of official policy and should be destroyed when no longer needed.

IRD also had relations with the External Services of the **BBC**.

THE ROLE OF SOCIAL DEMOCRACY (1947)

According to Sir Hugh Greene, head of the Eastern European Services in 1949-50, IRD was known as "an anti-communist department for propaganda." In 1949 a regional information office was set up in Singapore. In a letter from the head of IRD in London to the British Embassy in Singapore it was stated that: "The Commissioner General attaches considerable importance to the project, which has become even more necessary now that the communists look like becoming masters of at least most of China." There is a copy of this letter in the US archives.

"Although the Americans were not involved in any way with IRD's founding," says Lyn Smith, "they very soon, according to Mayhew, 'started their own show' with the formation of the CIA and the US Information Agency."

After the fall of the Labour government in 1951, IRD expanded rapidly, moving from modest offices in Carlton House Terrace to a 12-storey block in Millbank but here we are only concerned with the extent of its operations under a Labour Foreign Secretary. Had anything been known about these covert operations there would most certainly have been objections that the non-attributable information being circulated was calculated to deceive the public and in some cases "journalists and other opinion formers." For, as Lyn Smith put it in her article: "In the process of selection, negative features of communism only were reported resulting in a distorted picture of eastern Europe." In an interview with Lyn Smith, sometime in the 1970s, Mayhew defended the need for secrecy as follows:

> There was a large Labour Party majority in the House of Commons and quite a number of "fellow travellers" and people with Stalinist illusions inside the Labour Party. I think that had they known about IRD they would have attacked it as being contrary to Labour Party policies. So in a sense we had to keep it confidential for political reasons. It would not be politically dangerous now [in the 1970s] but in those days so many people made excuses for Stalin that what we were doing would have looked to them [had they known] to be contrary to the interests of peace and friendship with the Soviet Union. That was the political reason for secrecy. But it is difficult to make out that there was anything sinister about it. We were ahead of our time in fighting Stalinism; we were certainly taking great political risks, and quite right too. It was not underhand, unless it is underhand to brief up anti-Stalinist writers, broadcasters

and trade unionists. I don't consider that underhand: it was confidential, but it wasn't underhand.

Lyn Smith thinks that although the British public were in ignorance of the Department, the Russian government probably knew about it from the start. Guy Burgess, one of Britain's post-war defectors was on the staff of IRD for a few months at the beginning of 1948 until he was dismissed for "unsatisfactory work;" he may have been instructed to get himself recruited.

The department was curtailed in 1976 by Anthony Crosland, then Foreign Secretary and finally closed down in May, 1977, by his successor, Dr. David Owen. Its activities were no longer considered appropriate in the "balmy atmosphere" of *détente* that was developing on the eve of impending changes in the Soviet Union. But let Lyn Smith have the final word:

> IRD was born under a Labour government, it achieved vigorous maturity under the Tories, and then it died, as it was born, with Labour in control. But it was a lingering death. Dr. David Owen, who was the Foreign Secretary when IRD was disbanded, prefers not to discuss the department.... The Overseas Information Department (OID), which replaced IRD was set up as a much smaller department.... OID was to be less aggressive in it rebuttal of communist propaganda, and would concentrate less on getting its views heard behind the Iron Curtain... In the cooling climate of the 1980s, one can't help wondering: will there be life after death?"

Students of the cold-war, and of the role of social democracy in general, owe a debt of gratitude to Lyn Smith for her meticulous work in unearthing the facts in this sordid story. Her article should be made available to a much wider public.

It seem appropriate to conclude this chapter with a return to the article written by James Klugmann for the December, 1947 issue of *Labour Monthly* and to quote the following paragraphs from his conclusions:

> Thus in theory and practice the right-wing leaders of European social democracy become agents and instruments of the main reactionary force within the world - American imperialism, which in

THE ROLE OF SOCIAL DEMOCRACY (1947)

the field of world politics is receiving such strong and consistent support from the Labour government of Attlee and Bevin and the socialist government of Ramadier. In theory and practice the Socialist Parties of eastern Europe and Italy, though there are still, of course, difficulties and hesitation, move closer to their Communist comrades, unite the working-class forces, jointly combat reaction, foreign and internal, move towards ideological unity, and prepare the way to realise the ambition of all that is best in the European labour movement - organic unity, single parties of the working class....

In this struggle a heavy responsibility lies on the British labour movement to combat the influence of the right-wing leaders of the Labour Party who thus far have exercised so sinister an influence on the international social-democratic movement since the end of the Second World War.

Note: The above chapter was completed towards the end of 1994. On the 18th August, 1995, Richard Norton-Taylor and Seumas Milne reported in the *Guardian* that documents confirming the role of the British Labour government in setting up the Information Research Department (IRD), for the purpose of spreading "secret, MI6-financed, propaganda against Communism," had been released on the previous day at the Public Record Office. In a leading article in the same issue of the *Guardian* it was stated:

> The new documents also show that the IRD was less interested in the Soviet Union or its client governments in Eastern Europe than in those Communist Parties in Western Europe which might gain a share of power by entirely democratic means. This reflected the general aim, vigorously pursued by the US elsewhere and particularly in Japan, of frustrating left-wing challenges to pro-Western governments.

Chapter Eight
ECONOMIC DISASTER

AT THE BEGINNING OF 1948, the British Labour government stood at the crossroads. Europe was beginning to polarise. There were those countries that were taking the road to socialism; and those that were unable to turn their backs on the old system of society. In the latter half of 1947, the Czechoslovak government, for instance, had been confronted with clear alternatives: either to apply for Marshall Aid and lose its independence, or to appeal for help from the Soviet Union.

In July, a Czechoslovak delegation had travelled to Moscow and put its problems before the Soviet leaders. The Soviet government, though with problems of its own, had agreed to step up its supplies of grain and other foodstuffs as well as industrial raw materials; and in December, 1947, a new five-year trade agreement had been concluded between the two countries. At the same time, Czechoslovakia had also signed trade agreements with Yugoslavia and Poland and opened negotiations with other people's democracies, leading to a closer union with the emerging socialist community of nations.

In February, 1948, the struggle for political power between the working class and the bourgeoisie in Czechoslovakia reached a climax. Klement Gottwald, General Secretary of the Communist Party of Czechoslovakia, had often warned that reactionary forces in the non-communist parties would attempt to sabotage the programme of the National Front and had prepared the people of Czechoslovakia for such a confrontation. He had also warned the leaders of the National Socialist Party, the People's Party and the Slovak Democratic Party that any attempt at counter-revolution would meet with a crushing response.

Heedless of these warnings, however, the reactionary leaders of the above-mentioned parties strove to bring about a government crisis over the question of additional payments to civil servants.

In the afternoon of the 20th February, 1948, the Ministers of the National Socialist Party handed in their resignations; later in the same afternoon the Ministers of the Slovak Democratic Party handed in theirs; and that evening the Ministers of the People's Party also resigned. But groups of ordinary deputies representing these parties expressed their

ECONOMIC DISASTER (1948)

disagreement with the conduct of their leaders and contacted Klement Gottwald, informing him that they were ready to offer replacements for the Ministers who had resigned.

On the following day Gottwald addressed a huge rally of the people in Prague's Old Town Square and gave a report on the government crisis. He explained that in place of the Ministers who had resigned, new Ministers had been nominated who would be true to the cause of the people's democratic system and to the original spirit of the National Front. He called upon the entire people to set up Action Committees throughout Czechoslovakia in order to prevent provocations.

Later that day, Gottwald went to see President Benes at Prague Castle. He conveyed to him the demand of the people that he accept the resignations of the reactionary Ministers and appoint those who had been nominated to replace them by their respective parties. The President refused.

On Sunday, the 22nd February, Gottwald addressed 8,000 delegates to the Congress of Works Councils and Trade Union Organisations in Prague's Industrial Palace. The delegates gave an enthusiastic welcome to his statement, including his proposals for the replacement of those Ministers who had resigned by more faithful representatives of the people. Later that day he made a similar statement to the Congress of the Czechoslovak-Soviet Friendship Society in Prague's National Theatre. He pointed out that those who had brought about the crisis, not only desired an internal upheaval but also a change in foreign policy that would destroy their alliance with the Soviet Union.

On the 23rd February, Gottwald again met President Benes and urged him to accept the resignations that had been tendered. In spite of Gottwald's arguments that an overwhelming majority of the population was opposed to allowing Ministers who had resigned to return to the government and that other representatives of the parties involved had been nominated to replace them, President Benes again refused and further demanded that Gottwald reopen negotiations with the leaders of the political parties whose Ministers had resigned. This time it was Gottwald's turn to refuse.

Next day President Benes once again called upon Gottwald to negotiate with the reactionary leaders of the three parties concerned and to seek reconciliation. Again Gottwald refused.

On the 25th February, President Benes bowed to the will of the majority of the people and informed Gottwald that he had accepted the resignations of the Ministers and appointed the newly-nominated ones in their places. That evening Gottwald addressed a huge demonstration in Wenceslas Square and informed the people that the President had now accepted his proposals.

The Action Programme of the Government of the reconstructed National Front was presented to the National Assembly on the 10th March. Its main tasks were to carry out as soon as possible those sections of the government's programme adopted after the 1946 elections that had not yet been implemented and to meet the demands raised by the Congress of Works Councils and Trade Union Organisations, and by the Congress of Farmers' Commissions in February, 1948. All these tasks were duly completed within the term of office of the National Assembly, including the adoption of the 9th May Constitution.

As a result of the defeat of the reactionary Ministers, President Benes resigned from his office; and on the 14th June, 1948, Klement Gottwald was elected President of the Czechoslovak Socialist Republic.

A few weeks earlier, the body of Jan Masaryk, Czechoslovak Foreign Secretary, had been found in the Cernin Palace in Prague. The enemies of the Socialist Republic had spread the rumour that he had been murdered; but secret US State Department documents released 26 years later confirmed that he had committed suicide.

By the New Constitution of the 9th May, 1948, the question of power was settled in favour of the workers and farmers of Czechoslovakia. The multi-party system continued to exist but the non-communist parties were now led by reliable representatives of the National Front pledged to a progressive policy. The strategy and tactics of revolutionary change were charted and the country set out on a course for socialist construction.

The choice for Britain was equally clear: either American domination and economic subjection, or national independence and economic recovery through co-operation with the Soviet Union and the new people's governments of central and eastern Europe.

In a statement made at the beginning of the previous year, Morgan Phillips, Secretary of the Labour Party, had repudiated the idea of a Western Bloc on the grounds that the aim must be "the strengthening of collaboration between Russia, America and Britain;" and the *Daily Herald* had pleaded, on the 17th January, 1947: "Do not let us build on a bloc which divides western and central Europe from the east." But, according

ECONOMIC DISASTER (1948)

to the 8th January issue of *The Times*, Hartley Shawcross, the Labour Attorney-General, had already stated on behalf of the government: "The political conflict in Europe today is not between Conservatism and Socialism; it is between Social Democracy and totalitarian Communism."

There had been a partial Tory come-back in 1947, with modest swings against Labour in Liverpool, Edge Hill, West Islington and Gravesend. 1947 had also seen the re-emergence of Oswald Mosley and the advance of General de Gaulle. But there were strong Communist Parties in Belgium, France and Italy, standing guard over democracy and national independence. In these circumstances an American offensive was launched with the immediate task of removing the communists from these governments.

In March the Truman Doctrine was proclaimed, bringing with it financial support and military aid for any government that was prepared to maintain hostility to communism and to the Soviet Union. By May, under dollar pressure, Belgium, France and Italy had expelled the communists from their governments. In June the Marshall Plan had been announced, drawing sixteen victim nations, including Britain, into its economic net.

By the second half of 1947, economic disaster was already looming in those countries that had agreed to the conditions laid down by the Americans for the receipt of Marshall Aid. In Britain the collapse of convertibility and the exhaustion of the American loan gave rise to desperate measures: cuts in food imports, reductions of rations, cuts in capital construction, increased taxation and attempts to freeze wages while prices continued to rise.

But the key to the ultimate fate of Europe lay in Germany. Having failed to unite that country under the Marshall Plan the Americans set about the task of detaching the western zones and forming them into a separate country under American tutelage.

In face of the threatened division of their country into two separate states, the Socialist Unity Party of Germany had adopted "An Appeal for a German People's Congress for Unity and a Just Peace." This had been strongly supported in all four zones and on the 6th and 7th November, 1947, the First People's Congress had met in Berlin. Although the leaders of the bourgeois parties in the western zones (including the reformed Social Democratic Party under Schumacher) refused to take part, 650 delegates from the western zones had participated. It was the first all-Germasn representation since the end of the war. The Congress had demanded a plebiscite on democratic unity and the formation of a central government. It had also named a delegation to present its viewpoint to the ill-fated Conference of Foreign Ministers held in London from the 25th November to the 15th December, 1947; but the Conference had refused to receive the delegation.

On the 17th and 18th March, 1948, the Second People's Congress met in Berlin. Again there was a big representation from the western zones (more than 500 delegates) despite difficulties arising from the opposition of the western powers. This time the Congress decided to hold a referendum for a plebiscite on the unity of Germany. The referendum was conducted from the 23rd May to the 13th June. Despite the banning of the referendum in the American and French zones, and serious impediments in the British zone, 14,776,000 (about 40 per cent of those eligible to vote) demanded a plebiscite.

Meanwhile, the increasing burden of Bevin's foreign policy was placing an ever-increasing strain on the financial resources of Britain. In November, 1947, Hugh Dalton had resigned from the Treasury over a minor indiscretion, to be replaced by Stafford Cripps. His message for the British people in the New Year was clear: "The first and most important objective in 1948 is to earn more dollars." But he warned: "Our expansion of exports has hitherto taken place in a sellers' market. Many of our products are now beginning to meet competition."

Commenting on the Cripps plan in the February, 1948 issue of *Labour Monthly*, Palme Dutt wrote:

> Dollar exports must be raised 50 per cent., i.e., from £190 million to £285 million. But even if this formidable target is achieved (a considerable 'if'), the result will still be a £300 million dollar deficit for 1948. How is this £300 million deficit to be met? Existing gold and dollar reserves are stated to be £500 million. By the end of the year they are expected to fall to £250 million. But long before this figure would be reached, it is widely anticipated that a financial crisis would follow from the reserves falling below the minimum necessary operating level. What solution does Cripps offer?

Cripps had already pre-empted that question in his New Year speech. "We should not be able to get through," he had stated, "without further cuts of imports of food and raw materials from the western hemisphere

ECONOMIC DISASTER (1948)

essential to support our present production."

According to the *Economist* of the 17th January, 1948, "Direct aid for Britain appears to involve about £625 million spread over four and a half years," or about one-third of Britain's visible deficit. And most of that would have to be spent in America. This condition applied to all the countries in receipt of Marshall Aid. There was a warning against a proposal for the increased production of Greek and Turkish tobacco, on the grounds that this would interfere with the American hold on the European tobacco market; and there was a veto on European shipbuilding programmes in order to promote the expenditure of dollars by the Marshall countries on American shipping. As a result, the British Labour government had obediently cut down steel allocations for shipbuilding by 20 per cent, with disastrous consequences for British production, for employment and for the export programme.

In order to see that the conditions imposed in return for aid were complied with, American supervisory agencies were set up under an American Administrator General with local offices in each country. Other conditions included special rights for American firms establishing factories in European countries; and the reservation of strategic raw materials for American requirements.

On the 9th January, 1948, *The Times* noted that "the standard of living in the sixteen nations would be lower in 1952 (at the end of the Marshall Plan) than it had been in 1938." On the following day, in direct contrast, it further noted that "by 1949, each of the countries in eastern Europe hopes to have reached or exceeded by a big margin the level of the national income before the war." This despite that eastern Europe suffered far more destruction in the war than did western Europe; and that eastern Europe was achieving this without "American aid."

Over all this loomed the shadow of an impending economic crisis in America itself. In his New Year message to Congress on the 7th January, Truman had confirmed it thus:

> Already inflation is undermining the standards of living of millions of families. Inflation holds the threat of another depression, just as we had a depression after the unstable boom of the first world war.

He underlined this with a further warning in his Economic Report to Congress on the 14th January:

We stand in great danger that runaway prices, over-extended credit and unbalanced developments will lead to an economic recession. We cannot be sure that the economic recession would not be severe, and recovery slow and painful.

On the following day, the *Daily Herald*, in an editorial devoted to "Truman's Economic Report to Congress," drew attention to the seriousness of the situation in America:

President Truman cannot be accused of being an alarmist. As the *Daily Herald* has already pointed out, when he utters a warning of trouble ahead, it is well-founded and usually comes true. America's dominating economic position in the world today makes the prospect outlined by the President one of urgent importance to all other nations, including ourselves. A serious depression in the United States would lead to reduced production there and to a cutting down of overseas aid programmes.

In his *Notes of the Month* for February, 1948, Palme Dutt warned that this would lead to increased competition between Britain and America in the markets of the world:

American and British imperialism may co-operate in the common tasks of counter-revolution, in hostility to the Soviet Union and to the rising democratic anti-imperialist camp from China to eastern Europe. But even the co-operation conceals conflict in the fight for rival spheres of interest (the squeezing out of Britain in the Far East, in the Ruhr, in Greece and the Middle East); and the economic conflict grows daily more open.

In his speech on the economic prospects for 1948, Cripps declared that the costs of production had to be lowered if Britain was to compete in the export market. Wages had increased, he said, while prices had remained stable, and these wage increases were "a source of concern amid the increasingly competitive conditions under which we were selling our manufacture abroad." In fact, prices were by no means stable. And to peg wages while prices continued to rise meant a reduction in real wages.

On the 17th March, a western Military Pact was signed in Brussels, binding Britain, France, Belgium, Holland and Luxembourg in a close alliance under American control. On that same day, President Truman called for conscription in the United States and for large increases in the armed forces. In so doing, he specifically named the Soviet Union as the enemy. On the 25th March, Kenneth Royall, Secretary for War, explained to a Senate Committee how some of the money was to be spent:

> No part of the central Eurasian land mass could be effectively reached by strategic bombing from bases on or near the North American continent or in the Philippines. It follows that offensive bases with the consent of the nations involved must be on the mainland of the overseas land mass much nearer to the enemy than our own country.

Secretary for Air Symington contended that planes based in Alaska or Labrador could "bomb any part of Russia;" and Walter Lippmann wrote in the *New York Herald-Tribune* of the 25th March: "Japan is in a position from which Soviet Siberia, Manchuria, Korea and North China can be dominated at relatively modest investment of strategic air power." Even so the USA wanted bases nearer to the European areas of the Soviet Union.

Four months later, in the month of July, the British Labour Government allowed the United States Air Force to establish a base in East Anglia from which the Soviet Union could be threatened with an atomic attack.

The 47th Annual Conference of the Labour Party opened in the Grand Spa Hall, Scarborough on the 17th May, 1948, with Emanuel Shinwell in the chair. During the course of his address he deplored the fact that three years after the end of hostilities there was talk of another war. He considered it "an insult to the memory of those who gave their lives in the struggle against fascism and aggression." Nevertheless, he discounted the "fallacy" that Marshall Aid "would place European countries at the mercy of the United States," and commented:

> America may feel she is entitled to tell this and other countries how to run their affairs. However, neither in this country nor elsewhere is it likely that the people will accept harsh conditions or strings attached to any offer of material assistance.

But that was precisely what was happening as he spoke, and had been happening ever since the introduction of Marshall Aid. As for our relations with the USSR, Shinwell was proud to say that the Labour Party had always sought "to give the vast social experiment in the Soviet Union our support and to defend Soviet Russia when menaced even in its earliest days." This may have been true in the "earliest days," but was it true now? Less than six months had passed since the secret anti-Soviet Information Research Department had been set up by the Labour Foreign Office and only two more months were to pass before the airfields in East Anglia were to be handed over to the United States Air Force for the express purpose of threatening the Soviet Union.

In the various debates that followed the opening of the Conference, it was soon revealed that not everyone was satisfied with the performance of the Labour leadership in the past year. Among the various rank and file delegates who spoke on the morning of the first day was Mrs. H. Lane of the St. Pancras South-East Divisional Labour Party. Moving the reference back of the paragraph on Individual Membership in the Report of the National Executive Committee, she expressed alarm at the fact that within a year 40,000 members had been lost to the Labour Party.

"I live in an area," she said, "where if you put up a broomstick they would vote Labour; yet I find difficulty in the doorstep canvassing for members." She found that working people believed they were no better off than when the Labour government first came into power.

Seconding the reference back, H. Ratner of the Salford North Divisional Labour Party, agreed with the mover. "The drop in membership coupled with other items," he said, "such as local government results, arises because of the failure of the government to solve the economic crisis in a socialist manner."

There were no other speakers on this subject, which was in itself a depressing display of apathy, and after a few conciliatory remarks from the Chairman of Conference, the reference back was lost.

In the afternoon there was a debate on the international situation. A lively, if controversial, start was made by Koni Zilliacus of Gateshead Labour Party and Trades Council, who said:

> We are now on officially good terms only with the Social Democratic Parties of Scandinavia and Benelux and with the MacDonaldite Socialists of France and Italy, who are working as minor partners in capitalist coalitions and have practically no

working-class support, plus Dr. Schumacher's little lot in western Germany. All the rest of the European working class, beginning with the overwhelming majority of the French and Italian workers and trade unionists, are today, under the leadership either of the communists or of left-wing socialists, the two working together or fusing into new working-class parties....

We should recognise the right of the working-classes of Europe to choose whatever leadership is best suited for their conditions. If we do not do that, then where are we going? Are we going to remain on bad terms indefinitely, or are we going to begin talking with them again? Why are we on bad terms with them today, when it is impossible to achieve socialism in Europe, democracy in Europe or peace in Europe without the co-operation of the workers in Europe as they are today, and not as Transport House wants them to be? There is no alternative, short of joining Truman and Churchill in waging cold war with hot air on the workers of Europe.

Dr. H.B. Cardew, of the Bath Divisional Labour Party, drew attention to the second paragraph of the NEC Report, which stated that Czechoslovakia "has for the second time in ten years fallen victim to aggression from without aided by treachery from within." Dr. Cardew did not in any way support the action of the Czechoslovakian Communist Party "in turning out the other parties," a view that was in any case at odds with the facts, yet he saw no evidence that Russia had intervened. He agreed with the platform that social democrats could not work with communists, but asked what was the alternative on the continent of Europe? Answering his own question, he said:

> Logically, the only one is that they work with the capitalists. It has been the teaching of our party throughout and the lesson of history that whenever social democratic parties have tried to co-operate and compromise with capitalist political parties, the socialist party has been weakened for generations. The Report says: 'Socialism is meaningless without democracy.' That is undoubtedly true. But what we have all been taught, and taught by the official literature published at Transport House for the last fifteen or twenty years, is that democracy is meaningless without socialism.

Referring to the situation in Czechoslovakia, T. Gittins of the

PEACE AND THE COLD WAR I

Spelthorne Divisional Labour Party pointed out that "other peoples have achieved their form of government through different historical processes, and therefore it ill becomes a National Executive to put forward a statement of the vituperative, ill-balanced and unkind nature of this one towards our nominal ally, the Soviet Union." He then quoted the sentence that had given him offence:

> All their democratic phrasemongering and parliamentary facade are only temporary means to the dictatorship of a single totalitarian party at the behest of a foreign police state.

He said he was waiting with great interest to hear evidence produced that Soviet Russia had indeed intervened in Czechoslovakia, and added for good measure: "It is certainly true that our American friends, against whom and against monopoly capital there is no statement, intervened in the Italian elections."

T.H. Williams, a delegate from the Union of Shop, Distributive and Allied Workers, made the following reasoned appeal to the rest of the assembled delegates:

> Czechoslovakia has determined the form of government that she wishes to have in a constitutional manner. The constitution of Czechoslovakia allowed for a change of government. The people who were resigning from the governemnt in February were people who were trying to prevent the development of socialism, and because they were trying to prevent the development of socialism the workers of Czechoslovakia rose in their might and said: "You are not to wreck that for which we have fought; that which we in 1945 accomplished is not going to be wrecked by a handful of people who are now wanting to put back in the saddle capitalist control over a nation that achieved nearly 80 per cent nationalisation." President Benes accepted the resignation of these men and a new government was formed to which President Benes gave his consent.

There was a protest from Professor C.E.G. Catlin of Bury Divisional Labour Party who took exception to the fact that Zilliacus had referred to Saragat in Italy and Blum in France as Macdonaldites. Like H. Hynd of Hackney Central, he thought the Labour Party should have been represented at the Congress of Europe held in The Hague on the 21st

ECONOMIC DISASTER (1948)

February. "If we are not to back anything with which the Conservative Party or Mr. Churchill are associated," he said, "we should not be sending our representatives to the meetings of the International Labour Organisation, the United Nations Organisation, or any other international organisations."

In replying to the discussion on behalf of the National Executive, Hugh Dalton first dealt with the reasons why the NEC could see no reason to vary the decision of the previous year's Labour Party Conference on the proposed United States of Europe. One of the leading members of the movement was a Mr. van Zeeland who, before the war, had advocated lending money to Hitler and Mussolini in the hope that they would make good use of it. "I do not think our people do themselves credit in mixing with that sort of folk," said Dalton.

He suggested that the right people to associate with were democratic socialists. "The National Executive thinks that it is much better that we should have a continuing and permanent organisation with our fellow democratic socialists in western Europe than that we should, as it was said of old, 'go whoring after false gods' all over Europe and the known world." With regards to the socialists of eastern Europe, he assured his listeners:

> The plain truth is this, and much evidence can be given in support of it. In Czechoslovakia, Poland, Rumania, Hungary and Bulgaria, the democratic socialist movement has in each of those countries been absorbed under heavy pressure by the communists. In all those countries democracy has for the time being largely, if not wholly, disappeared.

The motion for the reference back was, of course, defeated. Shortly afterwards, under the heading of "Party Discipline," there was a discussion on a Supplementary Report relating to the exclusion of Messrs. Platt-Mills, MP, and Alfred Edwards, MP, from the party. Edwards was the right-wing Member of Parliament for the steel town of Middlesbrough who had expressed the view that strikes should be made illegal and that steel should not be nationalised. No voice was raised on his behalf.

Platts-Mills, on the other hand, had many well-wishers. His crime had been in being a signatory, along with 21 other Labour Members of Parliament, to a telegram of support sent to Pietro Nenni, socialist leader of the united group of socialists and communists in the Italian elections, instead of to Giuseppe Saragat, a small-time banker who had broken away from the main Socialist Party and formed a social democratic party that was, because of its anti-communist policy, favoured by the National Executive of the British Labour Party.

All 22 MPs had been warned about their behaviour and asked to sign a declaration as to their future conduct. All had signed except Platts-Mills, described by William Gallacher in his book, *Rise Like Lions*, as "one of the most outspoken, one of the most indomitable and courageous Members of the House of Commons." Platts-Mills had been expelled for his refusal to sign.

His case, however, had been taken up by the Haldane Society, represented at the Labour Party Conference by Edgar Duchin, who moved the suspension of Standing Orders to enable Platts-Mills to address the Conference in defence of his membership. The motion was formally seconded.

Opposing on behalf of the National Executive, Morgan Phillips, Secretary, rejected the arguments advanced and advised Conference to vote against the motion. On a card vote, the motion was lost by 2,563,000 to 1,403,000.

A little over a year later, there was another split, this time from Saragat's party. This split was led by a man called Romita, who accused Saragat of taking orders from the Americans. Saragat replied by calling Romita a stooge of the British. Wrote Gallacher shortly afterwards: "It may be well to issue a warning to Labour Members of Parliament: Don't send a telegram to Saraget. He isn't the white-haired boy any more."

In a discussion on the coming General Election, Herbert Morrison rightly said:

> The next General Election is more important than the election of 1945. If we win it, as I believe we can and will, the good work will go on. If we do not win it, we shall go backwards and it may take us quite a long time to return.

But there was no great rallying call to press on towards socialism, no answer to the deepening tension of world affairs and of Britain's crisis. The cost of trying to implement a Conservative foreign policy, of keeping British troops in Greece and Malaya; and of relying on America for conditional aid, had led, as everyone knew it would, to an economic crisis. Or, as Palme Dutt had put it earlier in the year: "The price of Bevin abroad is Cripps at home."

The 80th Trades Union Congress, which opened in Margate on the 6th September, 1948, represented a triumph for the cold-war warriors of the Labour movement. Every progressive motion and every prgressive speech was denounced as communist or Soviet inspired - starting with the dark hints and warnings given out by Florence Hancock in her Presidential Address:

> We are well aware that there exists in this country, as in many other countries, an organisation that tries by every means to provoke industrial troubles. It has been conclusively proved to be capable of using every opportunity and expedient to create artificial unrest, and to sabotage every constructive effort by which the free nations are striving to re-establish the institutions of democracy. All this has as one of its practical conquences the fomenting of unofficial strikes, and a constant and deliberate campaign is kept going with the object of undermining the solidarity of the unions and the discrediting of their elected officers and executive councils. We must rid our movement of these mischief-mongers. They derive their influence from those misguided trade unionists who allow themselves to be deceived and exploited by them.

No one who has ever taken part in an unofficial strike, with no strike pay and no official support from the union concerned, could ever believe that he or she had been the unwitting victim of the creation of "artificial unrest." Such industrial action was only ever taken in desperation, when conditions were no longer tolerable or when wages were such that it had become impossible to make ends meet.

But that was only a beginning. After appealing to trade unionists "to recognise and accept responsibilities;" and to "strengthen the spirit of solidarity," Florence Hancock went on to raise another communist bogey:

> It is not only within our national movement that difficulties have arisen of this nature. Our relations with the World Federation of Trade Unions have become a matter of serious concern.... If the World Federation founders it will be because attempts have been made to use the international organisation not for industrial but for

political purposes. We are not prepared to see the World Federation become the means by which a policy of aggression and of imperialist expansion is furthered in the interests of a single power or group of powers....

Propaganda in this country and in the communist-controlled and Soviet-supported countries everywhere, alleging that Anglo-American policy is calculated to provoke a third world war, is a wicked and dangerous falsehood.... If our government were party to a conspiracy with the United States government to go to war with the Soviet Union, enough pretexts could have been found in the last few months.

The fact that brooks no denial is that they have entered upon a great effort to preserve the peace of the world by carrying into effect a plan to restore the European economy based upon the offer of American financial and economic aid.

But as Harry Pollitt stated in an article in the October, 1948 issue of *Labour Monthly*:

> The Margate Congress was held at a time when the economic crisis in Britain is rapidly deepening; when increasingly the workers are expressing discontent over their wage rates and higher cost of living.... The grip of the USA on Britain's economy is tightening and a barbarous colonial war is being waged in Malaya; while Cripps bemoans the fact that there is no new manpower to draw upon, thousands of British young men are sent to murder colonial peoples fighting for their independence.

In the introduction to the Report of the 80th Annual Trades Union Congress it was stated: "The livliest debates of the week took place upon the question of the relations of the British TUC with the World Federation of Trade Unions." Harry Pollitt described these debates as "the most sordid in the history of the British TUC:" debates that, unless the existing policy were changed, the TUC would have "very deep cause to regret."

The scene had already been set in the President's Address. It was developed a stage further when Vincent Tewson, General Secretary of the TUC, arose to announce: "It has been impossible to conclude arrangements for the attendance of a fraternal delegate from the World

ECONOMIC DISASTER (1948)

Federation of Trade Unions." After the cries of "Why?" had subsided, Tewson tried to justify the extraordinary fact that the General Council of the TUC had actually wanted to decide who the delegate from the WFTU would be:

> Having in mind the evidence that was before them of a very crowded programme and the possibility of a record number of resolutions, they thought it would be desirable, in order to save the time of translation ... that an English-speaking person should attend. So, merely as a suggestion, they put forward the idea that either Comrade Nordahl from Norway, or Comrade Jensen from Denmark, might be invited to attend. The point was put over informally by myself by phone to the Secretary of the World Federation of Trade Unions and I was informed by the Secretary that he himself had decided to attend our Congress.

This had proved too much for Vincent Tewson who had then made the further point that "it might be an advantage if the person came from a country which was associated with the European Recovery Programme." This did not go down particularly well with the Secretary of the WFTU who pointed out that the WFTU ought "to be able to take measures to secure official representation at your Congress." In other words, that the WFTU ought to be able to decide themselves who their representative would be. In the end the matter was "talked out" and no invitation was sent.

Following this extraordinary explanation by Tewson, A.E. Bowden of the Amalgamated Union of Operative Bakers, Confectioners and Allied Workers, moved the following composite motion:

> This Congress re-affirms its support for the WFTU and urges its representatives to resist attempts to destroy unity inside this body. It further recognises the value of the WFTU in preserving world peace and defending the world's workers from aggressive monopoly capitalism. With this in mind, we urge the delegates of the British Trade Union Congress to make every possible effort for the removal of whatever barriers there may be which are retarding the development of the WFTU.

A.E.G. Bowden said that he had no intention of speaking at length on the motion but explained that it was expected, when the World Federation of Trade Unions was organised, that "international capitalism would be active in attempting to bring about the sabotage and final destruction of that organisation." If that happened he thought that the only people who would gain would be "the natural enemies of the of the working class of the world – monopoly capitalism."

Seconding the motion, P. Belcher of the Tobacco Workers' Union said: "I for one pass no criticism at all on the representatives of the British Trades Union Congress to the World Federation, but let it be said and let our General Council understand that it is being rumoured and strongly rumoured that it is the British Trades Union Congress who are attempting to split the World Federation."

Opposing the motion, Will Lawther of the National Union of Mineworkers complained of the "woolliness of the speeches" of those supporting it. "We want to suggest," he said " that if there be an example of mischiefmaking it is the action of the people who have been urged to withdraw this and have refused to do so."

Replying for the General Council, Arthur Deakin immediately launched himself into an attack on the Communist Party. "Who is responsible for for this resolution?" he asked. "It stands in the names of two unions, but I am going to suggest to you that if the Communist Party had not decided the policy line we should have been able to persuade those union representatives responsible to withdraw the resolution." At this there were a number of interruptions from the floor of the Congress. "Some of the people with whom we have been discussing this resolution," he continued, "are members of the Communist Party and are not free agents." Later in his speech he drew political lines as if they were lines of battle:

> When this organisation was constituted, when the Executive Bureau was set up, there was a definite alignment of interests. On the one side there were representatives of the non-communist countries; on the other there were the representatives of the communist countries in equal balance. There were four representatives of the USSR, France, Italy and Latin America who could be guaranteed to follow the communist line. On the other side the United States, Britain, Holland and China[17] would take the other point of view. But gradually that balance has been altered to the extent that it now stands in the ratio of five to three. There are five

representatives of the communist interest and three representatives of the non-communist countries. If you persue it and balance the representation on the Executive Committee of the General Council you find this, that the balance is much more heavily weighted against us to the extent that if an issue is pressed to the vote it virtually becomes a communist dominated organisation.

What really rubbed Arthur Deakin up the wrong way, however, was the implied criticism of the colonial policy of the British Labour Government by some WFTU delegates. "It was suggested," said Deakin, "that we were reactionary, that we were opposed to the principles of bringing relief to and raising the standards of life of people in those countries."

"Who sent the 50,000 troops to Malaya?" called out a delegate from the floor of the Trades Union Congress. But that only added fuel to the fire kindled by Deakin in his speech.

Another cause for complaint was the attitude of the majority of the WFTU delegates to Marshall Aid, which they rightly saw as a deliberate campaign to remove communists from coalition governments and to prevent similar coalitions being formed elsewhere. In his reply to the discussion, A.E.G. Bowden said:

> It has been suggested from the platform that this resolution emanated from the Communist Party. That is just not true ... but I want to point this out ... that even if it had come from a communist element inside my organisation ... it takes nothing at all away from the sense of the resolution itself.

The TUC then turned its attention to the situation in Greece. W. Nicholas, of the Union of Shop, Distributive and Allied Workers spoke on the General Council's Report. "I was a soldier in Greece," he said. "I landed in Greece with that force that is supposed to have liberated the country from Nazi tyranny.... It is obvious in Greece at the present moment that anyone who does not agree with the present government is labelled as a traitor and is liable to deportation and even death."

---

[17] This, of course, was the China of Chiang Kai-shek. The People's Republic of China did not yet exist.

G. James of the National Union of Railwaymen drew attention to the conditions of Greek workers outside Greece, namely the Greek seamen:

> The Greek seamen are in the very unfortunate position, as any workers would be away from their homeland, and with the smashing of the trade union movement in Greece, there is no free trade union centre in Greece that can be affiliated to the World Federation of Trade Unions.... The Greek shipowners have carried on, in this last eight months, a terrific attack on these Greek seamen; and backing the Greek shipowners are the Greek government....
> The Greek shipowners ... sponsor a state trade union called the Pan-Hellenic Federation ... they make their approach to the various governments of the world including our own government.
> In this struggle when these Greek seamen resist, what happens? They are immediately black-listed. Over 2,000 are black-listed at the moment, and when they are black-listed their papers are taken away from them, with the result that they cannot get a job in the Pool. They are the orphans of the storm, and the only thing that is open to them is to go to the Consul. When they go to the Consul he presents them with one of two alternatives: join the Pan-Hellenic Trade Union movement, or get a free ride back to Greece....
> I come from Cardiff, and the headquarters of the Greek Maritime Union are in Cardiff. As a result of the efforts of the Trades Council in Cardiff a long and traditional relationship has come about between the two, and the appeal I want to make here is the appeal of Cardiff Trades Council, through the delegates of all unions in Cardiff, that this Trade Union Congress, through the General Council, through whatever means they like, will see to it that those Greek seamen fighting under conditions that no one can ever properly determine, shall have the full support of the British Trade Union movement until such time as they are allowed to organise freely in Greece itself.

The President then said he would take Composite Resolution No. 4, standing in the name of the Transport and General Workers' Union, which read as follows:

> This Congress, being gravely concerned with regard to the recent executions in Greece, endorses the representations made by the

ECONOMIC DISASTER (1948)

British government to the Greek government and places on record its view that all forms of persecution should cease and that there should be every reasonable opportunity for freedom and liberty within a properly constituted democratic Greece.

Congress therefore asks the General Council to use their influence with the Labour government further to prevail upon the Greek government to take steps to establish a full measure of freedom and democracy in Greece.

The resolution was to have been moved by Arthur Deakin but he was not in the hall when it was called. "I am sorry," said the President, "but if there is no one here to move it, it will have to fall."

At that, a coal-trimmer from Newport, by name D.J. Bale, who it was later revealed suffered acutely from a chest disease caused by his employment, came to the rostrum in obvious distress and said: "I must apologise to this Congress because the mover of this motion has not come forward. I understood that arrangements had been made for this motion to be moved in our name, and seeing no one else coming forward, I took the liberty of coming, just to move this motion formally rather than see it fall." But he added: "In my opinion, comrades, this is a very pious motion. It is not at all a motion that I would wish to move."

He was supported by W. Mowbray of the Scottish Union of Bakers who nevertheless thought that "the problem of Greece can only be settled by the Greek people themselves."

John Horner of the Fire Brigades' Union, obviously agreeing with the mover that the motion was little more than a pious gesture, then moved an amendment to replace the whole of the motion in the following more forthright terms:

> Congress, deploring the situation in Greece, where a reactionary and fascist government has introduced repressive measures against the democratic and trade union movement, calls upon the British government to withdraw its support of that government and remove British armed forces from Greece. Congress also urges the General Council, by means of the World Federation of Trades Councils and through such other measures that are open to it, to work for the restoration of the democratic rights of the Greek people whereby they may elect a government of their own choice.

Horner said he believed it was time to do more on Greece than pass pious resolutions. "This is the fourth consecutive Congress where we have had the sorry question of Greece on our agenda, and ... it is time to let the world Labour movement and our government know, in unmistakeable terms, what we think about the royalist, fascist government in Greece and its anti-trade union activities." He then went on to say:

> We all know that the first act of this tragedy was played out in 1944, when Churchill directed the British armed forces in Greece to attack and to destroy the left-wing and progressive forces there, in order to prevent them from coming to power as the only alternative to the return of reaction. That tragedy has been played out, scene by scene and act by act in this last three years by our government. By economic help and by military assistance this country has maintained successive Greek governments which have moved more and more towards the right, and now we have the spectacle of a king back on his throne and fascists who collaborated with Metaxas and the Germans running their country, this time under Anglo-American domination....
>
> Britain has poured out scores of millions of pounds, and has maintained its armed forces, in support of this anti-trade union government ... our amendment asks for a change in that policy.
>
> It is true that visits to the Foreign Secretary and previous declarations by the Congress have perhaps saved the lives of one or two of the more well-known trade unionists in that unhappy country. It is true, for example, that the law passed last December introducing the death penalty for all strikes has been rescinded, but our government is still party to the maintenance of this fascist government in Greece. There are still British troops there. Our amendment demands that this no longer be. Our amendment puts beyond a shadow of doubt to the Labour movement and the world that in not the slightest degree will this Congress remain an accessory to the horrible events in Greece.

The motion was seconded by E.J. Turner of the Electrical Trades Union, who informed Congress that in October, 1946, his organisation had written to the Foreign Secretary protesting about the arrests and the murders of Greek trade unionists and that they had received a reply stating that the trade union position in Greece was receiving continual attention. Unfortunately, instead of things getting better they had become worse. "A year later, in 1947," he continued, "following arrests, murders and persecutions, my organisation again wrote to the Foreign Office, and on this occasion they pointed out in their reply to us that already they had intervened in this matter. They said that of the 17,500 people arrested, already 4,639 had been released. But the letter itself seemed to accept the principle that all was well, that 17,500 trade unionists could be arrested, exiled and so on, and that so long as we could get some released the position was satisfactory."

Another approach had been made in February, 1948, when the Minister claimed that "the position was being made somewhat difficult owing to the interference of neighbouring nations." E.J. Turner rounded off his speech with the following words:

> We might agree that neighbouring nations should not interfere, but I question the right of this country to be the one country that can interfere in the affairs of another nation.... Therefore I feel that this Congress should make an immediate approach to the government, to ask that our troops should be withdrawn from Greece and that we should allow the Greek people the job of solving their own problems.

Replying on behalf of the General Council, Vincent Tewson asked Congress to accept the original motion, the pious one, and turn down the amendment. Coming to the crux of the matter, he said:

> The amendment differs from the resolution on two points. First of all, it seeks the withdrawal of British troops and it also seeks the withdrawal of British support from the Greek government.... There is one point with regard to the amendment that has never been mentioned ... that there is in Greece at the present time a civil war.... I would ask you, in this question of the persecutions which are taking place, not for a moment to believe the general propaganda that the people who are being persecuted are being persecuted on account of their trade union activities.... Do not forget that an independent United Nations Balkan Committee has stated that attacks on Greek territory are being organised outside Greece.

PEACE AND THE COLD WAR I

In the face of the insinuation that it was really the communists who were causing all the trouble in Greece, the amendment was lost and the pious resolution was carried. In his article on *The Margate Conference* in the October, 1948 issue of *Labour Monthly* Harry Pollit noted:

> There is one very important point to remember when comparing the Labour Party Conference at Scarborough with the Trades Union Congress at Margate. There was no effective opposition at Scarborough, but there was a splendid fighting opposition at Margate, which is going to make its effects felt throughout the factories and trade unions. We are quite confident that in the shipyards, engineering factories, steel mills and coal mines the workers will not have allowed to pass unnoticed the fact that it was the "reds" who spoke up against wage freezing and for higher wages, who fought for more effective working-class control of Nationalisation Boards, who fought for the nationalisation of steel, who exposed the dangers of the Marshall Plan for the British people, who brought out such striking facts in relation to the urgency of the housing situation, who championed the cause of the heroic peoples of Greece, Spain and Malaya, and who fought for international working-class unity.

In the middle of April, 1948, I rejoined the Communist Party of Great Britain. I cannot remember why I applied to rejoin nor why it was that I was allowed to rejoin; but I have a Membership Card stamped from the middle of April, 1948 to the end of the year, and another stamped from the beginning of January until the end of February, 1949, when I decided to resign. I did not find the comradeship that I had enjoyed in the old pre-war days and I never felt comfortable after rejoining. So I opted out.

I did not expect the comrades to be pleased about this but I was, nevertheless, surprised to receive a letter from George Hardy, Sussex District Secretary of the CPGB, some six or seven months later, actually dated the 2nd September, 1949, and couched in the following terms:

> I am informed that some time ago you sent in a note to the Brighton Branch stating you wished to resign from the Party. The fact that you have not functioned as a Party member and particularly in view of your past record the West Brighton Branch has decided to

ECONOMIC DISASTER (1948)

recommend your expulsion and have adopted the following resolution:

"That this Branch recommend to the District Committee that Comrade E. Trory, in view of conduct unworthy of a Communist, be expelled from the Party."

This will come before the District Committee on Sunday 18th September. Although you have put yourself outside the Party and therefore will not be present when the final decision is taken, you can if you desire send in a statement to give reasons why the recommendation of the branch should not be carried out.

I immediately wrote back drawing the attention of George Hardy to the fact that I had resigned from the Communist Party some months previously and that since I was no longer a member, his letter was quite meaningless to me. To which I received the following reply dated the 19th September:

The recommendation by the West Brighton Branch that you should be expelled from the Communist Party was adopted unanimously by the Sussex District Committee at their meeting yesterday.

However, they felt that the branch terms of expulsion were not severe enough and decided to amend them to include the fact that you had been previously expelled for action unworthy of a communist,[18] and as you had also held the important position of Sussex District Secretary you had therefore not only proved yourself unworthy of membership but had shown yourself to be thoroughly politically unreliable and a downright self-centred opportunist.

In arriving at the decision to include these points the District Committee members mentioned the charges for which you were expelled previously, your subsequent entry into the Labour Party, your "resignation" therefrom and afterwards applying for re-entry into the Communist Party and your failure to carry out your elementary Party duties.

Your letter of the 3rd September was read to the District Committee. You will understand that a person who has a position in

---

[18] For details of this sorry story see Chapter II of *War of Liberation* by Ernie Trory.

relation to our Party such as yours is not allowed to resign. Therefore the only course open to the branch was to recommend your expulsion.

And there the matter rested. I did not join another political party until July, 1977, when I became a foundation member of the New Communist Party, of which I remain a member to this day.

Meanwhile in Germany the political situation was coming to a head. On the 7th June, 1948, the foreign ministers of the USA, Britain, France and the Benelux countries had taken a joint decision to set up a separate West German government. Eleven days later, on the 18th June, the American, British and French military governments issued a joint ordinance "concerning the re-organisation of currency matters" in their respective zones.

Under this ordinance, with only three days notice, the Reichsmark currency, then in circulation throughout the whole of Germany, was to be replaced by a new Deutschmark currency in their three zones. In the three western-controlled sectors of Berlin, a new special currency (the "B" mark) was to be introduced. The new money had been secretly reprinted in enormous quantities in the USA. This action of the western powers threatened to split, not only Germany, in terms of money and finances, but also Berlin, situated in the centre of the Soviet zone.

Faced with this new contravention of the Potsdam agreement, the Soviet military government was forced to take similar action. As no new notes had been printed for the Soviet zone, the old notes were revalued by means of postage stamps pasted on them. Steps were also taken to restrict traffic in order to safeguard the normal economic life of the Soviet occupation zone and the Soviet sector of Berlin. It was obvious that guarantees were needed against the use of normal traffic for illegal currency and black market trading operations.

Restrictions were therefore introduced by the Soviet authorities on the 19th June to prevent their zone from being flooded with devalued banknotes from the western zones, but never at any time did the Soviet administration place any restrictions on freight traffic. On the 24th June, however, the western powers stopped the entire freight traffic from west to east and set up an airlift. Instead of west Berlin receiving its food and other supplies from the surrounding Soviet zone, it was forced to get its food by air at enormous cost.

ECONOMIC DISASTER (1948)

On the 1st July, the German Economic Commission offered to supply the whole of Berlin from the Soviet zone. The offer was not accepted. On the 20th July, the Soviet occupational authorities made a similar offer, but this was rejected. On the 22nd July, the Soviet government offered to provide 100,000 tons of wheat and an appropriate quantity of other foodstuffs to meet the requirements of Berlin, including the western sectors. The commandants in the western sectors ignored the offer. On the 23rd July, the German Economic Commission offered to supply electricity to the AEG-Turbine in the British sector so that power-cuts could be avoided in west Berlin. The western commandants would not accept the offer. Also in July, the Soviet commandant offered to continue delivering milk for west Berlin under the old conditions, but even this humanitarian gesture was spurned.

These facts prove that there was no blockade and that all talk of "starving out west Berliners" was pure invention. All the restrictions imposed upon them were solely due to the attitudes taken by General Clay, Military Governor and Commander-in-Chief of the US zone, and by his British counterpart.

The airlift, which had been set up on the 24th June, continued until the 30th August, when the four powers reached an agreement providing for the introduction of the Deutschmark of the Soviet occupation zone as the only currency in Berlin; the establishment of four-power control of all financial measures in Berlin; and a discontinuation of the traffic restrictions between Berlin and the western zones of Germany.

There was dismay in the capitalist press at what the social-democratic *Telegraf* called "the abandonment of Berlin, through the introduction of east currency, to the political forces behind it." In less than two months, the western powers had repudiated the agreement, allowing the so-called "blockade" to continue until May 1949.

The airlift is said to have cost the people of the western-occupied zones of Germany more than a hundred million marks. According to the January, 1949 issue of *US News & World Report*, "the real reason for the airlift" was to get "bigger profits for the aircraft factories and oil companies of the USA'" In reality that was just a spin-off. General Clay came nearer the truth when he talked of the invaluable experience that had been gained in the use of air transport for military and civilian purposes. *The Times* described the airlift as a strategic manoeuvre that had completely revised all previous notions about the possibility of flying in supplies.

PEACE AND THE COLD WAR I

On the 1st July, 1948, while the Berlin crisis was still on, the military governors of the western zones handed the prime ministers of the provinces in their respective areas the directives that had been worked out in London. As a result, a so-called "Constituent Assembly" met on the 1st September. Of the 65 deputies delegated from the provincial parliaments, only three were workers - two communists and one social democrat. Max Reimann, one of the communists, created an uproar by moving that "discussions on a separate west German constitution cease." The motion was rejected.

Chapter Nine
MOVING TO THE RIGHT

ON THE 27TH JANUARY, 1949, Premier Stalin expressed his willingness to meet President Truman in order to discuss outstanding differences that would lead towards the realisation of a peace pact and to gradual disarmament. This was not to the liking of members of the Attlee government in London, who were opposed to direct talks between Truman and Stalin. In a cable dated the 2nd February and published in the *New York Herald Tribune* on the following day, its London correspondent wrote:

> Premier Josef V. Stalin's invitation to President Truman for a meeting in Russia, Poland or Czechoslovakia was received here with evident anxiety. The British government does not want an exclusive Soviet-American conference on European or world issues. Although British official spokesmen declined to comment on Mr. Stalin's move today, they indicated growing alarm at the fact that the Soviet Premier appeared to be holding the initiative in the new Russian peace offensive. They admitted that they thought President Truman had been put in an awkward position and they even ackowledged privately that they feared Mr. Stalin might agree to go to Washington to see the President. The thought alarmed them.

There was general relief, both in government and press circles, when it was learned that Truman had declined Stalin's invitation and that he would not enter into talks with Stalin "outside the framework of the United Nations."

At a session of the Security Council, held on the 8th February, the Soviet delegation, after noting the growing menace of aggressive circles, the rapid increases in all types of armaments, the swelling of military budgets and the intensification of war propaganda, introduced a motion calling upon the Security Council "to entrust the Commission of Convential Armaments to work out, as a first step, a plan for the reduction of the armaments and armed forces by the five permanent member states of the Security Council by one-third by the 1st March,

1950," and to entrust the Atomic Energy Commission to submit a draft convention for the prohibition of atomic weapons and for the control of atomic energy; both the plan and the draft convention to be submitted to the Security Council by the 1st June, 1949.

These proposals received very little coverage in the British press and were, in any case, opposed by the western powers, who continued their policy of encircling the Soviet Union in the belief that the USA would continue to hold a monopoly in atomic bomb production for several years to come.

On the 9th February the *Daily Worker* reported that Professor Blackett, the noted atomic scientist and Nobel Prize winner, had said in a speech in Cambridge on the previous day: "The view that atomic bombs alone can defeat a major power in a very short time, by the use of a few aircraft and a few bombs, is inane and ludicrous." He had also expressed the view that when the Soviet Union acquired the atomic bomb the balance of power would shift because of the huge Soviet land forces.

In the House of Commons, on the 24th February, Hector McNeil, Under-Secretary of State for Foreign Affairs, was asked whether the proposed North Atlantic Treaty was not, in fact, in breach of Article VII of the Anglo-Soviet Treaty of 1942, which stipulated that each party undertakes not to conclude any alliance or take part in any coalition against the other party. The questioner was assured that the North Atlantic Treaty would not be in breach of this article because it was completely defensive in intention and character. On the same day the *Manchester Guardian* reported that Henry Wallace had appeared before the House of Representatives Foreign Affairs Committee in Washington to testify against the North Atlantic Treaty. He had said:

> The core of the North Atlantic Pact means that we are going to arm western Europe and establish military bases around the periphery of the Soviet Union from Norway to Turkey. These moves will seriously undermine and weaken our national security. They will lead to economic bankruptcy for western Europe and for the United States. They invite a war which no nation can win.

But Winston Churchill thought otherwise. At a public meeting in Brussels on the 26th February, he stated: "The Atlantic Pact will give us all a guarantee that the cause of freedom will not be aggressively assaulted without effective help coming from the great American republic."

MOVING TO THE RIGHT (1949)

If Henry Wallace had given us some idea of the extent of the encirclement of the Soviet Union in the west, it was left to General MacArthur, the Supreme Allied Commander in the Far East, to enlighten us on the extent of the encirclement of the Soviet Union in the east. This he did in an interview with G. Ward Price, which was published in the *Daily Mail* on the 2nd March:

> The Pacific has become an Anglo-Saxon lake and our line of defence runs through the chain of islands fringing the coast of Asia. It starts from the Philippines and continues through the Ryukyu Archipelago, which includes its main bastion, Okinawa. Then it bends back through Japan and the Aleutian Islands chain to Alaska.

Many promminent Americans were against the proposed North Atlantic Treaty. Even John Foster Dulles was opposed to the idea and was quoted in the *Manchester Guardian* on the 9th March as having said at a conference of the Federal Council of Churches, held in Cleveland, that "the Russians do not mean to start a war under conditions now prevailing, but might do so if they feel their homeland is imminently and seriously menaced." On the 10th March, a sectional meeting of the conference, representing 35 million Protestants, carried a resolution stating: "No defensive alliance should be entered into which might well appear as aggressive to Russia as a Russian alliance with Latin America would undoubtedly appear to us." Also reported to be opposed to the treaty was the Secretary-General of the United Nations, Trygve Lie, who refused to comment on it or upon Truman's opinion that it strenghtened the United Nations.[3]

On the 1st April a Soviet note was delivered to the British Foreign Office and simultaneously to the other countries of the North Atlantic Treaty. The note to the British government read as follows:

> The North Atlantic Treaty contradicts the principles and aims of the United Nations Organisation, and the commitments that the governments of the United States of America, Great Britain and France have assumed under other treaties and agreements. The treaty violates the Anglo-Soviet Treaty, the Franco-Soviet Treaty and the Yalta and Potsdam Agreements. Such powers as the United States, Great Britain and France are parties to the North Atlantic Treaty. Thus the treaty is not directed either against the United

States of America, or Great Britain, or France. Of the great powers, only the Soviet Union is excluded from among the parties to this treaty, which can only be explained by the fact that it is directed against the Soviet Union.

But the Soviet protest was in vain. The treaty was signed on the 4th April by the United States, Canada, Belgium, Denmark, France, Iceland, Italy, Luxembourg, the Netherlands, Norway, Portugal and the United Kingdom. It was quickly ratified by the governments of the various signatories and became effective on the 24th August, 1949. The group of countries that signed the treaty comprised the North Atlantic Treaty Organisation, or NATO.

The day after they had signed the treaty, the European signatories, including Britain, asked the United State government for military assistance. In reply to a question in the House of Commons on the 8th April, the British Prime Minister announced that the US government had replied that it was prepared to recommend to Congress that such assistance should be given.

According to the *New York Herald Tribune* of the 9th April, the programme was expected "to call for around $1,250 million worth of military supplies and equipment over twelve months." For good measure, President Truman threw in a promise that he would not hesitate to order the use of the atomic bomb if it were necessary for the welfare of the United States or if the fate of the democracies of the world were at stake. It had been reported in *The Times* on the previous day.

At a meeting of the General Assembly of the United Nations, held on the 13th April, the Soviet delegate, Andrei Gromyko, repeated the charges he had already laid at the doors of the signatories of the North Atlantic Treaty and said that the governments of Great Britain and France must "bear full responsibility for violating the obligations assumed by them on the strength of treaties with the Soviet Union."

Meanwhile, Churchill was in America, where he had made an extraorinarily virulent anti-Soviet speech, on the 31st March, in Boston. Here is a part of it:

> We are now confronted with something quite as wicked but in some ways more formidable than Hitler, because Hitler had only the Herrenvolk pride and anti-Semitic hatred to exploit. He had no fundamental theme. But these 14 men in the Kremlin have their

MOVING TO THE RIGHT (1949)

hierarchy and a church of communist adepts, whose missionaries are in every country as a fifth column, awaiting the day when they hope to be the absolute masters of their fellow-countrymen and pay off old scores. They have their anti-God religion and their communist doctrine of the entire subjugation of the individual to the state. Behind this stands the largest army in the world, in the hands of a government pursuing expansion as no Tsar or Kaiser had ever done.... Is time on our side? That is not a question that can be answered, except within strict limits. We have certainly not an unlimited period of time before a settlement should be achieved. The utmost vigilance should be practised, and I do not think myself that violent or precipitate action should be taken now.

On the 9th April, the *New York Herald Tribune* carried an article written by the two well-known American commentators, Joseph and Stewart Alsop, who used the whole of the space available to them to analyse Churchill's speech. They asked: "What did he mean by denying that we had 'an unlimited period of time before a settlement should be achieved?' To what was he referring when he said he did not think 'violent or precipitate action' should be taken now?" Obviously he was referring to the American possession of the atom bomb, the secrets of which were expected to be in Soviet hands by 1952. As the Alsops saw it:

> In Mr. Churchill's opinion, it is apparent that we have only two ways to survival. Either Russia will change radically and soon, or, when the "not unlimited period" of our safety begins to run out, we must force a preventive struggle, leading if need be to preventive war, in order to secure a settlement with the Kremlin.

The case for war on the Soviet Union was put even more clearly in the USA on the 13th April by a member of the House of Representatives, Clarence Cannon, who was Chairman of the House Appropriations Committee. He said:

> If there should be another war, which God forbid, the outcome could be decisively determined by atomic warfare in three weeks or less.... With the signing of the North Atlantic Pact we could have ample land bases and within a week we could blast every nerve centre.... Of course, a war could not be won by air power alone.

There must be troops for occupation.... But under the Marshall Plan and North Atlantic Pact we will have allies with troops and ships.... Why not let them contribute some of the boys necessary to occupy enemy territory after we have demoralised and anihilated it from the air? We followed that plan in the last war.

In a book entitled *If Russia Strikes?* written by a well-known military analyst and reviewed in the *New York Herald Tribune* on the 18th April, it was argued that some time before 1952 the USA should send an ultimatum to the Soviet Union on the following lines:

Either you will immediately accept international control of atomic energy and open your borders to agents of a world atomic authority, or we shall proceed to the destruction of your atomic plants and supporting elements (such as major power stations) by use of our own air atomic weapons.

The military analyst, a man named Eliot, believed, as did many others, that the western powers would maintain their superiority in arms until about 1952, and that thereafter any war would be one of mutual anihilation. Once the Soviet Union had the atomic bomb the western powers would have to think twice about using their own.

At home, on the 20th March, 1949, there was a comparable lurch to the right following a provocative fascist march in north-east London which had resulted in clashes between the large forces of police used to protect it and the indignant crowds that resented the presence of fascists in their area. To the surprise of everyone the Chief Commissioner of Police, with the consent of the Labour Home Secretary, Chuter Ede, imposed a ban on "all public processions of a political character in London" for three months, under powers given in the Tory Public Order Act of 1936. This meant that all May Day marches in London, on what was to be the sixtieth world anniversay of May Day, were made illegal.

The London Trades Council immediately decided to hold May Day meetings at all of the assembly points originally fixed for the march, plus a central meeting in Trafalgar Square. On the day, large crowds gathered and some of those present attempted to march. But a strong force of police broke up the demonstrators and arrested several of them.

Commenting on the ban in the May, 1949, issue of *Labour Monthly*,

MOVING TO THE RIGHT (1949)

written on the 15th April and so released for publication before the actual events of May Day itself, Palme Dutt wrote:

> For a parallel to such a ban on May Day by Labour's leaders, it would be necessary to go back to the ill-omened example of the ban on Berlin's May Day by the social democrat Severing, which preceded Nazism.

In May, 1949, there were strikes of miners, railwaymen and dockers. This was not surprising, one has to say, after fifteen months of an official "wage freeze;" though none of them were over the question of wages.

The miners' strike concerned "concessionary coal," that is coal supplied to miners at reduced rates. It was confined to Lancashire, where the "concession" did not apply. The miners put in a claim for it. The claim was refused. The miner's put a ban on overtime and the management retaliated by setting members of another union to do the work usually done by members of the National Union of Mineworkers. The men came out and by the 10th May every pit but one in Lancashire was idle. The management, faced with this situation, quickly found "a basis for negotiations" and the men went back to work having secured substantial grants of concessionary coal.

The railway strike, arose over the fixing of "lodging turns" without proper consultation with the men. The strikes were confined to strikes on Sundays throughout a number of weeks in the summer.

The dockers' strike was a much more serious affair. It developed out of a Canadian strike of merchant seamen, members of the Canadian Seamen's Union, who struck against a demand for large wage reductions. The shipowners responded by recognising a rival union, the International Seafarers' Union, whose members accepted the conditions rejected by the Canadian Seamen's Union.

According to D.N. Pritt, who happened to be in Canada at the time, the shipowners "hired strike-breaking crews, who, as is not uncommon in North America, were recruited not from the industry but from professional gangsters." These gangsters "made their way on to the ships by violence and beat up the members of the Canadian Seamen's Union who were on board."

On the 14th May, a Canadian ship arrived in Avonmouth with a strike-breaking crew; and the Avonmouth dockers refused to handle her.

PEACE AND THE COLD WAR I

On the 16th May, the dockers were threatened with a lock-out; whereupon the whole dock labour force struck. A few days later, 600 men in neighbouring Bristol came out in sympathy.

It should be explained that the Avonmouth dockers were only refusing to unload the "black" Canadian ships. On the 27th May, troops were brought in to unload a banana ship in Avonmouth.

In Liverpool 45 men were suspended for refusing to handle a "black" Canadian ship sent on from Avonmouth. This brought a thousand men out on strike; on the 30th May, another 1,400 Liverpool dockers joined them. By the 3rd June the number of dockers on strike in Liverpool had risen to 11,000.

On the 6th June, 1949, with the dock strike in full flood, the Labour Party met in Conference at Blackpool. The Chairman's address was delivered by the Rt. Hon. James Griffiths MP who, seemingly oblivious to the plight of the miners, railwaymen and dockers, noted that it was the Jubilee year of the foundation of the Labour Party and spoke of "the new and splendid chapter written into the history of our country by the massive programme of economic and social advancement we have carried through." He painted the same rosy picture of the situation abroad:

> In Europe the first instalment of Marshall Aid has produced remarkable results both in recovery and co-operation. With the creation of the Council of Europe the foundations of Western Union have been securely laid. The Atlantic Pact has established a new community of democratic nations united to defend their right to social progress.
>
> In the Commonwealth Britain has carried through a transformation unprecedented in the whole story of civilisation. I think future generations may well consider our government's handling of the Indian problem as the greatest of all its many contributions to world progress. Not least of the credit goes to our Prime Minister, Clem Attlee. The free association of Europe and Asia within the Commonwealth is a happy symbol of that international brotherhood to which our great movement is dedicated.

He recognised that "to ensure the success of these policies we have had to make heavy calls upon all sections of the community. We are conscious of the fact that the mothers of Britain are carrying a heavy burden.... During these four years we have kept inflation at bay. Now we have to secure that prices are reduced.... We shall also work with a will to secure a home for every family...." He outlined the advances made in the sphere of national health. Then, towards the end of his speech, he reverted to the well-worn theme beloved of all cold war warriors:

> Let me emphasise the lesson to be drawn from our experience for it is of supreme importance that the country should learn it in time before the next election. It is the lesson that the only bulwark against communism in these days is the return of the Labour government and the further development of Labour's policy.

Later, on the same morning, Jack Stanley of the Constructional Engineering Union, moved the following composite motion:

> This conference, in the light of experience since the inauguration of the government's policy on personal incomes, costs and prices, is firmly of the opinion that this policy has reacted unfairly against the workers, and has had little or no effect on the reduction or control of profits.
> Conference therefore calls upon the government to remedy this matter by removing the restriction on wage increases, by increasing the tax on profits, preventing the distribution of reserves and bonus shares, checking company reconstruction designed to increase capital and personal, tax-free fortunes, and continuing control of prices of commodities essential to the well-being of the workers.
> Conference calls upon the government to introduce an interim budget in the autumn based on these demands.

In support of the motion, Jack Stanley quoted figures for nine companies in the construction industry that had shown a 50 per cent increase in their combined profits. In one instance, he told the conference, the net profits were 69 per cent. "In regard to wages," he said, "is there anyone here who can justify a wage of 94s.6d. per week for a worker?"

On the question of prices, he said: "Official figures are no criterion of the general position. As soon as controls are taken off, up go the prices according to demand, in many instances rising above 100 per cent. It is no use the Ministry of Food saying that if there is price control the goods disappear and there is a black market. Increased prices cause them to disappear from the place where they should be - that is the worker's table - and the shopkeeper flourishes."

J. Thorpe of Brightside recalled, "I was one of those individuals who attended the Central Hall conference in 1948 when we came to an agreement or an understanding that we would not put in any application for increased wages on the condition that there should be a stricter review of prices and profits. The results of that appear to be that so far as the workers are concerned, wages have been frozen.... In comparison with the 100 per cent index for prices in 1947, prices are now 109...."

The motion was opposed by Arthur Deakin of the Transport and General Workers' Union and by Roy Jenkins MP, both of whom challenged "the suggestion that the government policy on prices, profits and wages has not been to the advantage of the workers of this country."

Winding up the debate, Sir Stafford Cripps MP, Chancellor of the Exchequer, recognised the "very real anxieties of the party and of those whom we especially represent in the country." Continuing, he said: "We want to arrange the country's economic and financial affairs so as to give us, and particularly the ordinary men and women of the country, the highest possible standard of living, bearing in mind that we must also provide for the general security of our country in a troubled world." But soon he was on the old familiar hobby horse:

> A sort of pincer movement is going on at the moment to depress the people of this country and to make the people feel miserable. One jaw is the Tory machine and the other is the Communist.

After a seemingly interminable speech containing all the old platitudes, he came to his peroration:

> Let us then cling, comrades, to those wise and unselfish policies of socialism that we have followed with so large a degree of success throughout the period of this Parliament, and which we are determined to make the basis of our return to power at the next General Election.

Predictably, the speech was greeted with loud applause and the composite motion was defeated.

MOVING TO THE RIGHT (1949)

On the morning of Wednesday, the 8th June, Herbert Morrison introduced the debate on the policy statement, *Labour Believes in Britain*. To the list of successes in Europe outlined by the Chairman in his opening address, Morrison added "the coming of the German Federal Republic." After Morrison came Rhys Davies MP, representing USDAW, who said of *Labour Believes in Britain*:

> I regret there is nothing at all in this document about the colossal expenditure on armaments. I wish there was something in it about the abolition of military conscription. The hearts of the mothers of this country are heavy when their boys are called up and their careers broken by military service.... We have at this moment 750,000 men and women in military uniform, costing £700 million per annum. Can you tell me, therefore, how you are going to close the gap; where are you going to get the money from for education and housing when you are wasting the substance of the nation in that fashion?

Rhys Davies was followed by A. Alman of South East Hackney CLP who had this to say:

> We often hear complaints from working people that there seems to be little change in the life of the West End, under "fair shares for all," from the position before the war, and we think that is probably true. We ask that in the final draft of our policy there will be an assurance that we do not trust the capitalists to be fair.

On the same theme, Mrs. Helen McCarthy of Finchley and Friern Barnet CLP said:

> Speaking of private enterprise this morning, Herbert Morrison said: "Anti-social conduct will be pulled up short and sharp, and people with vested interests will be required to mend their ways." These are fine words and brave words that we expect from the principal architect of this fine document, but I want more evidence of the certainty that this is to be done. On this important point there is no evidence of concrete action. The pamphlet is quite unconvincing and, I think, nebulous and some of us in that respect fear the worst. We want a complete assurance that the government

will be prepared to act drastically with the capitalists.

The discussion on *Labour Believes in Britain* went on for two whole days during the course of which the points already mentioned were elaborated. There were also a number of complaints about policies in the nationalised industries that seemed to be as far beyond the reach of workers' control as they were when they were in private ownership. There were, in addition, some suggestions for the nationalisation of other industries, in which respect the following, from Graham Thomas of Monmouth, was of the utmost importance:

> I would like to ask the Executive to grasp the nettle of the Imperial Chemical Industries, of which I have had some experience in a managerial capacity.... There is not a single thing in this building today which at some time during its life has not come into contact with a product produced by ICI. There are very few things that you can go and buy across the counter that are marked "ICI" but, nevertheless, this giant combine deals with metals, explosives, plastics, nylons, fertilisers, dye-stuffs and a whole host of about 100,000 products.

He could also have appealed for the nationalisation of all the drug companies, especially those that were eventually to have such a devastating effect on the efficiency of the National Health Service.

On the following day Ernest Bevin came into the discussion. He had little new to say on the situation in Europe, in the Commonwealth or in the Far East. Nor did he have anything *new* to say on the subject of communism. But that did not deter him:

> I want to pay my tribute to the great work that the Executive and this party did in collaboration with their fellow socialists of the continent, to help to bring hope and spirit to the resistance to the onrush of communism at that time.

Later in his speech he recapitulated:

> For the government to have achieved the Dunkirk Treaty, the Brussels Treaty, the Atlantic Pact and the European Assembly, all inside two and a half years, is not a bad record in foreign affairs.

MOVING TO THE RIGHT (1949)

Not everyone would have agreed with that. But there was more:

> Before I leave Europe, there is this vexed problem of Russia. Somehow this awful difficulty of dictatorship by the minority or the veto seems insurmountable. We cannot sacrifice democracy. They apparently feel that they cannot sacrifice unanimity.... Therefore I do not know what will happen.

Dealing with the situation in the British Commonwealth, he noted that "in Australia, New Zealand, India, Ceylon, Pakistan or the great territories of Africa or South Africa, there is a common attitude now on this question of aggression and on the maintenance of peace." He claimed that "in Malaya we have restored government, and it has contributed enormously to the consolidation of peace in that area." Indonesia, he thought, was a problem for the Dutch. But who deserved the credit for the rosy situation he had portrayed? Said Bevin:

> And so you get a picture of unity gradually developing from the Americas throughout Western Europe, right through the Middle East, through our Commonwealth to Asia, where there is a great and common bond.

At the end of Bevin's speech, the Chairman, James Griffiths MP, was moved to say: "Thank you and God speed you in your great work."

On the Thursday afternoon, R. H. Crossman MP, whilst purporting to agree with Bevin, let drop a few words of homespun wisdom that were certainly calculated to give food for thought:

> I was in Czechoslovakia just after the purge [sic]. There was not a Red soldier there. Communism does not follow the Red Army; it goes in advance of it, and it comes every time where socialism has failed to hold the confidence of the workers. Our first job in foreign policy is to make it possible for the workers to be held by the socialists. That means giving them a decent standard of living. The first line of defence against communism is not military armament, it is socialist policy."

But, generally speaking, the main body of the conference seemed bemused by the arguments of the big guns on the platform in the face of an imminent General Election. Towards the end of the day, Hugh Dalton was moved to observe:

> One of the most remarkable features of this debate has been an almost complete absence of criticism of Ernest Bevin, and that is new. In these conferences, year by year since he went to the Foreign Office, there has generally been criticism, sometimes from one angle and sometimes from another. Although at the end of the debate the conference has always by overwhelming majorities endorsed the policy of the government and of its Foreign Secretary, yet criticisms have often on previous occasions been voiced.

Could this have been due, at least in part, to the expulsions and threats of expulsion extended to those who had criticised in the past? In his book, *Rise Like Lions*, Gallacher wrote:

> "1949 was a bad year for the Lefts. There was an election not far away, and what was going to happen when it came along occupied the most part of their thought. They began to look for cover. Only a few remained steadfast in their opposition to the American war policy being pursued by the government and loyal to the cause of peace. Emrys Hughes, Tom Braddock and Leah Manning were ordered to appear before the "inquisition" and after a harsh and anything but comradely interrogation, were warned what would happen if they didn't modify their attitude. Lester Hutchinson, Leslie Solley and K. Zilliacus were expelled from the party. In the course of his examination Leslie was accused of referring to the Tories as "warmongers." "What's wrong with that?" he asked. To which the chief inquisitor sharply replied: "That's communist language."

Writing in the June, 1949 issue of *Labour Monthly* before the Blackpool Conference, Gallacher had described the document, *Labour Believes in Britain*, which had already been made available, as "an insult to the intelligence of the working class it represents." Writing in the July, 1949 issue of *Labour Monthly*, after the Blackpool Conference, D.N. Pritt asked:

> How did a conference with so many delegates drawn from the

rank and file of a good mass party lend itself to such action as, for example, the approval of the wage freeze against which their brothers in the trade unions are threatening to strike, and the acceptance of the fundamentally unsocialist policies stated in *Labour Believes in Britain?*

Meanwhile, the dock strike continued. On the 6th June, the crew of the British ship *Trojan Star* refused to sail her out of Avonmouth because the lock-gates were manned by troops. Two days later another British ship was similarly affected.

On the 13th and 14th June respectively, the Liverpool and Avonmouth dockers returned to work on a guarantee of no victimisation; but they still refused to handle the cargoes of Canadian ships that had been "blacked."

The scene then moved to London, where an attempt was made to trick the dockers into unloading Canadian ships that had been diverted there by making out that the strike had been settled. But on the 27th June, when it was realised that this was not so, 4,000 men stopped work. By the 5th July, the figure had risen to 8,484 leaving 44 ships lying idle.

On the 7th July, the government sent in troops to unload the ships. This brought the drivers of meat haulage firms and of fruit and vegetable firms out rather than carry goods unloaded by troops. On the 8th July, the government threatened to proclaim a state of emergency. As a result 400 watermen and bargemen struck. By the 12th July, when the government put their threat into action, there were 13,296 men out. Two days later the number had risen to 14,289.

As D.N. Pritt put it in his book on *The Labour Government, 1945-51*: "The tragic spectacle continued of a Labour government using troops to help British employers to defeat, by a lock-out, workers who were observing the simplest and most fundamental loyalty and solidarity; and all this to help Canadian employers who were using strike-breakers to defeat their own workers."

Throughout the period of the dockers' strike, the trade union leadership in general, including in particular Arthur Deakin, was doing all it could to discourage strike action. The Transport and General Workers' Union held an inquiry, which resulted in six out of the seven strike leaders being disciplined. In his book, *Labour in Power, 1945-1951*, Kenneth O. Morgan records that Jack Dash, who was one of the six strikers disciplined, had noted that all six were communists. Predictably, the TGWU inquiry declared that the strike "was part of a wider plan, inspired from communist sources, the object of which was to dislocate the trade of the country and so add to our economic difficulties." But, as Morgan put it:

> Communism was not the root cause at all.... There were genuine fears about the the working of the Dock Labour Scheme, with employers' demands that dockers work long periods of overtime.... What had begun as a well-meant institution during the war to end the old problem of unregulated casual labour was breaking down. The TGWU was too vast and remote to handle local grievances, especially with Deakin so closely bound up with government policies as almost to be identified with the employers rather than with his own members.

On the 19th July, the National Dock Labour Board ordered the dockers to return to work by 7.45 a.m. on the 21st July, saying that "failure to return to work will jeopardise the very existence of the scheme." But the government, fearing that this might be interpreted as a threat to deprive the dockers of the security provided by the dock-labour scheme, and so lead to a general strike of dock labourers all over the country, announced that the statement issued by the National Dock Labour Board had been issued without consultation with the Emergency Board and that there was no intention of ending the dock-labour scheme. By this time, there were 15,505 men on strike.

On the 22nd July, the Canadian Seamen's Union withdrew their pickets from the affected ships and announced that they were terminating their dispute so far as Britain was concerned, whilst maintaining it for the rest of the world. This enabled the dockers in British ports to return to work on the 25th July.

But now a more serious crisis was looming. There was no longer a shortage of manpower in industry. As Palme Dutt wrote in his *Notes of the Month* on the 15th August, for publication in the September, 1949 issue of *Labour Monthly*:

> Within America official unemployment has passed the four million mark. In country after country of Marshall Europe unemployment is soaring. The decline of Britain's export markets

has brought in view the prospect of spreading unemployment in the basic industries, shown already in extending dismissals for "redundancy," short time and the closing down of factories for lack of orders....

After four years of inglorious existence as a pensioner government on the dollar dole, the Labour government is approaching bankruptcy. Toryism, whose policy of dollar dependency has been obediently carried out by the Labour government, is equally involved in the bankruptcy. Desperately the Labour Ministers are making the pilgrimage to their Mecca of Washington to beg for more dollars as their only idea of a solution. But an icy blast is meeting them from Washington.

There was, of course, as Palme Dutt explained, an alternative policy: one that was becoming more and more widely recognised by all on the left who were opposed to the ruin of dollar dependence. That policy was set out in the then newly-published Draft of a General Election Programme of the Communist Party: *The Socialist Road for Britain*,[19] which signposted, in the words of Palme Dutt, "the alternative path forward for the British people to conquer the crisis and become masters of their fate, in unity with the peoples who have already dared to be free, and have found their way to independence, recovery and rising prosperity *without dollars.*"

There was, of course, a third programme already before the electorate, the Conservative Party *Right Road for Britain.* Commenting on this on the 25th July, *The Times* remarked:

> Critics have been quick to point out, with perfect truth, that a great deal of what it says is common to Labour policy and that whole passages would fit comfortably into the rival statement, *Labour Believes in Britain.* There would be serious reason for disquiet if this were not so. Democracy in general and the British two-party system in particular can work only so long as there is a wide measure of agreement between the parties.

---

[19] Not to be confused with *The British Road to Socialism*, the first edition of which was not published until 1951.

PEACE AND THE COLD WAR I

When the Marshall Plan was introduced in 1947, the Soviet Union, the People's Democracies, and the communists in western Europe had warned that it was not a plan for recovery but for the economic subjection of Europe to dollar control. At that time, the communists were denounced as the enemies of recovery whose aim was economic ruin and mass misery in order to promote their revolutionary aims.

But the fears of the communists had since been justified. Whereas the Marshall Aid countries had shown poor recovery figures, the Soviet Union and the People's Democracies had forged ahead. Industrial production in the Soviet Union, according to the United World Economic Report of 1948, was 71 per cent above the level of 1937, as against 70 per cent for the United States and 10 per cent for Britain. France was barely level with its 1937 figures and Belgium was still 9 per cent short but Poland was 41 per cent ahead and Bulgaria 79 per cent.

The communist alternative plan for ending Britain's dollar dependence and developing east-west trade was now admitted to be economically feasible. But this would have meant ending the "cold war" and that was not desirable, as witness the *Observer* on the 22nd May:

> Increased east-west trade in Europe would reduce the dependence of western Europe on American foodstuffs, and therby the dollar deficit. All this sounds tempting. But if we fall for the temptation, the political result will be disastrous.

On the 3rd July, the *Observer* returned to the subject with the following explanation for its rejection of the obvious solution to the problem of dollar deficiency:

> It becomes increasingly possible to find elsewhere things for which during and immediately after the war we were absolutely dependent on America.... While this policy saves dollars ... it inexorably widens the division of the western world.... This might balance the books, but it would nevertheless be a measureless calamity.... For it is doubtful whether there is any alternative source except Russia and eastern Europe for the massive bulk supply of grain and other staple foods.

Such was the political and economic situation confronting the delegates assembled in Bridlington on the 5th September for the 81st

MOVING TO THE RIGHT (1949)

Annual Trades Union Congress.

The seriousness of the situation was immediately admitted by Sir William Lawther in his Presidential address:

> A full decade of storm and struggle lies behind us. What lies before us is essentially a continuation of the effort we have been called upon to make to maintain our freedom and our democratic way of life....
>
> Our capacity to carry the staggering burden imposed upon us as a nation by six years of war has been put to a stern test in the last four years. Much heavier task yet await us....

A new factor, noted by Lawther in his address, was the growing disenchantment of the British Labour Government in the United States of America:

> An impression seems to be growing over there that the British workers are being pampered at the expense of the American tax-payers. It is asserted that our welfare services are, in effect, subsidising the British people's standards of life and labour at America's expense. Such industrial troubles as we have had lately are interpreted across the Atlantic as evidence of the unwillingness of British workers to accept any responsibility in helping our country to solve its economic problems, and as proof of the government's failure to influence the action of its trade union supporters.

Later in his address he laid the blame for these "industrial troubles," not on the directors of the mines and railways and docks but on a more familiar enemy:

> Not a little of the industrial trouble we have had recently has been caused by trade unionists who have allowed themselves to become involved in stoppages of work deliberately engineered by communist agitators. In view of the way in which communist influences are at work in our movement, I say to those of our members who have been deceived and misled in regard to the rights and wrongs of recent industrial disputes, that they are playing into the hands of those who seek to subvert our trade union organisation.

PEACE AND THE COLD WAR I

Towards the end of his address he invoked the Soviet-German Pact of Non-Aggression, signed in 1939,[20] and the activities of the World Federation of Trade Unions as examples of problems that had confronted the movement in its struggle to defend democracy.

After hearing a violently anti-communist, cold war speech from Arthur Deakin, a composite motion was moved endorsing action of the General Council in withdrawing from the World Federation of Trade Unions. It was moved by M. Hewitson MP of the National Union of General and Municipal Workers. Neither he nor his seconder, A.G. Tomkins of the National Union of Furniture Trade Operatives had anything new to say, relying on the old threadbare arguments of the right-wing leadersip. But F. Bullock of the Amalgamated Union of Foundry Workers, speaking against the motion, said:

It is the view of all thinking trade unionists that the 18th January, 1949, will rank in the history of our movement as our blackest day.... When the walk-out took place a great blow was struck at the hopes of the workers, a blow of grievous extent, but, happily, not fatal. In its depleted form the World Federation carries on its struggle for the realisation of its Charter.

In support of this view, R. Anderson of the Civil Service Union said:

It is clear that even prior to the 1948 Congress one or two members of the General Council were already preparing the betrayal of international trade unionism. The smokescreen of anti-communism was being created to blind the minds of rank and file delegates in Congress to the real aims that inspired these leaders of the General Council. At the Margate Congress the debate centred not on withdrawal from the World Federation but on strengthening the World Federation. No hint was given in the lengthy statement by the General Council spokesman that withdrawal was in their minds, but clearly the intention at that time was to smash the World Federation....

---

[20] For a full description of the events leading up to the signing of the Soviet German Pact of Non-Aggression, its content and subsequent events, see Chapter I of *Imperialist War* by Ernie Trory.

MOVING TO THE RIGHT (1949)

I should like as an antidote to the statements that have been made this morning to read a few lines from the manifesto of the World Federation. These lines, I am certain, will echo in your hearts as workers. "The whole history of Labour and trade union life demonstrates," says the manifesto, "that the most effective weapon in the hands of the workers fighting to ensure emancipation rests in their unity. To break unity is to break that weapon. It is this that the enemies of the working class have sought to do at all times. This has always been the aim of the forces of capitalism." Those words will be remembered by everyone in this hall in the months and years to come. I second this resolution in the name of my union ... We refuse absolutely to be led up the garden by Mr. Deakin or Mr. Tewson, or any other communist-haters who are in the ranks of our trade union movement.

It was inevitable that reference would be made to the dockers' strike during the course of the debate. This came in the speech of L. McGree of the Amalgamated Society of Woodworkers:

Those who desire to split the international trade union movement also desire to split militant trade unionism in this country. Mr. Deakin is supposed to be the leader of the dockers and in splitting the World Federation he now launches an attack upon the London dockers for one of the most magnificent struggles for trade union solidarity that this country has ever witnessed.... The Canadian seamen were fighting the Canadian shipowners - something Mr. Deakin does not want to tell you. They were resisting a cut in wages of 25 per cent. And if Mr. Deakin and members of the General Council cannot recognise international trade union solidarity, 20,000 London dockers can. They repudiated Mr. Deakin because they were standing by the principles of trade unionism.

At the end of the day, however, the composite motion was carried by 6,258,000 votes to 1,017.000.

On the Tuesday afternoon, there was a full scale debate on Trade Unionism and Communism, which left none of the delegates in any doubt as to whom the right-wing leadership of the TUC considered to be the main enemy of organised labour.

On the following Wednesday morning, the Prime Minister graced the

Congress with his presence. But he had little cheer to offer the delegates who had already been informed, by means of a Supplementary Report on the Economic Situation, that "the adverse economic and financial conditions have been worsened in recent months as shown by the further and serious drain on our already low reserves of gold and foreign currencies, occasioned by the increasing gap between the value of our exports and the cost of imports indispensable to the maintenance of our standards of living and employment." To which problem a permanent solution could only be found "in a greater volume of production at lower costs."

It was left to L. Cannon of the Electrical Trades Union to supply a ray of hope by drawing attention to the fact that whereas under capitalism there would always be economic crises in one country or another, under socialism there could be no crisis but only "an expanding economy which is met by an expanding purchasing power of the people...." He went on to say, "Many things can be said from this platform about the Soviet Union, Czechoslovakia, and so on, but it can never be said that the Soviet Union is confronting an economic crisis...."

On the 18th September, nine days after the end of the Bridlington Trades Union Congress, the pound was devalued by 30 per cent. In announcing the devaluation in a radio broadcast, Sir Stafford Cripps explained that the decision to devalue had been taken by the Cabinet before he left for Washington, that is to say before the Trades Union Congress met. This information was withheld from the Congress delegates. Wrote George Allison in the October issue of *Labour Monthly*:

> The main decisions of Congress add up to a dangerous line of policy that is far removed from the aims and aspirations of the rank and file. By the endorsement of the General Council's resolution on profits, prices and wages, and the supplementary report presented by Vincent Tewson, Congress now finds itself tied to a policy which can lead to the most devastating results for the working class....
>
> In the international field, Congress was prevailed upon to endorse the General Council's line on walking out of the World Federation of Trade Unions and seeking to form a new trade union "international" with the CIO and the AF of L. No one who heard this debate and the speeches of Deakin can be under any illusion regarding the direction in which the General Council seeks to drag

MOVING TO THE RIGHT (1949)

the British trade union movement. The extent to which this policy is applauded by the reactionary forces the world over, the glee with which this decision has been welcomed by those who are now frantically preparing for World War III, are in themselves grave warning to every British trade unionist.

Immediately after the decision had been reached on international trade unionism, the Congress Secretary made his speech against communism in this country, and particularly against communists working loyally and energetically in their respective trade union organisations. These decision sum up precisely the work of the Bridlington Congress.

But it was not all gloom and doom. On the 23rd September President Truman, in a statement from the White House, announced: "We have evidence that within recent weeks an atomic explosion occurred in the USSR. We always expected it. Ever since atomic energy was first released by man, the eventual development of this new force by other nations was to be expected. This probability has always been taken into account by us."

On the following day, the military correspondent of *The Times* wrote: "The recorded explosion of an atomic bomb on the territory of Soviet Russia brings to an end many speculations and surmises. Varying estimates have been made about the time it would take the Russians, with the aid of a number of highly trained German scientists, to produce the bomb. One which had the backing of a good deal of competent opinion, was eight years. Four years is certainly below the average estimate."

On the same day, the *Manchester Guardian* commented: "If ever there was any sense in talking about preventive war, there is none now. This is not a bad thing. There have been some irresponsible people in the United States ... who might have been tempted to start such a war ... this danger is unlikely to recur."

The obvious implication was that the Soviet atomic bomb was a deterrent, and that it was now no longer practical for the western imperialist powers to consider using their own atomic bomb against the Soviet Union. Konni Zilliacus put the matter very clearly in a press interview that was published in the *New York Herald Tribune*, also on the 24th September:

I have long believed that the atom bomb in Russian possession would be the best guarantee of world peace. This may disabuse the powers that be in the United States of any idea that because they alone had the bomb they would dictate to the rest of the world."

If we accept that "the atom bomb in Russian possession" was "the best guarantee of world peace" then men like Alan Nunn May and Dr. Klaus Fuchs, convicted of passing atomic secrets to the Soviet Union, must be seen in a new light. Both May and Fuchs were convicted of conveying at least a part of this information to the Soviet Union while the war was still on and while the Soviet Union was one of our two major allies. How this was any worse than handing over the complete results of all our atomic researches to our other major ally, the United States, is difficult to appreciate.

On the 1st October, the *New York Herald Tribune* quoted Walter Lippmann as having said: "We could not start a preventive war while we had a monopoly ... because we did not have enough bombs to win such a war." And on the 4th October, in the continuation of an earlier article in the *New York Herald Tribune*, Joseph and Stewart Alsop remarked: "the trance-like reception of the news that the Soviets have exploded an atomic bomb is a bitter commentary on the quality of American leadership.... And the plain truth is that the United States and the western world are totally unprepared for the new situation that has now arisen."

On the day that Truman had announced the explosion of the Soviet atomic bomb, Vyshinsky, the Soviet Foreign Secretary, called upon "all nations to settle their disputes peacefully and for the five great powers to conclude among themselves a pact for the strengthening of peace."

Referring to Truman's announcement on the 22nd September, that the USSR now had an atomic weapon, J.D. Bernal, Professor of physics at Birkbeck College, wrote in the January, 1950 issue of *Labour Monthly*:

> Before then it could be argued that the Soviet Union, lacking an atom bomb, had as good a reason for insisting on its prohibition as the United States had for retaining it as a blackmailing weapon. The fact that, having the bomb, the USSR still insists as vehemently as ever on its policy of destroying stocks and of controlling any further military use of atomic energy, is an earnest of its desire for peace. On the other hand, the response of the government of the United States, ably seconded by the government of Britain and all other satellites, in refusing all compromise, show plainly that they have

MOVING TO THE RIGHT (1949)

learned nothing and are still bent on war.

The People's Republic of China was proclaimed in Peking on the 1st October, 1949. The Soviet Union immediately recognised the new government of China and established diplomatic relations. Later in the same month, the erstwhile Dominion of India (constituted in 1947) became the Republic of India and opted for a policy of non-alignment. These two events, following in the wake of the explosion of the Soviet atomic bomb, changed the world balance of power in favour of the USSR. The US policy of encirclement of the Soviet Union had come apart in the Far East.

Chapter Ten
THE 1950 GENERAL ELECTION

ON THE 10TH JANUARY, 1950, the government announced that the House of Commons would be dissolved on the 3rd February; that the General Election would take place on the 23rd February; and that the formal State Opening of Parliament would take place on the 6th March.

Kenneth O. Morgan, in his *Labour in Power 1945-1951*, informs us that: "There had been much debate amongst Ministers about its timing." Cripps and Bevan and the "Tribunite Left" had favoured an early election "on tactical grounds," whereas Morrison had favoured a late election, delayed until the summer, "so that the economy could recover its equilibrium after the shock-treatment of devaluation and the latest round of expenditure cuts." Gaitskell had favoured an election in November, 1949, before the higher import prices after devaluation had greatly affected the cost of living. Bevin, however, declined to express an opinion - on the grounds that since he was "no politician," he had no views on the subject.

In the event, Attlee went with the majority. So, as Morgan remarks in his book: "For the first time since 1906, a General Election was to be held during the depths of winter."

The Labour Party Election Manifesto was the first to appear, being published on the 18th January, 1950, under the title: *Let Us Win Through Together*, an abbreviated version of *Labour Believes in Britain*, but, as D.N. Pritt observed in his *The Labour Government 1945 - 1951*, "with one or two significant differences. It was silent, for instance, on wages policy." Nor did it make any direct mention of "defence" or of its policy in relation to the atomic bomb, although it did include the following rather vague reference to the Soviet Union:

> We will continue, if returned to power, to work realistically for peace. We will stand firm against any attempt to intimidate us or to undermine our position in the world. But we will remain ready to co-operate fully with Russia, as with any country that is prepared to work with us for peace and friendship.

Just how vague this was can be guaged from the paragraph that followed it:

> Labour believes that the purposes of the United Nations are best served by still closer associations between friendly countries within the Charter. The Labour government has put particular energy into strengthening the associations of the Commonwealth, the Atlantic community, and western Europe. These associations are, we believe, not only compatible but necessary to each other as bastions of world security.

To say that the "association of the Atlantic community" was formed within the Charter of the United Nations, which specifically forbade the formation of such *blocs* directed against other member countries, was patently untrue. But if the Labour Party Election Manifesto was vague, the Conservative Party Election Manifesto, *This is the Road*, was anything but vague. It contained a vicious attack on communism in general and on the socialist countries in Europe, as well as on China in particular. Here is part of the section headed "Britain and the World:"

> Socialism abroad has proved to be the weakest obstacle to communism and in many countries of eastern Europe has gone down before it. We are not prepared to regard those ancient states and nations which have already fallen beneath the Soviet yoke as lost for ever. In China 500 million people have been submitted to communist dictatorship, and in the new countries of south-east Asia democracy is under heavy communist pressure.

The Liberal Party, in its Election Manifesto, *No Easy Way,* also added its mite to the perpetuation of the cold war, rounding off its policy statment with the following:

> Until we can trade freely with communist countries, we must strengthen the interests of democracy throughout the non-Soviet world, wiping out the economic misery on which communism thrives.

Only the Communist Party, in its Election Manifesto, *The Socialist Road for Britain,* warned of the dangers to peace of the anti-Soviet and anti-communist policies of the three main parties:

> The foreign policy of Mr. Bevin and the Labour government is the foreign policy of Churchill and Toryism.... In return for arms and dollars, British lads are to die for the aggressive aims of American millionaires. It is a repudiation of Labour's 1945 election programme, *Let Us Face the Future*, which promised friendship with socialist Russia and with the working class of all countries. It ranges Britain with reaction all over the world to maintain a fascist dictatorship in Greece, bring the Nazi monopolists back to power in Western Germany, give economic support to Franco Spain, and wage colonial wars against the peoples of eastern Asia. It is a violation of all the wartime treaties between the Allies reached at Teheran, Yalta and Potsdam. It is a violation of the British-Soviet Treaty of Friendship. It is a violation of the Charter of the United Nations.

So what had been the consequences of "the Churchill-Bevin foreign policy" for Britain? In the first place it had disrupted the United Nations and replaced it with the Atlantic Pact - "a sectional military alliance." Secondly, it had involved Britain in shameful and costly wars, as in Malaya, "draining Britain's resources and throwing away British lives to maintain imperialist rule...." Thirdly, it had bankrupted Britain's budget, "leading to cuts in social legislation." Fourthly, it had brought Britain under American economic domination and military occupation.

The Communist Party called for the repudiation of all sectional war *blocs* like the Brussels Pact and the Atlantic Pact; the ending of the military occupation of Britain by American troops and bombers; friendship with China and the Soviet Union; prohibition of the atom bomb and a reduction in the stocks of conventional arms; an ending of the present colonial wars and a return to Britain of British troops in Greece, Malaya and the Middle East.

The election campaign, according to Morgan, "was a less intense or memorable affair than the campaign of 1945." Pritt admitted that it had, "on the surface at any rate, a certain mildness." Churchill called it "demure." It seemed almost as though the main parties had agreed to avoid discussing the vital issues of foreign policy. That is, except when the Communist Party candidates brought them up, a lead that was followed by constituents at both Labour and Conservative Party meetings.

Then, out of the blue, at a Conservative Party meeting in the Usher

Hall, Edinburgh on the 14th February, Churchill unexpectedly said:

> I have not, of course, access to the secret information of the government, nor am I fully informed about the attitude of the United States; still, I cannot help coming back to this idea of another talk with Soviet Russia upon the highest level. The idea appeals to me of a supreme effort to bridge the gulf between the two worlds, so that each can have their life, if not in friendship, at least without the hatreds and manoevres of the cold war.

Churchill's speech, which took the Labour leaders by surprise, was loudly cheered by a crowded audience. On the following day, Bevin hastened to reply in a radio broadcast. After blaming the Soviet Union for failing to reach an agreement in the past, he went on to say, somewhat grudgingly:

> If Russia shows the slightest change of attitude and indicates her readiness to settle these relationships and give the world complete peace, then we shall be ready to enter into discussions with the object of abolishing the possibility of war and enabling all nations to co-operate with each other.

Rather more enthusiastically, Clement Davies, leader of the Liberal Party, in a statement issued on the following day, declared: "I warmly endorse Mr. Churchill's proposal that a new and supreme effort should be made at the highest level to bridge a gulf between the western world and Russia."

Herbert Morrison, however, speaking on the 16th February, referred to Churchill's speech as "soap-box diplomacy" and said: "In the light of what our Foreign Secretary said on the wireless on Wednesday night it is clearly his view, as it is certainly mine, that such an effort in the spirit of electoral stunting would be anything but useful." Attlee also supported Bevin's view on the matter. But on the 17th February, A.J. Cummings, a well-known columnist, wrote in the *News Chronicle*:

> It is deeply to be regretted that Mr. Attlee and Mr. Bevin made so chilly a reply to Mr. Churchill's suggestion for a new approach to Stalin on the highest level in order to reach agreements on the hydrogen and atom bombs. To dismiss it as an election stunt was a

gross error of judgment. I believe it was something more than an election stunt. By his proposal Mr. Churchill has committed himself to a major proposal from which he knows they cannot withdraw. If Mr. Bevin had had a flicker of imagination in his soul he would have used the occasion to accept the idea whole-heartedly and to expand it with all the force at his command.

It would seem that Churchill was more in touch with the mood of the country than either Bevin or Attlee; and he was not slow to follow up his advantage. In a radio broadcast that very day, he reiterated the proposal he had made at Edinburgh amd then asked:

> Why should it be wrong for the British nation to think about the supreme question of life or death, perhaps for the whole world, at a time when there is a General Election? Is that not the one time of all others when they should think about them? What a reflection it would be upon our national dignity and moral elevation, and indeed upon the whole status of British democracy, if at this time of choice we find nothing to talk about but material issues and calculations about personal gain or loss.

Churchill was nothing if not pragmatic. While the USA had a monopoly of the atomic bomb, he had never ceased to call for its use in a "preventive war" against the Soviet Union. But after Truman's announcement that the Soviet Union had itself exploded "an atomic device," Churchill had accepted that a nuclear blitz on the Soviet Union was no longer a practical proposition, a belief he clung to until his dying day.

In the last broadcast of the General Election, on the 18th February, Attlee, who was obviously not completely convinced of the new situation, said:

> The discovery of atomic energy loosed a new fear in the world. So impressed was I with its dread potentialities that within a few weeks of taking office, I went to Washington to discuss with President Truman and Mackenzie-King [the Canadian Premier] how we could harness this new power for the peaceful purposes of mankind. The hydrogen bomb has even more dreadful possibilities. The machinery of the United Nations is still there ready to be used to

the full. We on this side of the iron curtain have the will to discuss with the Russians, this with all other outstanding difficulties.

It was a far cry from the attitudes struck by the Labour Party leaders during the General Election of 1945, when Bevin had said: "With a Labour Government in office, which could be believed and understood by Russia and other countries, a new atmosphere would be created and the whole international situation would be changed." Now it was: "We on this side of the Iron Curtain...."

On the whole, with the leaders of both parties still nevertheless trying to convince the electorate that they were better placed to reach an agreement with the Soviet Union, it was Churchill and his cronies who took the honours. Certainly, the Soviet Union seemed inclined to accept Churchill's change of policy at face value. Broadcasting in English from Moscow on the 22nd February, M. Federov, referring to Churchill's proposal for a top-level meeting with Stalin, said:

> He was hinting rather transparently that should he come to power he would arrange such a meeting. His statement caused quite a stir. The Labour leaders, who had been so zealously conducting Churchill's foreign policy, were taken aback. They tried to ridicule this proposal as an election stunt, not worthy of attention.... Beyond all doubt this proposal is designed to catch votes. However, it is something more than an election trick. Unwittingly, Churchill's speech is a confession of the failure of that policy, which he himself formulated in his ill-famed Fulton speech almost four years ago. Churchill rejected the very idea of post-war co-operation among the three great powers. The aggressive course mapped out by Churchill in Fulton has been diligently implemented by the Truman administration and the Labour leaders alike.... But the policy of Fulton, aimed at establishing world domination of the Anglo-American monopolies, has failed completely; and the election manoeuvres of Winston Churchill are surely proof of this failure.

On the 23rd February, 1950, the people of Britain went to the polls. The final figures showed that the overall majority of 146 seats that the Labour Party had held after the General Election of 1945, had now been reduced to five!

The result, which was predictable, was nevertheless disappointing.

The total poll was 84 per cent as compared with 74.5 per cent in 1945. The Labour vote had risen by 1.3 millions but the Tory vote had risen by 2.5 millions. The difference in votes was 773,772.

Generally speaking the traditional working-class strongholds, despite misgivings over such policies as the wage-freeze and cuts in social services, remained true to the Labour Party. They did, in fact, vote to keep the Tories out. But in the rural constituencies and in the suburban areas it was a different story.

In an article in the March, 1950 issue of *Labour Monthly*, Hyman Fagan noted that the petty bourgeoisie had "swung over to the Tories." Whereas in the 1945 election large numbers of them had voted for Labour's relatively left-wing programme, they had not been inspired with the almost-Tory programme presented for their approval in the 1950 election. "The completeness of this swing over of the petty bourgeoisie," wrote Fagan, "is shown in the constituencies where there are large concentrations of lower middle class:"

> Thus in borough constituencies round London, like Finchley, Harrow, Richmond and Twickenham, whilst the Labour vote increased by 5.4 per cent over 1945 (or only in proportion to the total increase in the electorate), the Tory vote on the other hand increased by 42 per cent. In 1945 Labour won seven seats out of 15 in such constituencies. In 1950 it won one seat out of 17. It is estimated that in Middlesex alone there was an 8.5 per cent swing against Labour and an 8 per cent swing in outer Essex.

It was a mistake to think that middle class voters could be won on the basis of a pseudo-Tory manifesto. In the former "feudal" strongholds of southern England and in the eastern counties, on the other hand, the Labour vote actually increased, though not by enough to win seats.

The Communist Party put up 100 candidates; not one was elected. Even the two sitting members, Gallacher in West Fife and Piratin in Stepney, both lost their seats, as did the "independent" Labour candidates: Pritt in North Hammersmith, and Platts-Mills, Zilliacus, Solley and Hutchinson in their respective constituencies. These candidates had the right policies, but the workers voted to defeat the Tories, even though, in their view, that meant voting against their most loyal Members of Parliament. "We've got to vote Labour," one elector told Gallacher, "It's the only way to keep the Tories out."

THE 1950 GENERAL ELECTION

In his report to the Executive Committee of the Communist Party, made on the 8th July and unanimously adopted, Harry Pollitt quoted the following from a political letter issued shortly after the General Election, giving the reasons for the poor showing of the Communist candidates:

> First, the fact that our Party is not yet sufficiently deeply rooted amongst the masses of the workers, especially in the factories and trade unions. This is the main reason why we were not able to break through the confusing propaganda of the right-wing Labour leaders and win the workers for active support for our policy and candidates.
> Second, the fear of a return of the Tories, and the elementary class hatred of the Tories, which has not yet advanced to the political level of an equal class hatred of right-wing Labour as the agents of capitalism and Toryism in the Labour movement.
> Third, there is no doubt that a large number of workers voted Labour because they felt that, with all its weaknesses, the policy of the Labour government was responsible for the comparatively full employment that exists, for the benefits they feel they have received from the National Health Service, for Family Allowances etc.
> Fourth, the anti-Communist propaganda, which has been carried through during the past five years by the Labour leaders and the Tories.

Pollitt confirmed his belief in the correctness of these conclusions but thought that the Executive Committee had not been sufficiently self-critical. "Our greatest mistake and weakness in the General Election," he maintained, "was our neglect of arousing the masses in defence of peace."

Whilst defending the decision of the Communist Party to field 100 candidates, a view not held by everyone, he conceded that the party had adopted "a sectarian attitude, which objectively denied the need for any attempts at united action against the Tories and right-wing Labour leaders...."

This had led the party to accept, as Pollitt put it, "a position of self-imposed isolation, which made it appear that we looked upon all workers in the Labour movement as one reactionary mass, because of the wrong policy of their leaders, and saw no possibility of making any differentiation between them."

When the new parliament opened on the 6th March, it was noticeable that although the King's Speech contained many references to foreign affairs, it did nor contain a single reference to Anglo-Soviet relations. The opening of Parliament coincided with the publication of a statement indicating that "defence" would cost £780 million in the then current financial year. £20 million more than in the previous year.

During the month of April, 1949, Clarence Cannon, Chairman of the US House of Representatives' Appropriations Committee, was reported as having said: "The United States must be prepared to equip the soldiers of other nations and let them send their boys into the holocaust, so that we don't have to send our boys. That's what the atom bomb means to us." Much later, in Washington on the 19ty May, 1951, Senator Taft was to echo that sentiment when he said: "It is cheaper to fight with soldiers of foreign nations even if we have to equip them with American arms; and there is much less loss of American life." There was never any doubt as to how the USA felt about rearming Germany.

Opening the debate on "defence" in the House of Commons on the 16th March, 1950, Emanuel Shinwell, Minister of Defence,[21] said in reference to the atom bomb:

> We cannot, and do not, ignore in our defence planning the appearance of this new and terrible weapon nor its more deadly development, the hydrogen bomb, which now appears to be within the range of scientific development. We know that Soviet Russia has made progress more rapidly than at one time seemed likely; we also know that the Americans have continued to develop the industrial technique as well as the basic scientific knowledge required to improve on the bombs used in the last war and at Bikini. We ourselves, within the resources which we can allot to the task, are following our own programme.

Shinwell was followed in the debate by Churchill. The latter, having realised the futility of a nuclear exchange with the Soviet Union, had turned once more to the policy of building up a vast conventional capability and was now insisting on the formation of "a front in Europe

---

[21] Note that the "Minister of War" had now become the "Minister of Defence."

against a possible further invasion by Soviet Russia and its satellite states."

Without having explained what he meant by "a possible further invasion by Soviet Russia" he added: "I say without hesitation that the effective defence of the European frontiers cannot be achieved if the German contribution is excluded from the thoughts of those who are responsible."

Replying to the debate, a startled Clement Attlee said of Churchill's speech: "I am bound to say I was astonished by the Right Honourable gentleman's irresponsible reference to the rearmament of Germany." On the 18th March, the *Daily Herald* announced: "The British government stands by the allied policy of keeping Germany disarmed;" and reported that:

> This was underlined by the Foreign Office spokesman last night. "Only last November," he said, "the Foreign Ministers of Britain, France and the United States reaffirmed their intention to enforce German disarmament and oppose all forms of remilitarisation."

In the House of Commons on the 28th March, Churchill returned to the subject of the rearming of Germany and said: "I see no reason why the Germans should not aid in the defence of their own country and of western Europe, or why British, American, French and German soldiers should not stand in the line together on honourable terms of comradeship as part of a common system of defence."

Later in the debate, when Bevin was referring to this speech, Churchill interjected to say that he had never used the expression "rearming" or the "rearmament of Germany." Subsequent events, however, were to expose this interjection for the quibble that it certainly was.

Churchill also tried to explain, in the same debate, why he had pressed for high-level talks with the Soviet Union during the General Election. "I was most anxious," he said, "that the return of a Conservative government to power, which was a possibility, should not be taken as involving an exacerbation of the already tense situation that exists." He agreed that the position of the Soviet Union was much stronger than it had been and that, with regard to the new developments in atomic weaponry, "there is no doubt now that the passage of time will place these fearful agencies of destruction effectively in Soviet hands."

He appealed to the government to make "a further effort for a lasting and peaceful settlement" with the Soviet Union. But he failed to to explain how such an effort was to be achieved at the same time as the entry of Germany into a so-called system of European defence that was obviously aimed at the Soviet Union and her allies.

Winding up the debate for the government, Bevin attacked Churchill, saying that, as he understood the Fulton speech, "it was a preventive war that the honourable gentleman had in mind." He also reasserted that Britain, France and the United States had set their faces against "the rearming of Germany."

Commenting in the *Daily Herald* of the 31st March on Churchill's speech in Parliament Michael Foot had this to say:

> Seventeen months ago the settlement was to take the form of an ultimatum. Today Mr. Churchill almost succeeds in capturing the terms of affection with which he greeted the Russian warlord in the days of the common fighting. Stalin may marvel to himself what wonders a little atom bomb may do in improving diplomatic manners.

Writing in the April issue of *Labour Monthly*, E.H. Burghope, Secretary of the Atomic Sciences Committee of the Association of Scientific Workers, stated:

> The threat of the use of atomic weapons plays a key role in the implementation of American foreign policy. It is aimed at discouraging the great social transformations that are taking place in eastern Europe and the Far East. Although the threat has lost a good deal of its effectiveness since the announcement that the USSR has had atomic weapons at its disposal since 1947, it still remains a major instrument of cold war. The most important step in the struggle against weapons of mass destruction would involve bringing the cold war to an end and returning to the principles of foreign policy advocated by President Roosevelt, who believed in the peaceful co-existence of different social systems.

That the threat of atomic war still played a key role in American foreign policy had been confirmed only two months earlier by General Howey, the former US Commander in Berlin. Anticipating the successful manufacture of the hydrogen bomb by at least three years, he had proclaimed on the 6th February, 1950: "Now that we have got a head start on the H-bomb we should lay down the law ... not as diplomats, but as soldiers.... We have got to act while we have the advantage."

On the 8th April, 1950, the Co-operative Party, at its Annual Conference in Great Yarmouth, unanimously resolved to give its full support to any initiative of the Labour government "to end the cold war and outlaw weapons of mass destruction." Moving the motion on behalf of the National Committee, Tom Williams MP said:

> Britain should be prepared to declare that it will have no part or parcel in the production or use of instruments of mass destruction. I believe a lead will have to be given to the nations of the world, and Britain is the nation that has sufficient moral authority to give it.

During the second week in April, the Annual Delegate Meeting of the Union of Shop, Distributive and Allied Workers called upon the Labour government "to assume the moral leadership of the world" and went on to say that it was of the opinion that "the present crippling burden of armaments, which arises from the cold-war situation, is the biggest contributory factor to the growing economic crisis and the danger of war." In the name of humanity, it called upon the powers concerned to adjust their differences and lift the twin shadows of war and unemployment from mankind.

In an article in the *Public Employees' Journal* at about that time, Bryn Roberts, General Secretary of the National Union of Public Employees, after referring to a recent statement made by the President of the British Atomic Association to the effect that the area of destruction of a hydrogen bomb would probably be larger than the area covered by Greater London, went on the ask the following questions?

> What are we to do in the face of this? Should Britain, in its extremely vulnerable geographical position, support a policy of stockpiling atomic and hydrogen bombs as a means of defence and in the hope of ensuring peace; or would the best policy be to outlaw these beastly things and make it known to the world that while we shall continue atomic research for industrial purposes we shall not manufacture, or assist others to manufacture, either atomic or

hydrogen missiles, or co-operate in any military operations with any nation that does not cease the manufacture of such deadly instruments.

On the 19th April, the Scottish Trades Union Congress urged the Labour government to appeal to the United Nations "with the passion and energy which the danger demands" to secure mutual agreement between east and west for: 1. a ban on the manufacture of the hydrogen bomb and all atomic weapons; 2. the destruction of all existing stocks of atomic weapons; 3. international control of the sources of atomic power and its utilisation for peaceful purposes."

Two days later, on the 21st April, the *News Chronicle* reported that the British Council of Churches had decided at Cardiff to ask the Labour government to "take the lead in renewing international negotiations on the control of atomic energy."

On the 18th May, M. Podushkin, a fraternal delegate from the Soviet Power Workers' Union, addressed the Annual Conference of the Electrical Trades Union and declared:

> War and peace is the main question of our time. The Soviet Union is a most consistent fighter for peace. There is nothing aggressive in its policy and desires. Peace is essential to the happiness of the Soviet people and to the development of their socialist economy. Responsibility for the present situation rests squarely on the shoulders of the American imperialists and reactionaries who attack the Soviet Union with frantic fury. Evidence of the fact that the policy of the Soviet Union is a peace policy is seen in the overwhelming support now forthcoming from workers in all parts of the world.

On the 26th May, the Annual Conference of the Union of Post Office Workers called upon "all governments and all peoples to end the cold war." Moving the motion, Charles Geddes, the General Secretary, said: "Faintly but insistently the trumpets of war are sounding again." George Douglas, who seconded the motion, said: "the tragedy of the times is that the friendship between Russia and Britain, built during the war, is gradually receding."

But for all the resolutions of the trade union and labour movement, the cold war continued. Addressing the General Assembly of the Church of Scotland in Edinburgh on the 27th May, Hector McNeil, who was then Secretary of State for Scotland, said: "There can be no expectation of an early end to the cold war." This view was also affirmed by Sir Alexander Cadogan, the British delegate to the United Nations, in a speech made in Montreal on the 28th May, when he said: "It might take generations to put an end to the cold war."

On the 19th June, in his address to the Annual Conference of the Amalgamated Union of Foundry Workers, its President warned: "Britain cannot fail to be right in the centre of any future war. To talk about being neutral when we are committed to the Brussels and Atlantic Pacts is absurd. The atom bomb must be destroyed and its production banned for ever." His remarks were loudly cheered by the delegates and it was recorded by W.P. and Z.K. Coates in the second volume of their *A History of Anglo-Soviet Relations* that in their judgment these remarks "were widely representative of British trade union opinion at that time."

Meanwhile, in the USA, tension continued to mount. On the 1st June, Truman had allocated nearly a billion and a quarter dollars for the second year of the Mutual Defence Assistance Programme, of which one billion dollars was earmarked for NATO. In a cable date-lined Paris, the 5th June, 1950, Joseph Alsop noted: "We are imperceptibly passing into another period of acute crisis. One cause of this new crisis is the new tempo of Soviet rearmament." At a press conference, held on the 7th June, Secretary of State Dean Acheson said that "there is no magic" for ending the cold war, and that the western powers must go ahead with their plans to create "conditions of strength" to prevent Russian aggression. This in spite of the fact that there was absolutely no evidence of any Soviet attempt to commit aggression nor any evidence that the Soviet Union desired anything more than parity with its self-styled enemies in the rearmament race.

On the 13th June, in a major foreign policy speech, Dean Acheson, apparently apprehensive of the growing opinion in some circles in Europe that war on the Soviet Union was being aggressively organised in the USA, declared:

> There is a third course of action which might have been considered in earlier times and by another type of government and people than ours - that is, we should drop some atomic bombs on the Soviet Union. This course is sometimes called by the euphemistic phrase of "preventive war."

This could only have been a reference to Churchill's speech at Fulton, when he thought the secrets of the atom bomb were to be safe in the keeping of the United States for another five years at least. Dean Acheson hastened to add, no doubt in the light of the knowledge that the Soviet Union now also possessed and had experimentally exploded a small atom bomb: "Such a war would be incredibly destructive. It would not solve the problems, it would simply multiply them."

The sponsors of the Atlantic Pact lost no opportunity to proclaim that "the strength of the free world will never be used for aggressive purposes." Hitler had said the same of his Anti-Comintern Pact, which he described as merely "a defensive arrangement against the threat of Soviet aggression and the menace of Communism." In the June, 1950 issue of *Labour Monthly*, Palme Dutt carried the analogy a stage further when he wrote:

> In the path of the aggressive plans of the old Hitlerite war camp, the Covenant of the League of Nations represented a certain obstacle. Hence they denounced the Covenant ... and finally built their Axis military coalition outside the League of Nations. So today the new Anglo-American heirs of the Axis, the planners for a third world war, find the Charter of the United Nations a certain obstacle.... Following the example of the Axis and the Anti-Comintern Pact, they have built their sectional military coalition or Atlantic Pact outside the United Nations.

In justification of America's aggressive role, John Foster Dulles, foreign policy adviser to the Secretary of State, Dean Acheson, urged the planning of a general conference to review the United Nations Charter. According to a report in *The Times* on the 28th April, Dulles had declared in a speech to the American Society of International Law: "The Charter and membership of the United Nations are already dated.... Many new forces have emerged. An atomic age has dawned."

Chapter Eleven
THE INVASION OF NORTH KOREA

UNDER THE MOSCOW AGREEMENT of December, 1945, it had been agreed by Britain, the USA and the USSR that after its liberation from Japanese rule, Korea would become a unified, independent, democratic state. In violation of this agreement, the government of the USA took advantage of the provisional military occupation by the victorious powers to set up a regime in South Korea subservient to Washington.

The USA poured money into South Korea together with weapons and military advisers. In spite of the economic crisis that was beginning to make itself felt in the USA, more than a billion dollars was invested in South Korea. The New Corea Company, whose assets were formerly owned by a Japanese trust, was floated and its shares marketed by the National City Bank. Among its assets, the New Corea Company claimed half the mines, railways, banks and arable land in North Korea! The Oriental Consolidated Mining Company, also formerly Japanese but now in American hands, claimed ownership of the Unsan gold mines. These too were in North Korea and said to be the richest in the whole of Asia.

The President of North Korea was Syngman Rhee, a man who had spent 30 years in the United States and who had been brought back to South Korea to head the puppet government set up by the Americans. Syngman Rhee abolished the press and liquidated the political opposition with brutal violence.

In an interview with the *United Press*, on the 7th October 1949, Syngman Rhee boasted that the South Korean army could take the North Korean capital of Pyonyang within three days. On the 1st November, 1949, the *New York Herald Tribune* reported that Syn Sung Mo, the South Korean War Minister, had declared that his armies were ready and waiting to push into North Korea. There had already been a number of provocative border incidents.

At a conference with his divisional commanders in Seoul during October, 1949, General Roberts, Chief of the American Military Mission in South Korea, admitted that there had been "many attacks on the territory north of the 38th parallel on my orders," but added: "From now on, the invasion by the land forces of the territory north of the 38th parallel is to be carried out only on the basis of orders from the American Military Mission."

This is quoted in the book, *Thus Wars Are Made* by Albert Norden, who also tells us that three months later, in January, 1950, General Roberts announced: "The campaign against the north has been decided upon, and the date for carrying it through is not very far off." Documents of the Syngman Rhee government, captured during the subsequent occupation of Seoul by the Korean People's Army and published by the North Korean government, confirmed the systematic preparations for the invasion of North Korea from the south.

On the 28th April, the *Melbourne Sun* published a cable from its correspondent in New York reporting an address given by the correspondent of the *New York Times*, Ricard Johnston:

> He told the Overseas Press Club today that the South Koreans are fanatic in their desire to attack North Korea. Johnston was for many years stationed in South Korea as the *New York Times* correspondent. He declared that it is a matter of indifference to the South Koreans whether their civil war led to a third world war of not.

When Johnston spoke of "the South Koreans," he spoke as if they were a united people. But this was patently not so. On the 14th March, a correspondent of the *New York Times* named Sullivan had reported from Seoul that 13 deputies of the National Assembly of South Korea had been sentenced to imprisonment for periods ranging from one and a half to ten years for violations of the Security Act. Each was found guilty on five charges, of which the fourth was "opposing the invasion of North Korea by the South Korean forces."

In the South Korean elections of the 30th May, Syngman Rhee suffered a crushing defeat and his support in the new National Assembly was reduced to less than a quarter of the seats. The overthrow of his hated regime seemed certain and its impending collapse was openly predicted. The general opinion was that only a victorious war could raise his prestige enough to save him.

On the 5th June, the *New York Herald Tribune* published an interview with Brigadier-General W.L. Roberts, commander of the American military overseers in South Korea, conducted by the paper's correspondent, Marguerite Higgins.

Anticipating the forthcoming invasion of North Korea, the General

THE INVASION OF NORTH KOREA (1950)

declared that the American military group in South Korea was a living example of how, by the sensible and intensive use of 500 American officers and men steeled in fighting, it was possible to train 100,000 men to look after the shooting for the Americans. "In South Korea," he said, "the American taxpayer has an army which is a fine watch-dog for the capital investments made in that country."

Later that month, Secretary of State Acheson's adviser, John Foster Dulles, who was a member of the Board of Directors of the National City Bank, which had marketed the shares of the New Corea Company, appeared in South Korea. His photograph, taken on the border between South Korea and North Korea in the company of high American and South Korean officers by *Associated Press* on the 19th June, was flashed round the world. On that same day, in an address to the South Korean National Assembly, Dulles prophesied that the Communists would soon lose their rule over North Korea. On the 20th June, the Swiss paper *Züricher Zeitung*, said:

> There is no lack of people in South Korea who see the solution of the problems weighing heavily upon the country in a military attack on the North. The American have outfitted 150,000 men with American weapons, have put them under the command of American instructors, and have long been preparing for war.

On the 25th June, the day of the invasion of North Korea, John Gunther, the American writer, found himself in MacArthur's private railway car on a pleasure trip in the vicinity of Tokyo. MacArthur's chief political adviser was to have accompanied him but he had had to cancel his plans as MacArthur needed him elsewhere. He was replaced by two other high officers who travelled with Gunther instead.

According to Gunther, one of them was "unexpectedly called to the telephone just before dinner." When he returned, he told Gunther: "A tremendous story is just coming out. The South Koreans have attacked North Korea."

This was confirmed by General MacArthur himself on the 30th July, when he told press correspondents assembled at his headquarters in Tokyo: "When the war began on the 25th June, the North Korean army had not yet carried out its mobilisation plan. Only six divisions were ready, although the North Korean plans called for 13 to 15 divisions in case of war."

It had been stated by field observers of the United Nations on the 24th June, a few hours before hostilities had begun, that "no reports have been received of any unusual activity by North Korean forces that would indicate any impending change in the general situation along the frontier." But officers of the South Korean forces captured after the outbreak of war insisted that on that particular day, their regular Saturday leave had been cancelled and that on the following day they had been ordered to begin "the full phase of the attack north of the 38th parallel."

Kim I Sek and some other South Korean leaders were captured at the very beginning of the war. They gave valuable information. A number of documents were also captured. These showed quite clearly that the South Koreans, backed by the Americans, were the aggressors. According to Kim I Sek, the final instructions given to Syngham Rhee by Dulles went as follows:

> Start the aggression against the North, accompanied by propaganda on the grounds that the North has invaded the South first. If you can but hold out for two weeks, everything will go smoothly, for during this period the United States, by accusing North Korea of attacking South Korea, will compel the United Nations to take action, in whose name land, naval and air forces would be mobilised.

The invasion started in the early hours of the 25th June. According to a captured front-line officer, Lieutenant Han Su-whan, formerly of the 17th Regiment of the South Korean army:

> Though the 24th was a Saturday, officers of the regiment were not allowed to go out; they were ordered to be on the alert. We all stayed up that night in a tense mood, and by daybreak of the 25th a secret order reached us from headquarters to launch an attack on the region north of the 38th parallel line. All the units that had launched the sudden attack from the Ongjin area broke through the 38th parallel line, and their advance covered from one to two kilometres.... Soon after we had launched our attack, we were confronted by a fierce counter-offensive of the Constabularies of the People's Republic.... We, who had been so proud of being equipped with American arms of an ultra-modern type, collapsed

immediately everywhere before the Constabularies of the People's Republic; even the 53 rocket guns we had were of no use."

In his book, *New Light on Korea*, D.N. Pritt wrote:

> Within eight hours of the first news of the hostilities reaching Washington, the Security Council was summoned.... Its members were called from their sleep at 3 a.m. and twelve hours later, in the absence of the Soviet representative and of any representative of China (the nominee of the defeated bandit Chiang Kai-shek still sitting in China's seat), they had passed what appeared to be a resolution of the Security Council.

But, according to the Charter of the United Nations, all five permanent members of the Security Council had to concur before any resolution could be said to be valid. The representaive of the USSR, objecting in principle to China's being represented by the nominee of a government that had ceased to exist, did not attend. The resolution was, therefore, totally void. It nevertheless condemned "the invasion of the Republic of Korea by armed forces from North Korea" and recommended its members to give military aid to South Korea.

In reaching its decision, the Security Council neither asked the North Korean government to give *its* version of the outbreak of hostilities nor took into consideration its claim that the South Koreans were the aggressors.

On the 2nd July, the *Observer* boasted: "The Security Council, overnight, was transformed into the executive authority of non-Communist world opinion," adding that it had "suddenly begun to work as it was intended to work." On the same day, the West Berlin *Telegraf* told its readers that South Korea, which it described as "the last corner of democratic freedom on the Chinese mainland," had been subjected to the "cowardly attack of Communism."

In a statement made on behalf of the Soviet government on the 4th July, Gromyko accused the Security Council of acting "not as a body invested with the main responsibility for the maintenance of peace, but as an instrument employed by US ruling circles with the object of unleashing war." But, unlike the USA, whose President was already threatening to occupy Formosa and the nominally independent Philippines, as well as sending a military mission to Indo-China and calling for a crusade against every socialist country in the world, the USSR remained calm.

Within three days of the outbreak of war, the People's Army of North Korea had driven back the South Korean invaders and liberated Seoul. But the Americans had anticipated this possibility and had already landed three infantry divisions, one armoured division and one marine division in South Korea. This was, of course, in violation of all international agreements. On the 26th and 27th June, the US forces bombarded North Korean cities and villages, shot up harbours and landed transports under the protection of the Pacific and Seventh fleets, which pushed into North Korean territorial waters.

On the 5th July, the Federal German radio announced that the Americans had "rounded up the South Korean troops, who were retreating in panic, and brought them back into position." It was to be another three years before the USA, with official losses of 25,000 dead and 100,000 wounded, were forced to agree to an armistice.

The peoples of the USA and of Korea paid for the war with their lives but the industrial-military complex of the USA reaped its profits in dollars. The industrialists of the Federal Republic of Germany also raked in the dollars. In 1950 West Germany increased its exports to the USA from 46.5 million dollars to 102.4 million dollars; and in 1955 its exports to the USA reached 356.3 million dollars. This was the basis of the post-war recovery of the Federal Republic of Germany, then being described as an economic miracle.

The main products exported from the Federal Republic of Germany to the USA were steel pipes, machine tools and rolling equipment. Parallel with the rapid rise in the war profits of the West German capitalists went the rise in its slanders against the Communist Party of Germany, the only party in that country that dared to raise its voice against the American crimes in Korea and against their collaborators in Bonn.

The Chancellor of the Federal Republic of Germany, Konrad Adenauer, used the Korean conflict to create a German army in secret, without the knowledge even of his own government, but in conspiracy with the rulers of the USA. Like Hitler before him, he later justified this by repeatedly declaring that the purpose of the new German army was to wage a war against the East.

In his autobiography, *As It Happened*, Clement Attlee sums up the situation, simply but inaccurately, as follows:

THE INVASION OF NORTH KOREA (1950)

In July 1950 occurred the aggression by the Noth Koreans on South Korea. I had no doubt that it was our duty to give full support to the United Nations and in this we had the agreement of the Opposition, but the the Korean attack was not an isolated episode. It showed that Communist forces were prepared, if occasion offered, to resort to war. It became necessary, therefore, to strengthen the armed forces of the democracies.

Strange that Attlee should have dated the so-called "aggression by North Korea" as being in July when his own Cabinet had agreed, on the 27th June according to the official Cabinet Records, "to endorse US action in opposing Communist aggression in Korea."

In his book, *Labour in Power*, Kenneth O. Morgan writes: "The British government at once released naval forces from Hong Kong in support of American troops in Korea," and indicated, on the 30th June, that "there would be a more useful demonstration of the United Kingdom's capacity to act as a world power with the support of the Commonwealth." This in spite of the Labour government's already-existing military commitments, which were also described as being "against the Communist threat."

On the 5th July, the left-wing Labour Member for Methyr Tydfil, S.O. Davies, moved in the House of Commons: "That this House expresses its deep concern at the alarming situation in Korea, and recognises the possibility of another world conflict arising therefrom. It therefore calls upon the government to withdraw all British naval forces from the affected area; to give, in accordance with the Cairo Conference in 1943 and the Moscow Conference in 1945, full recognition to the claim of the Korean people for the unification and independence of their country; to repudiate all British commitments which involve on our part any obligations to maintain the present division of the world into two powerful and dangerously poised hostile groups; and to declare in conformity with the government's socialist principles our determination to give every encouragement to all people aspiring for freedom and self-government." In moving this motion, S.O. Davies said:

> The government have allowed themselves to be drawn into this tragic situation by the wholly irregular action of the United States and in direct violation of the letter and the spirit of the United Nations Charter.... I should have expected a socialist government

to be a little more deliberate and cool-headed in such a situation as this and not to have plunged headlong in support of the reckless irresponsibility of the United States.

On the 25th July, the Air Minister announced that Royal Air Force policy was to be reorganised. Already, in the previous May, it had been decided that large extensions to some service aerodromes in Britain were to be carried out by engineering units of the United States Air Force, in order to make them suitable for dealing with the large American B36 bombers, and with a new range of US bombers, shortly to arrive, requiring runways three miles in length.

On the following day it was reported that land reinforcements were to be sent to Korea, and that another £100 million was to be made available for defence. All these measures were approved by Parliament. On the 28th July, the release of members of the Regular Army was suspended and a limited selective recall of reserves was announced. Parliament then adjourned until the 17th October.

On the 3rd August, while Parliament was in recess, the government assured the US Ambassador in London that Britain would increase its defence expenditure to £3.4 billion over the next three years. This figure was later increased to £3.6 billion.

On the 11th August, it was decided to recall Parliament on the 12th September, to discuss defence. On the 30th August it was announced that National Service would be extended from 18 months to two years, and that the US Bomber Force in Britain was to be increased from 180 to 1,000 involving the use of 30 airfields instead of three, with a minimum of 50,000 American troops stationed here. On the 10th September, two days before Parliament reassembled, the Tory opposition stated it would support the government's defence proposals.

Hugh Gaitskell, Minister for Economic Affairs, emphasised that the workers would bear the brunt of the cost of stepping up defence spending, which was "bound to have an effect on the cost of living." But the wage freeze was to stay. At its conference that September, however, the TUC, by a narrow majority, withdrew its support for the wage freeze.

At its Annual Conference in Margate, held during October, the Labour Party, nevertheless, endorsed the British involvement in Korea by a considerable margin. A motion criticising Bevin's foreign policy was defeated by 4,861,000 to 881,000.

THE INVASION OF NORTH KOREA (1950)

On the 18th September, it had been announced that Bevin, after full consultation with the government, had accepted in principle the eventual formation of a West German Army, and, on the following day, that Britain, France and the USA had agreed that any attack on West Germany would be treated as an attack on themselves.

In response to this agreement, Ministers of the People's Democracies in Europe met on the 20th October, calling for: "A four-power declaration against the remilitarisation of Germany and for the carrying out of the Potsdam Agreement; the development of Germany's peace economy, while the restoration of its war potential is prevented; a Peace Treaty, the restoration of German unity, and the withdrawal of occupational troops within a year after the the conclusion of a Peace Treaty; and the formation of an all-German Constituent Council on a party basis, to prepare the way for a provisional democratic peace-loving all-German government."

These proposals were rejected by Dean Acheson on the 25th October; talks on German rearmament were begun in Washington on the 28th.

Attlee, however, though anxious to please the US government with a view to maintaining US aid to Britain, nevertheless drew the line at extending the war into the territory of the Chinese People's Republic, recognised *de jure* by the British government on the previous 6th January, or allowing the war to develop into a military confrontation with the Soviet Union, as some Americans seemed to want. A statement made by Truman, at a press conference in the White House, to the effect that the US government was prepared to use the atomic bomb in Korea if necessary, sent Attlee flying off to Washington to inform the President of the USA that the British government was opposed to this absolutely.

Attlee reached Washington on the morning of the 4th December and managed to convince Truman that the proposed bombing of Chinese industrial cities would be counter-productive. At a private meeting, quoted by Francis Williams in *A Prime Minister Remembers*, Attlee asked Truman if he were really giving active thought to the use of the atomic bomb in Korea, a possibility that had appalled public opinion in Britain and in most other European countries as well. Truman replied that his statement should not be taken as having any new significance.

Attlee's talks with Truman and Acheson went on until the 8th December, during the course of which Attlee urged the need for an early cease-fire in Korea and the folly of excluding China from the United Nations. Acheson was not impressed. He spoke of the danger to Japan

PEACE AND THE COLD WAR I

and the Philippines if Korea and Formosa went Communist.

Nevertheless, when Attlee returned to Britain on the 11th December he was able to assure his Cabinet that Truman had said he had no intention of using the atom bomb in China or Korea and that the Americans had heeded his warning that war with China would mean war with Russia also. Attlee was hailed in Parliament as the bringer of peace.

It had been planned to hold the Second World Peace Congress in Sheffield from the 13th to the 19th November. The first had been held in Paris in April, 1949, but in order to accomodate delegates from the socialist countries who had been refused visas by the French government, a parallel congress had been held in Prague. These two congresses had led to the formation of the World Peace Council. Association with it had been immediately banned by the Labour Party.

Despite this, when pressed by the Americans to ban the Congress in Sheffield, the Labour government had insisted that it had no power to do so; and that individual delegates would only be refused visas if they were *personae non gratae*. What the Labour government did not say was that it considered anyone of importance in the peace movement to be *personae non gratae*. At a Foreign Press Association dinner, on the 2nd November, Attlee had claimed that the aim of the World Peace Movement was "to paralyse the efforts of the democracies to arm themselves." In the House of Commons the Home Secretary subsequently admitted that up to the 10th November, 561 application for visas had been received, 300 granted and 215 refused. Even some of those who had been granted visas were refused entry on arrival, as were many of those arriving from countries whose citizens did not require visas. Among those refused entry on arrival were Professor Joliot-Curie and the Soviet composer Shostakovitch.

On the 12th November, the organisers of the Congress were compelled to change the venue to Warsaw, where *all* the elected delegates were welcomed without question. The result was a very successful Congress. First and foremost of the demands in the finally-agreed document was an end to the war in Korea and the withdrawal of all foreign troops, with a final settlement in accordance with the will of the Korean people, under the supervision of a Security Council on which the Chinese Peoples' Republic would have taken its rightful place.

Chapter Twelve
THE RETURN OF CHURCHILL

IN JANUARY, 1951, the USA commuted the death sentences passed on 21 Nazi war criminals, reduced the sentences on 70 others, and cancelled the decree confiscating the millions accumulated by Alfred Krupp during the war. This left him free, as Pritt remarked in his book, *The Labour Government 1945-51*, "to apply those millions to the rearmament of Western Germany."

In the February, 1951 issue of *Labour Monthly* Robin Page Arnot declared: "This is the grand outcome of the Marshall Plan, the Western Union and the Atlantic War Pact, and all the other fetters by which the Labour government, operating a Tory foreign policy, tied this country hand and foot to Yankee imperialism."

On the 24th February, the Soviet Union addressed another Note to the Western Powers on German rearmament, describing it as a violation of the Potsdam Agreement. Then, at a meeting of the deputies of the Foreign Ministers of the Four Powers held in Paris on the 5th March to discuss the agenda for a proposed Conference of the Foreign Ministers themselves, the Soviet Union suggested, as subjects for discussion: the demilitarisation of Germany; a Peace Treaty with Germany and the withdrawal of all occupation forces; and reductions in the armed forces of the Four Powers.

On the 29th March, the Washington correspondent of *The Times* reported: "The United States went into the meeting in a half-hearted mood, convinced that a Conference of Foreign Ministers, even if it could be arranged, would achieve nothing."

On the 14th April, Ernest Bevin died. He had been ill for some time and had been relieved of his duties as Foreign Secretary a month earlier to become Lord Privy Seal. In his place, Attlee had appointed Herbert Morrison - to the chagrin of Aneurin Bevan, who had coveted the post himself.

In a broadcast tribute, Attlee, after referring to General Marshall's original speech on aid to Europe, said of Bevin: "His welcome for that speech may well have saved Western Europe from Communism." Later in his speech Attlee said: "Bevin always stressed the point that prevention of war was not enough. There must always be a positive policy of raising standards of living throughout the world so as to destroy the conditions in which Russian Communism thrives."

The meeting of the deputies of the Foreign Ministers came to an end on the 21st June without having agreed an agenda for a conference of their Ministers. The representative of the Soviet Union wanted the meeting of deputies to stay in session until it reached agreement but the representaives of the three Western Powers insisted that "continuance of the talks could have no practical utilities."

On the 3rd April, while the agenda for the Conference of Foreign Ministers was still being discussed, West Germany was admitted into the European Coal and Steel Community under the Schuman Plan, originally put foward by the French government on the 9th May, 1950, in order to bring under control the production of coal and steel in Western Europe at a time when the end of the post-war shortage of coal was in sight and the rate of German steel production was rapidly rising.

It was welcomed by the USA as a step towards the economic integration of Europe and the creation of a single vast market, harnessing the coal and steel of the Ruhr to the armed forces of the United States. The Schuman Plan was, in fact, a forerunner of the Common Market. On the 9th July, 1951, the three Western Powers, no longer considering it necessary to consult with the Soviet Union, unilaterally declared the termination of the war with Germany.

On the 21st July, the *New York Nation* commented on a German rearmament plan, prepared by the Adenauer government and being considered by the American authorities, as follows:

> Some of the German proposals are startling. They include: (1) a German tactical air force of at least 2,000 planes, with a minimum air force personel of 40,000; (2) German armed forces to total about 250,000; (3) eventual re-introduction of conscription and a two-year period of compulsory military service....
>
> The proposed armada of 2,000 German war planes is almost exactly equal numerically to the tactical air force at Hitler's disposal just before World War II.

There were, of course, some areas of dissent among Labour Members of Parliament over the prospects of German rearmament. But, in the end, the need for loyalty to American imperialism was recognised as of

THE RETURN OF CHURCHILL (1951)

prior importance if further loans were to be relied upon.

Meanwhile in the colonies, and elsewhere abroad, Labour policy continued to be indistinguishable from Tory policy. In Malaya, new security measures had been introduced in November, 1950, giving powers to conscript labour and enabling mine and plantation owners to "group" their workers in "resettlement camps." A month later, rewards were being offered for the capture, *dead or alive*, of communists - £233 for ordinary party members and £7,000 for the Secretary-General. In his previously mentioned book, Pritt gives graphic descriptions of a number of unpleasant events that took place in Malaya, of which the following are but two typical examples:

> In January 1951, two villages were collectively fined £5,000 and £3,000 for refusing to give information about the killing of a planter; and in February a battalion of Gurkhas went to a village which had refused to give information as to the whereabouts of liberation forces, removed the entire population of Malay, Chinese and Indian inhabitants to a camp a hundred miles away, auctioned the belongings of the villagers, and burnt down all the houses. In March, 1951, it was announced that 11,630 persons were detained without trial in concentration (not resettlement) camps. By October, 1951, the war had been raging for two years, with many changes in British commands but no success, and no sign of an end.

In the Middle East, the Labour government continued to pursue the imperialist policy initiated by the so-called National government of Stanley Baldwin, Ramsay MacDonald and Sir John Samuel in 1936 when a Treaty had been signed between Britain and Egypt, under which British defences had been set up in the Canal Zone supported by 10,000 troops and 400 aircraft with ancillary personnel. After the Second World War, the popular demand in Egypt was for the renunciation of the 1936 Treaty and the evacuation of all British troops. In January, 1950, the Wafd Party had come to power, pledged to secure the abolition of the Treaty and the evacuation of all foreign troops. On the 20th November, however, Bevin had stated, in the House of Commons: "The British government has no intention of leaving the Middle East defenceless."

Almost eleven months later, on the 8th October, 1951, the Egyptian government denounced the Treaty of 1936. On the 16th, British reinforcements were sent to Egypt; a British army convoy was attacked on the 18th October and, in response, British troops took over key points on the Suez Canal. It was almost the last act of the Attlee Labour government.

Then there was the Iranian oil crisis. On the 7th March, 1951, the Iranian Prime Minister, General Razmura, said by Morgan in his book *Labour in Power 1945 - 1951* to have been "admired by the British as a supposedly progressive nationalist," was assassinated by members of an extreme Muslim sect, Fidayan-I-Islam. General Razmara was succeeded on the 27th April by Dr. Mussadiq, who promptly nationalised the Anglo-Iranian Oil Company together with its assets, including the oil refinery at Abadan, the largest in the world.

Notwithstanding that the Labour government in Britain had itself nationalised 20 per cent of its own native industry; and that the US State Department was urging the British Foreign Office to withdraw from Iran completely, Morrison considered the option of possible military intervention. Shinwell, Minister of Defence, was particularly belligerent, arguing that giving in to Mussadiq in Iran could lead to the nationalisation of the Suez Canal in Egypt. But as Morgan remarked in his book, Britain, heavily committed to military action in Korea and Malaya, had problems enough.

By the 21st June all negotiations with Mussadiq had broken down and military and naval action was being seriously discussed. But in the end common-sense prevailed and the British personnel in Abadan were evacuated.

On the home front, the year 1951 was a disaster. There were shortages of coal and of metals and other materials. Train services were cut to save coal, tinned food factories were closed down because of a shortage of tins, and 11,000 car and body workers were put on a four-day week because of the shortage of steel. Towards the end of January, another 2d. was cut off the already miniscule meat ration, due to a dispute with the Argentine over prices. By March the official cost of living index was up three points.

In April, the Budget revealed that the total share of expenditure on social services had dropped from 9s.3d. in the pound to 7s.7d. while expenditure on "defence" had risen from 4s.7d. to 7s. in the pound. Food subsidies were pegged at £400 millions and the increased costs

THE RETURN OF CHURCHILL (1951)

passed on to the consumers. Half the cost of spectacles and dentures were to be paid by the recipients.

On the 21st April, Aneurin Bevan left the Cabinet. In his letter of resignation to Attlee, Bevan wrote:

> The Budget, in my view, is wrongly conceived in that it fails to apportion fairly the burdens of expenditure as between different social classes. It is wrong because it is based upon a scale of military expenditure, in the coming year, which is physically unobtainable without grave extravagance in its spending. It is wrong because it envisages rising prices as a means of reducing civilian consumption, with all the consequences of industrial disturbance involved. It is wrong because it is the beginning of the destruction of those social services in which Labour has taken a special pride and which has given to Britain the moral leadership of the world.

Bevan's resignation was followed by the resignations of Harold Wilson from the Board of Trade, and John Freeman, from the Supply Department of the Treasury. Sir Hartley Shawcross took over from Wilson as President of the Board of Trade and Alfred Robens succeeded Bevan as Minister of Labour. On the 3rd May, 55 back-bench Labour Members refused to vote for the clause imposing charges for spectacles and dentures.

Noting these events in the June, 1951 issue of *Labour Monthly*, Palme Dutt wrote: "There is no indication here yet of either a new policy or a new leadership. But there is a very indubitable indication of the bankruptcy and crisis of the old policy and the old leadership." Later in his article, Dutt observed that if Bevan, who as recently as the previous January had appeared as the main protagonist of the £4,700 million rearmament programme, was now denouncing it and claiming to voice the sentiments of a considerable section of left opinion, it was legitimate to ask: "What is the political platform of Mr. Bevan on the main questions of the day - on rearmament, on the war policy, on the Atlantic Pact, on the anti-Soviet alignment with world reaction, on rearming Germany and Japan, on the wages fight etc."

Some of these questions were answered on the 14th July, when a "Keep Left" pamphlet entitled *One Way Only* was published with a Foreword by Bevan, Wilson and Freeman It contained some positive proposals, such as a scaling down of the rearmament programme and the need to restrain the USA in it's foreign policy, especially over the rearming of Germany. It emphasised the need to keep down prices at home and to increase expenditure on social services. It also called for negotiations with the Soviet Union. It wanted less dependence on the USA but did not oppose NATO or the American bases in Britain.

The pamphlet had a hostile reception from the capitalist press but still it sold 100,000 copies. On the 27th August the Labour Party replied with a policy statement under the title *Our First Duty Peace*, primarily a defence of the government's rearmament programme. This was reviewed in *World News* on the 8th September, by John Gollan, a leading member of the Communist Party of Great Britain and soon afterwards its General Secretary. The following substantial extract was quoted by D.N. Pritt in his *The Labour Government 1945-1951:*

> Despite the deceitful anti-Tory phrases with which each section concludes, its main purpose is the defence of the criminal right-wing policy and its disastrous consequences, against the growing opposition to that policy in the Labour movement.
>
> The agenda for the Labour Party Conference was unprecedented for the number and scope of critical resolutions tabled. They covered every aspect of policy, but the main target of criticism was the arms programme....
>
> Tied to the fatal American alliance and preparations for war, the Executive had nothing to offer the rank and file except reduced standards and rising living costs....
>
> Alarm at the growing danger of war is the outstanding feature in the trade unions and Labour Parties. There is no popular support for the American alliance, but on the contrary, the growing fear that the alliance will drag us into war. There is widespread opposition to the rearming of Germany and Japan, and the virtual alliance with Franco. They want a cease fire in Korea. There is concern about the developing tension in Persia.
>
> The statement avoids these central issues of discussion in the movement and the country.... To attempt to discuss them, to attempt to justify government policy, would be an exposure of the lie which forms the heart of this document ... that Soviet policy is the menace and that "the only aim of our rearmament is to prevent war...." The arms programme, it continues, is "the minimum required to deter aggression...."

THE RETURN OF CHURCHILL (1951)

But what is the origin of the arms programme? Its roots are to be found not in Korea or in Soviet policy, but in the Truman doctrine of 1947, the Marshall Plan and the signing of the Atlantic War Pact in 1949, which disrupted the United Nations.

From that date the war preparations have been speeded up and the American bases established. The armies were expanded and co-ordinated under Eisenhower, the arms programme worked out, the decisions taken to grab the whole of Korea as a base, rearm the Germans and Japanese and bring Franco and Tito into the war alliance....

"In diverting a part of our industrial effort towards rearmament," continues the statement, "it is vital that we do not endanger the economic and social structure.... The burden of rearmament ... can be carried by our economy without too great a strain."

This ludicrous assertion had already been laughed out of court by events. Rearmament has produced disruption and crisis.... The balance of payments ... has been destroyed.

Above all the rapidly rising cost of living, one of the main signs of strain in the economy, has produced nationwide revolt. All the unions are demanding wage increases....

With not a single new proposition for new social advance or attack on capitalism, with the statement itself declaring that the essence of socialism is a balance of priorities within present limits, *Our First Duty - Peace* ends up with the declaration that Labour's task has only just begun.

On the 21st September, *Tribune* published *Going Our Way*, which set out to justify the criticisms made by Bevan, Wilson and Freeman on their resignations. But the timing was all wrong. Two days earlier, Attlee had informed his Cabinet that he had decided to dissolve Parliament. The Labour Party had closed ranks in order to present its traditional united front to the electors.

The 83rd Trades Union Congress opened in Blackpool on the 31st August, 1951, 19 days before it was known that Attlee had fixed the date for another General Election. Unions with a total membership of more than five millions had passed resolutions at their annual conferences calling for higher wages, control of profits, and other measures to reduce the cost of living. Unions with a total membership of more than two millions, including the National Union of Mineworkers who were also calling for closer relations withthe USSR, were demanding Five-Power negotiations to end the threat of war. But in most cases the resolutions they had submitted to the TUC had been adopted in the face of strenuous opposition from their own right-wing leaders.

These cold-war warriors were soon in action. On the first day the President set the tone with a speech condemning the Soviet Union as the main reason why it was necessary to rearm even if it led to an unavoidable rise in the cost of living. He was followed by Hugh Gaitskell, Chancellor of the Exchequer, whose main concern appeared to be that too pressing demands by the workers might cause inflation, jeopardising "our position as a centre of world trade and finance."

"But how did the delegates react to these bludgeoning efforts of the right-wing Labour leaders?" asked Quæstor in the October, 1951 issue of *Labour Monthly*.

> An early sign was the cold and wary silence in which delegates heard the President's address, letting him down whenever he paused for cheers. Another was their failure to applaud the unashamed Liberal and Tory platitudes mouthed by Gaitskell, confining themselves to polite clapping at the end. But above all there was the series of important resolutions which in effect were votes of censure on the government: for its cuts in the health services, particularly on tuberculosis treatment; on housing and the need to reorganise the building industry; flagrant breaking of its pledges on questions like equal pay and toleration of yellow company unions in nationalised industries; and especially in allowing the heavy cuts in value of Old Age Pensions, sickness and injury benefits and the like by rising living costs. This last resolution, moved by a leading Communist, [John] Horner (Fire Brigades Union), in a fighting speech, was seconded by a leading non-Communist, F. Stilwell (Transport Workers and Chairman of the General Purposes Committee), and was adopted unanimously.

> Even in motions that were defeated, the message was there. A motion condemning charges for dentures and spectacles under the National Health Service was carried on a show of hands by an overwhelming majority; but the General Council imposed a card vote and

THE RETURN OF CHURCHILL (1951)

it was defeated by 3,775,000 to 3,272,000. It would have been even closer if the card of the National Union of Railwaymen, with another 391,000 votes, had not gone missing when the vote was taken.

Speaking against a resolution calling for trade with all nations, without discrimination against the USSR, China or the People's Democracies, Arthur Deakin argued against flour and timber from Russia because the price asked was "the sacrifice of our freedom and liberty."

In a long debate on a composite motion demanding a new initiative by the Labour government in the interests of world peace, in order to secure an end to the cold war, general disarmament, abolition of weapons of mass destruction, control of atomic energy for peaceful purposes and an increase of world food production, the General Council made it a vote of confidence by taking it as an amendment to paragraphs in its own report and thus secured its defeat.

By judicious use of the block vote, the General Council was able to forestall the passage of progressive motions condemning the arming of Germany and Japan, deploring the constant rise in profits at the expense of the cost of living, and demanding that compensation for former shareholders in nationalised industries be reduced. But in each case more than two million votes were cast in favour.

With Parliament scheduled to be dissolved on the 4th October and the General Election fixed for the 25th October the Annual Conference of the Labour Party, held in Scarborough on the 1st and 2nd October, was a truncated affair. It was, as Morgan put it in his book, "suffused by a profound mood of party unity," although, as he went on to point out, the effect was somewhat modified the next day when it transpired that Bevan's supporters had captured four out of the seven seats in the constituency section of the National Executive Committee.

Only the most necessary business was discussed at the Conference. There was no debate on specific motions, only a discussion on the Labour Party Election Manifesto that had been issued on the eve of the Conference. This listed the four major tasks facing the nation as being: "to secure peace; to maintain full employment and increase production; to bring down the cost of living; to build a just society."

In respect of the first stated aim, the Manifesto claimed that the Labour Party had "striven hard since 1945 to bring all the nations together in world-wide co-operation through the United Nations," but admitted it had had "grievous disappointments, particularly with the Soviet Union." Nevertheless it promised, in the words of the Manifesto, "to persevere," adding: "We do not for one moment accept the view that a third world war is inevitable. We arm to save peace."

This despite the virtual isolation of China and the Soviet Union from all serious discussions on matters of international importance, the wars that were raging in Malaya and Korea, and the crises looming in Egypt and Iran, in none of which could the actions of the Labour government be said to be in the interests of saving peace.

"Surely now," the Manifesto insisted, "it is vital to the fate of civilisation that the voice of Labour should be heard wherever and whenever the issues of war and peace are discussed between the spokesmen of the Great Powers." But the voice of Labour would not be vital if, subservient to the policies of the United States, it attacked the Soviet Union and the People's Republics of Europe and Asia on every conceivable occasion. The disappointment of the British Labour government with the Soviet Union must have been as nothing compared with the disappointment of the Soviet Union with the British Labour government.

On full employment and production, the Labour Manifesto was on safer ground; but on the cost of living, though this had increased less in Britain than in other capitalist countries, it had not matched the progress made in the socialist countries and in the Peoples' Republics.

As for social justice, as Pritt remarked: "The ownership of wealth was still concentrated in too few hands."

The Election Manifesto of the Conservative Party, which was signed by Winston Churchill, emphasised the need for a stable government and went on to say:

> In the wider world outside this island we put first the safety, progress and cohesion of the British Empire and Commonwealth of Nations. We must all stand together and help each other with all our strength both in Defence and Trade. To foster commerce within the Empire we shall maintain Imperial Preference. In our home market the Empire producer will have a place second only to the home producer.
>
> Next, there is the unity of the English-speaking peoples who together number hundreds of millions. They have only to act in harmony to preserve their own freedom and the general peace.
>
> On these solid foundations we should all continue to labour for a United Europe including in the course of time those unhappy

THE RETURN OF CHURCHILL (1951)

countries still behind the Iron Curtain.

Then came the only specific mention of the Soviet Union, or "Soviet Russia" as Churchill insisted on calling it, in the following revealing terms:

> These are the three pillars of the United Nations Organisation which, if Soviet Russia becomes the fourth, would open to all the toiling millions of the world an era of moral and material advance undreamed of hitherto among men. There was a time in our hour of victory when this object seemed to be within our reach. Even now, in spite of the clouds and confusion into which we have since fallen, we must not abandon the supreme hope and design.

In spite of the above, however,, the Conservative Party supported the Labour Party's rearmament programme whilst believing, nevertheless, that better value could have been obtained for the money.

The Conservative Election Manifesto promised to repeal the Iron and Steel Act, and reorganise publicly-owned rail and road transport. But coal would remain nationalised. And then this: "Subject to the needs of rearmament, the utmost will be done to provide better housing, water supplies, and drainage, electricity and transport in rural areas."

The Election Manifesto of the Liberal Party opened with a fair description of the situation confronting the nation:

> There is still no peace between nations. Hanging over the whole world is the fear that some governments [unnamed] are planning aggression. There is still war in Korea, and the dispute in Persia [Iran] is an immediate danger. We have begun a giant programme of rearmament, which will affect the living standards of all of us. At the same time, the Dollar Gap has again opened and that, together with a shortage of all foreign currencies, brings the ugly threat that we may not be able to buy raw materials we must have to keep up the employment of our people. On top of all this is the fact, which comes home to every housewife every day: the cost of living keeps going up.

Of course, the recommended solution was more Liberals in Parliament, to "act as a brake on class bitterness and create a safeguard against the deadening power of the great political machines."

Peace would be maintained through the rule of international law by "collective security among the free nations." Support would be given to the rearmament programme. The Liberals recognised the British Commonwealth, which they claimed to have created, to be one of the greatest forces for peace. The Council of Europe, which they described in their Manifesto as an old Liberal conception, they also believed was essential to the peace of the world – as well as partnership with the United States,

The Communist Party, which contested only 10 constituencies instead of the 100 it had contested in the 1950 General Election, stood on a policy of peace and friendship with the Soviet Union and with the socialist countries in Europe and Asia; an end to British participation in the wars in Korea and Malaya; reductions in armament expenditure so as to increase social amenities in health, education and housing; measures for the redistribution of wealth, including higher taxation for the rich and lower taxation for working people as well as a resumption of the nationlisation programme. It also stood for independence from the United States.

The main strategy of the Communist Party was directed towards creating a demand in the Labour movement for more progressive policies and for the defeat of the Tories.

Pritt described the election as "curious in a good many ways." All three major parties were agreed on all the main issues – support of the rearmament programme, hostility to the socialist world, subservience to the United States and their occupation of air bases in Britain for offensive atomic warfare, the rearming of Germany and Japan, participation in the wars in Korea and Malaya, and cuts in the social services to pay for them.

In some quarters it was suggested that the Labour leaders may well have been willing to lose the election in the face of the many problems that would confront the next government.

The Gallup Polls at the beginning of the campaign were depressing. On the 5th October there was a Tory lead of 7 per cent over Labour. Forecasts of a Tory majority of 150 were not uncommon. In an article in the December, 1951 issue of *Labour Monthly*, William Gallacher, ex-MP for West Fife, wrote:

> The Labour leaders did nothing to lessen the likelihood of those

THE RETURN OF CHURCHILL (1951)

prophecies coming true. They were without policy or programme. They gave no leadership whatever to the working class. Morrison, peddling cheap, smug impudence, handed out what he thought to be soothing syrup to the middle class, especially the Liberals, but only made it more certain that they would go over to the Tories. For only strength, not whining, will attract the wobblers; and effective leadership of the working class will, at any crisis, arouse the working class to a demonstration of strength that wins all except those who are quite definitely enemies of human progress....

It looked all set for a Tory victory by a wide margin. But, as polling day drew near, the situation began to change. Despite the disappointing performances of the Labour leadership, hatred of the Tories and their warmongering policies, symbolising all that was unacceptable in the system of capitalist exploitation, aroused the workers to action. Everywhere the cry went up: "Defeat the Tories." Wrote Gallacher in his article:

> A mighty factor in stimulating the men and women in the factories, the decisive elements in the election, was the *Daily Worker*. True it hasn't the mass circulation of the big capitalist dailies, but it goes into the factories and gives a lead to the shop-stewards and through them to the factories as a whole....
> Day after day it exposed the type of men who constituted the leadership of the Tory Party and the interests they represented - Stock Exchange speculators, armament makers, aristocratic landowners, and all the unholy crew that live in idle luxury at the expense of the working class. That was something the workers could understand, and it fanned their hatred of the Tories.

Throughout the country, members of the Communist Party were welcomed as helpers in the Labour Party committee rooms, where they brought a new spirit to the lack-lustre campaign of the reactionary Labour leaders who were not even sure whether they wanted to win the election or not. In most constituencies, Communist Party members and Labour Party members worked happily together in a common cause - the defeat of Toryism. If only they had been allowed to work together for peace and socialism. But it was not to be. The cold war warriors in the leadership of the Labour Party saw to that. They loosed off their best shots against an imaginary enemy in the socialist countries of Europe and Asia and against communists everywhere. As with the defences in Singapore during the Second World War, when the real attack came the big guns were facing the wrong way.

There was a decided swing back to Labour towards the end of the campaign, but it was not enough. When the results were announced, it was revealed that the Conservatives had won, not with a majority of 150 seats, as had at one time been forecast, but with the slender overall majority of 17. Even so, the Labour Party, with 295 seats, had polled 230,684 votes more that the Conservatives with 321 seats. The Liberal representation was reduced from nine seats to six.

The first political act of Churchill on regaining the premiership was to arrange a visit to Washington - to beg for a further loan. His next, to send Oliver Lyttleton to Malaya to beef up the war there. Support for the American aggression in Korea was to continue. All this meant more cuts in social services, an extension of the wage freeze and further rises in the cost of living.

Commenting on the result of the General Election, and the problems that lay ahead, in the December, 1951 issue of *Labour Monthly*, S.O. Davies, MP, said:

> Peace, the struggle for peace, is by far the most important question for all of us in Britain. The rising cost of living, the need for higher wages to meet it, the new restrictions imposed by the new Tory government, all of these things are subordinate to the supreme question of peace. For all of them are created by the injury done to the cause of peace, by the vast rearmament which drives, unless it be stopped, towards a more terrible war. Stop rearmament, stop the expenditure already begun of £4,700 millions on arms, stop the even more monstrous sums, which we are told the Americans demanded at the Ottawa meeting just before the dissolution of parliament, and you cut off at the root the evil growth of inflation....
>
> This was the chief lesson of the General Election campaign and of its results. But for reasons that should be understood the campaign within the Labour movement lacked its traditional *élan* and enthusiasm; lacked a distinctive and irreconcilable contrast, at this particular moment in our history, with immediate Tory policy. As stated the people feared war. Their daily worries about the increased cost of living and conscription tearing their sons away from their

THE RETURN OF CHURCHILL (1951)

homes, some of whom were the principal breadwinners, were all related to rearmament, and that to our foreign policy. Let it not be forgotten that this last General Election was fought in an atmosphere of war preparations and threatened war.

The Tory Party were not only in agreement with our foreign policy: in fact, they proudly claimed to have been the authors of it, and that they had succeeded in forcing its adoption on the Labour government. Many Labour candidates, I know, agree with me when I say that had Labour gone to the country with a socialist foreign policy, that is, a policy for peace, the Tories would have suffered a defeat more severely than that of 1945....

We have now the doubtful privilege of seeing Tory pre-election pledges being throttled by the same stranglehold of a mistaken foreign policy and its monstrous progeny of rearmament with all its social and economic consequences. The Tory government is, apparently, seeking the same solution, and that is to go cap in hand once again to the most dangerously predatory power in the world. More American aid is to be sought. This, I believe, will be given but at a price of further and deeper humiliation; a price that will inexorably spell the doom of Britain. Already we have paid heavily for so-called "American Aid." For it we have handed over Britain, with its 50 million men, women and children, as the principal base in the war strategy of American imperialism - bases for American atom bomb squadrons and thousands of American soldiers and airmen....

What is the lesson to be learned from all this? Immediately, there must be a review of policy, and this I understand to be the intention of those trade union branches that are demanding a recall of the Scarborough Labour Conference so that there can be a full democratic discussion both of what has been done in the past and what has to be aimed at in the future.

The British working-class movement is still based on our trade unions, and never have the rank and file been stronger and more militant than at present. They will, I am confident, not only resist any attempt of the Tory government to worsen their conditions but will also respond to a progressive policy that will break the shackles now fastened on us. Our first call will be to the workers of the world, acclaiming our solidarity with them; to revive our traditional hatred of imperialism with its tyranny and oppression; to declare the determination to expose and oppose the machinations of all warmongers; to extricate Britain from the threat of counter-revolutionary forces, and to identify the British Labour movement with the progressive forces of the world.

What more is there to say. We will leave the epitaph to Palme Dutt, who wrote in his *Notes of the Month* in the December, 1951 issue of *Labour Monthly.*

> After six years of a parliamentary majority, with full constitutional powers to carry through any change, no change has been made in the class structure of Britain. Capitalism and landlordism remain in possession, and Toryism returns to power.

In his article on *Constitutional Illusions,* published in *Rabochy i Soldat* during the summer of 1917, Lenin had insisted that "every capitalist country, including Russia, is basically divided into three main forces: the bourgeoisie, the petty-bourgeoisie and the proletariat."

Of the petty-bourgeoisie, Lenin had pointed out that it was economically impossible for them to pursue an independent line, and that they "involuntarily and inevitably" gravitated one minute towards the bourgeoisie and the next towards the proletariat.

The problem confronting members of the British Labour Party in 1945-51 was the fact that though it had always been, and still was in 1951, the mass party of the working class, its leaders were basically petty-bourgeois, and the majority of them could not help gravitating towards the bourgeoisie.

In doing so they accepted the Fulton programme of Churchill and united with the Tories in support of rearming, not only Britain but Germany and Japan as well. As Churchill had pointed out in a speech made in Liverpool on the 2nd October, 1951: "In the main lines of foreign policy the socialists have followed the course suggested to them by the Conservative Party."

The domestic policies of the British Labour Government were determined by its foreign policy. The wage freeze and the cuts in social services were necessary to pay for its participation in the wars in Malaya and Korea, for rearmament and for the high cost of trading almost exclusively with the USA. In the end it found itself in opposition to its own working class, and it paid the penalty..

BIBLIOGRAPHY

Acland, Sir Richard	Keeping Left. (1950)
Attlee, C.R.	As It Happened. (1954)
Balogh, Sándor & Jakob, Sándor	The History of Hungary after the Second World War. (1986)
Burns, Emile	Right-Wing Labour: Its Theory and Practice. (1961)
Churchill, Winston S.	The Second World War, Volume VI. (1954)
Coates, W.P. & Z.K.	A History of Anglo-Soviet Relations. Vol. II. (1958)
Craig, F.W.S.	British General Election Manifestos: 1900-1974. (1975)
Danilov, Leonid	Soviet Five-Year Plans. (1985)
Dutt, R. Palme	How to Save the Peace. (1948)
	Crisis of Britain and the British Empire. (1953)
Foster, William Z.	The Twilight of World Capitalism. (1949)
Gallacher, William	Rise Like Lions (1951)
Grechko, A.A.	Liberation Mission of the Soviet Armed Forces in the Second World War. (1974)
Hannington, Wal	An Engineer Looks at Russia. (1947)

PEACE AND THE COLD WAR I

Hobsbawm, Eric	Age of Extremes: The Short Twentieth Century. (1994)
Laski, Harold J.	The State in Theory and Practice. (1935)
	Reflections on the Revolution of our Time. (1943)
	Faith, Reason and Civilisation (1944)
Lenin, V. I.	Constitutional Illusions. (1917) Collected Works, Vol. 25, pp. 194-207.
	The State and Revolution. (1917)
	"Left-Wing" Communism - An Infantile Disorder. (1920)
Matthews, George	Food and the Nation. (1943)
Molotov, V. M.	Speeches to the Paris Peace Conference. (1946)
Moran, Baron Charles	Winston Churchill. (1966)
Morgan, Kenneth O.	Labour in Power: 1945-51. (1984)
Norden, Albert	Thus Wars Are Made! (1970)
Pollitt, Harry	Britain's Problems Can Be Solved. (March, 1947)
	Looking Ahead. (1947)
	Trade Unionists - What Next? (1948)
	Communism and Labour - A Call for United Action. (1949)

BIBLIOGRAPHY

Pollitt, Harry (Cont.)	Peace Depends on the People. (1950)
	After the Election. A Fighting Policy for Labour. (1951)
Pritt, D.N.	War Criminals. (1946)
	New Light on Korea. (1951)
	The Labour Government 1945-1951. (1963)
Rust, William	The Story of the *Daily Worker*. (1949)
Smith, Lyn	Covert British Propaganda: The Information Research Department: 1947-77. An article in *Millenium*, Vol.9, No.1. (Spring, 1980)
Sykes, Greta with Helen Mercer and Jan Woolf	Deadly Persuasion, Teaching the Cold War: A Study of School History Textbooks. (1985)
Werth, Alexander	The Conflict of East and West. 9th Montague Burton Lecture on International Relations. (1950)
Williams, Francis	A Prime Minister Remembers. (1961)
Zhdanov, A.A.	The International Situation. Report made at the Conference of Nine Communist Parties. (September, 1947)
Zilliacus, K.	I Choose Peace. (1949)

Unattributed
Cabinet Papers for 1945-51.
(Released under the 30 Years Rule.)

Labour Monthly Vols. 27-35. (1945-53)

Recalling the Past for the sake of the Future: The Causes, Results and Lessons of World War Two. Novosti Press (1985)

Report on Czechoslovakia by the British All-Party Parliamentary Delegation. (1946)

Reports of Labour Party Conferences. (1945 to 1951)

Reports of Trades Union Congresses. (1945 to 1951)

The Socialist Road for Britain. General Election Programme adopted at the 21st National Congress of the CPGB. (1949)

The Fight for Peace and Working Class Unity. Report to EC of CPGB. (1950)

INDEX

Abadan, Iran, 238.
Acheson, Dean (US Secretary of State), 223, 224, 227, 233.
Acland, Sir Richard (Tiverton LP), 62.
Acorn Press, Brighton, 109, 110.
Adenauer, Konrad, 31, 230, 236.
Aftenposten, (Norwegian newspaper), 24.
A History of Anglo-Soviet Relations (Coates), 223.
Alaska, USA, 187.
Albania, People›s Republic of, 9, 12, 13, 25, 63.
Albania, Communist Party of, 12.
Albanian, Democratic Front, 12.
Albert Hall, London, 45.
Aleutian Islands, 187.
Allied Control Commission in Finland, 22.
Allied Control Commission in Hungary, 17.
Allied Control Council in Berlin, 29, 102.
Allison, George, 206.
Alman, A. (South East Hackney CLP), 195.
Alsop, Joseph and Stewart, 189, 208, 223.
Amalgamated Engineering Union (AEU), 114.
Amalgamated Society of Engineers (ASE), 114, 115.
American Commentary (BBC), 60.
American Federation of Labour, 151.

American Society of International Law, 224.
Amery, John, 51.
Amery, Julian, 51.
Amery, L.S., 51.
Amherst, Lord, of Hackney, 14.
Anders, General, 34, 35, 93, 94.
Anderson, R. (Civil Service Union), 204.
Anglo-American Military Alliance, 53, 61, 62, 123, 124.
Anglo-Iranian Oil Company, 238.
Anglo-Soviet Alliance (20 Years Treaty), 61, 62, 140, 186, 187, 212.
Anglo-Soviet Youth Friendship Alliance, 50.
A Prime Minister Remembers (Williams), 233.
Arnhem, Netherlands, 95.
Anschluss, 24.
Anti-Comintern Pact, 224.
Antwerp, Belgium, 51.
Arcos raid, 62.
Argentina, 34, 48, 143, 238.
Arnot, Robin Page, 48, 235.
Arrow Cross Party, Hungary, 19.
As It Happened (Attlee), 230.
Associated Press, 11, 31, 227.
Asturias, Spain, 112.
Athens, Greece, 39.
Atlantic Ocean, 123, 203.
Atlantic Pact. (See under North Atlantic Treaty.)
Atomic Authority, International, 40.

Atomic Development Authority, 41.
Atomic Energy Commission, 39, 40, 41, 42, 186.
Attlee, Clement, 30, 33, 40, 56, 61, 75, 77, 103, 105, 107, 108, 118, 153, 157, 185, 192, 210, 213, 214, 219, 231, 233, 234, 235, 238, 239, 241.
Australia, 197.
Austria, 24, 25, 124.
Austria, Communist Party of, 24.
Austrian Freedom Front, 24.
Avonmouth, Avon, 191, 192, 199.

Baldwin, Stanley, 237.
Bale, D.J. (T&GWU), 177
Balkans The, 33.
Bank of England, 56, 104.
Baruch Plan, 39, 40, 42.
Bateson, Mrs. Ward, 78.
Bavaria, Germany, 31.
Bazarin, Colonel-General, 28.
BBC Eastern European Services, 155.
BBC World Service, 154.
Beaverbrook, Lord, 76.
Belcher, P. (Tobacco Workers' Union), 106, 174.
Belgian Congo, 101.
Belgium, 31, 78, 150, 161, 188, 202.
Benelux Countries, 182.
Benelux Countries, Social Democratic Parties of, 166.
Benes, Dr., 15, 159, 168.
Benstead, J. (National Union of Railwaymen), 57.
Berlin, Germany, 26, 28, 29, 143, 162, 182, 183, 184, 191, 220.
Bernal, J.D., 208.

Between the Wars (Trory), 116.
Bevan, Aneurin, 210, 235, 239, 241, 243.
Bevin, Ernest, 11, 34, 35, 53, 55, 62, 63, 70, 107, 137, 142, 143, 145, 146, 147, 152, 153, 154, 157, 162, 171, 196, 197, 198, 210, 212, 213, 214, 215, 219, 220, 233, 235.
Bikini Atoll, 218.
Bishop, Reg (Editor, *Russia Today*, 1946), 51.
Bi-zone, 43.
Blackett, Professor, 186.
Blackpool, Lancashire, 192, 241.
Blum, Leon, 73, 74, 152, 168.
Blyton, William R., 14, 15.
Bonn, West Germany, 230.
Bormann, Martin, 51.
Bosnia-Herzegovina, 11.
Boston, USA, 188.
Bournemouth, Dorset, 54.
Bowden, A.E. (Amalgamated Union of Operative Bakers, Confectioners and Allied Workers), 173, 175.
Braddock, Tom, 198.
Bridgeport, USA, 66.
Bridlington, Yorkshire, 202, 206, 207.
Brighton 1st Branch, AEU, 112, 113, 114.
Brighton & Hove Labour Party, 112.
Brighton Dome, 78.
Brighton & Hove Gazette, 109, 115.
Brighton Labour Club (London Road), 114.
Brighton, Sussex, 51, 80, 96, 109, 113, 180.
Brighton Town Council, 115.

INDEX

Brighton Trades Council, 111, 114, 115.
Britain, Battle of, 95.
British Council of Churches, 222.
British-Czechoslovak Friendship League, 15.
British Empire Conference of Communist Parties, 117.
British Socialist Commonwealth, 90.
British-Soviet Friendship Houses, 50.
British-Soviet Friendship Society (BSFS), 50.
British-Soviet Society, 50, 130, 131, 132.
British-Soviet Unity, National Council of, 50.
Browder, Earl, 66, 67, 68.
Brown, Ernest (National Organiser, BSS, 1946), 51.
Brown, George, MP for Belper, 73.
Brown, Tom (Secretary, BSS, 1946), 51.
Brussels, Belgium, 164, 186.
Brussels Treaty, 196, 212, 223.
Budapest, Hungary, 19.
Bulgaria, 9, 21, 22, 150, 151, 169, 202.
Bulgarian Fatherland Front, 21.
Bulgarian People's Army, 21.
Bulgarian Workers' Party, 21.
Bullock, F. (Amalgamated Union of Foundry Workers), 204.
Burgess, Guy, 156.
Burgess Hill, Sussex, 110.
Burghope, E.H. (Atomic Sciences Committee of Association of Scientific Workers), 220.
Burma, 9, 47, 95, 123.
Byelorussia, USSR, 27.
Byrnes, James, 11, 32, 43, 53, 124.

Cable and Wireless Bill, 56.
Cadogan, Sir Alexander, 223.
Cairo Conference (1943), 231.
Cambodia, 9.
Cambridge, Cambs., 186.
Cambridge University, 127.
Canada, 47, 77, 188, 191.
Canadian Seamen's Union, 191, 200.
Cannon, Clarence (USA), 189, 218.
Cannon, L. (Electrical Trades Union), 206.
Cardew, Dr. H.B. (Bath DLP), 167.
Cardiff, South Wales, 176, 222.
Cardiff Trades Council, 176.
Cards on the Table (LP), 132.
Carlton Club, London, 142.
Carlton House Terrace, London, 155.
Castlereagh, Lord, 34.
Catlin, Professor C.E.G. (Bury DLP), 168.
Cavendish-Bentinck (Ambassador to Poland), 142, 143.
Centenary Celebration Committee (Brighton 1st Branch AEU), 113.
Centenary Exhibition (Brighton AEU), 114.
Central Hall, Westminster, 33, 50, 51, 194.
Cernin Palace, Prague, 160.
Ceylon, 9, 47.
Chadwick, Philip, 113.
Chamberlain, Neville, 26.
Channel Islands, 111.
Chiang Kai Shek, 117, 175, 229.
Chicago Tribune, 34.
China, 9, 20, 33, 40, 55, 110, 117, 123, 125, 155, 164, 165, 174, 175, 210, 212, 229, 234, 242, 244.
China, Communist Party of, 125.

China, National Liberation Movement of, 125.
China, People's Republic of, 208.
Chinese People's Republic, 233.
Churchill, Winston, 7, 31, 36, 37, 38, 39, 50, 60, 61, 62, 75, 76, 105, 132, 133. 152, 154, 167, 169, 178, 186, 188, 189, 212, 213, 214, 215, 218, 219, 220, 224, 244, 245, 248.
CIA, Formation of, 155.
Citrine, Sir Walter, 48, 83, 91.
City of London, 66.
Civil Aviation Bill, 56.
Civil Liberties, Council for, 98, 99.
Civil Service Commission, Committee of, 143.
Clay, General, 183.
Clay, Harold (NEC), 130, 131.
Cleveland, USA, 187.
Clout, Walter (Mayor of Brighton), 80, 115.
Coates, W.P. and Z.K., 223.
Cobden, Richard, 115.
Cologne, Germany, 31.
Commission of Conventional Armaments, 185.
Common Market, 236.
Communist Party. See under name of country.
Congress of Industrial Organisation (USA), 101.
Congress of Europe, 168.
Constitutional Illusions, (Lenin), 250.
Cook, E. (S.W. St. Pancras LP), 59, 60.
Co-operative Union, 45.
Co-operator, 114.
Corbett, W., DSO, 15.
Corn Laws, 115.

Council of Europe, 192, 246.
Councils of Action, 62.
Crabtree Arcade, Lancing, 109.
Crabtree Estate, Fulham, 109.
Crabtree Press, Brighton, 109, 113, 116.
Crawford, J. (Boot & Shoe Operatives), 82, 106.
Crimean (Yalta) Agreement, 187.
Crimean (Yalta) Conference, 34, 65, 66, 67, 125, 212.
Crimean War, 34,
Cripps, Stafford, 162, 164, 171, 172, 194, 206, 210.
Crosland, Anthony, 156.
Crossman, R.H.S. (Coventry East DLP), 132, 138, 141, 197.
Croydon, Surrey, 113.
Cummings, A.J., 213.
Curzon, Lord, 34.
Cyrankiewicz (Prime Minister of Poland), 151.
Czechoslovakia, 9, 13, 14, 15, 16, 49, 50, 70, 101, 150, 151, 158, 159, 167, 168, 169, 185, 197, 206.
Czechoslovakia, Communist Party of, 13, 14, 49, 158, 167.
Czechoslovakia, Congress of Farmers' Commissions of, 160.
Czechoslovakia, Congress of Works Councils and Trade Union Organisations of, 160.
Czechoslovakia, National Socialist Party of, 14, 158.
Czechoslovakia, People's Party of, 14, 158.
Czechoslovakia, Social Democratic Party of, 14, 49.
Czechoslovak-Soviet Friendship

INDEX

Society, 159.
Czechs and Slovaks, National Front of, 13, 14, 16, 158, 160.

D'Abernon, Lord, 34.
Daily Express, 11.
Daily Herald, 38, 45, 60, 115, 132, 160, 164, 219, 220.
Daily Mail, 187.
Daily Worker, 4, 45, 53, 68, 115, 125, 186, 247.
Daimler-Benz works, 28.
Daladier, Édouard, 26.
Dalton MP, Hugh (NEC), 132, 139, 162, 169, 198.
Danube Flotilla, 24.
Danube, River, 24.
Danubian states, 123.
Dardenelles, 142.
Dash, Jack, 199.
Das Reich, 36.
Davies, Clement, (Liberal Leader), 213.
Davies MP, Harold (Leek DLP), 131, 137.
Davies MP, Rhys (Union of Shop Distributive and Allied Workers), 195.
Davies MP, S.O.D. (Methyr Tydfil), 231, 248.
Davis, J.H. (Reviewer), 112.
Dawn Music (Chadwick), 113.
Deakin, Arthur (Transport & General Workers$ Union), 83, 174, 175, 177, 194, 199, 200, 205, 206, 243.
Decartelisation Dept. of the US Military Government in Germany, 31.
de Gaulle, General, 53, 161.

Denmark, 25, 87, 150, 173, 188.
Dien Bien Phu, Battle of, 59.
Dimitrov, Georgi, 21.
Dock Labour Scheme, 200.
Doenitz, Karl, 52.
Douglas, George (Union of Post Office Workers), 222.
Driberg, Tom, MP for Maldon, 79.
Duff Cooper, 142.
Duchin, Edgar (Haldane Society), 170.
Dukes, Charles (National Union of General & Municipal Workers), 80, 82, 87.
Dulles, John Foster, 124, 187, 224, 227, 228.
Dunkirk Treaty, 196.
Du Pont, 108.
Dutt, R. Palme, 10, 26, 30, 48, 52, 53, 117, 118, 146, 147, 162, 164, 171, 191, 201, 224, 239, 250.

East Anglia, 165, 166.
Eastern Front, 23.
East Grinstead, Sussex, 113.
East Prussia, People's Councils of, 27.
Economist, 30, 163.
Ede, Chuter, 45, 190.
Eden, Anthony, 35, 147.
Edge Hill, 161.
Edinburgh, Scotland, 214, 222, 223.
Edwards, Alfred (MP for Middlesbrough), 169.
Edwards, R.H. (National Union of Vehicle Builders), 141.
Egypt, 55, 58, 138, 237, 238, 244.
Eisenach, Germany, 27.
Eisenhower, General Dwight, 241.

Eliot (Military Analyst), 190.
Ellerby, W.J. (Civil Service Clerical Association), 98, 100.
Engels, Frederick, 110, 111.
Engels on Irish Affairs, 110.
Erfurth, General, 22.
Eton College, 127, 143.
European Coal and Steel Community, 236.
European Recovery Programme, 173.
Evans, The Reverend Stanley, 51.
Evening Argus, Brighton, 76, 77, 114.
Evening News, London, 37.

Fagan, Hyman, 216.
Falkingham, Edna (Union of Shop Distributive & Allied Workers), 134, 135.
Family Census (Royal Commission on Population), 109.
Federal Council of Churches, USA, 187.
Federov, M., 215.
Fidayan-I-Islam, 238.
Field, Peter, 30.
Financial Times, 121.
Finchley, London, 216.
Finland, 22, 24, 25, 101.
Finland, Communist Party of, 22.
Finland, Democratic Union of the People of, 22.
Foot, Michael, 220.
For He's a Jolly Good Fellow, 103.
Formosa, 229, 234.
Foster, William Z., 67, 123.
Foulkes, F. (Electrical Trades Union), 105, 107.
France, 9, 25, 31, 40, 70, 74, 101, 111, 117, 125, 150, 152, 161, 164, 174, 182, 187, 188, 220, 233.
France, Catholic Party of, 152.
France, Communist Party of, 53, 74, 117, 125, 152.
France, MRP, 152.
France, Popular Republican Movement of (MRP), 53.
France, Republican Liberty Party of, 53.
France, Socialist Party of, 49, 50, 53, 74, 152, 166.
Franco, General, 55, 58, 84, 86, 102, 107, 240, 241.
Franco-Soviet Treaty, 187.
Frank, Hans, 52.
Frankfurt-on-Main, 44.
Freeman, John, 239, 241.
Frick, Wilhelm, 52.
Friendly Society of Steam Engine and Machine Makers and Millwrights, 115.
Friends of Soviet Russia, 50.
Friends of the Soviet Union, 50.
Fritsche, Hans, 52.
Fuchs, Dr. Klaus, 208.
Fulton, Missouri, 7, 31, 36, 37, 38, 50, 152, 215, 220, 224..
Funk, Walter, 52.
Fyfe, Hamilton, 115.

Gaitskell, Hugh, 210, 232, 242.
Gallacher, William (MP for West Fife), 82, 170, 198, 216, 246, 247.
Gallup Polls, 246.
Gardner, G. (Amalgamated Weavers' Society), 99.
Gardner, Jim, (National Union of

Foundry Workers), 46.
Gdansk (formerly Danzig), Poland, 20.
Geddes, Charles (Union of Post Office Workers), 222.
General Assembly of the Church of Scotland, 222, 223.
General Strike (1926), 114.
General Motors, USA, 52.
George, Lloyd, 62.
German Economic Commission, 183.
German Economic Council, 144.
German Federal Republic (West Germany), 195, 230, 233, 235, 236, 239, 240, 241, 242, 246.
German Labour Front, 83.
German Officers' League, 27.
German People's Congress for Unity, 161, 162.
German People's Front, 30.
Germany, 9, 16, 17, 21, 24, 25, 27, 28, 29, 30, 31, 33, 43, 58, 60, 78, 85, 95, 101, 107, 108, 118, 123, 125, 143, 144, 145, 147, 149, 150, 161, 162, 167, 182, 212, 218, 219, 220.
Germany, Communist Party of, 25, 26, 27, 28, 29, 30, 32, 44, 49, 125, 149, 230.
Germany, Free, National Committee of, 26, 27.
Germany, Liberal Democratic Party of, 30.
Germany, National Peace Movement of, 27.
Germany, Social Democratic Party of, 30, 49, 149, 161.
Germany, Socialist Unity Party of, 44, 49, 149, 161.
Gibson, George (General Council TUC), 87, 89, 90, 92.
Gilbert, Captain, C.M., 52,
Gittins, T. (Spelthorne DLP), 168.
Goebbels, Dr. Joseph, 36, 37, 63, 105.
Goering, Hermann, 37, 51.
Going Our Way (Tribune), 241.
Gold Badge of Congress (TUC), 87.
Gollan, John (CPGB), 240.
Gottwald, Klement, 13, 14, 15, 16, 49, 158, 159, 160.
Grand Spa Hall, Scarborough, 165.
Gravesend, Kent, 161.
Great Britain, Communist Party of, 49, 63, 64, 65, 66, 68, 69, 70, 75, 117, 119, 120, 125, 128, 130, 131, 174, 175, 180, 181, 201.
Great Britain, Communist Party of, 18th Congress, 66, 67, 79, 104, 105, 108, 112; 19th Congress, 118, 124, 125.
Great Yarmouth, Norfolk, 221.
Greece, 33, 35, 39, 55, 60, 61, 78, 85, 86, 104, 105, 106, 107, 117, 118, 119, 121, 123, 125, 141, 142, 143, 146, 164, 170, 175, 176, 177, 178, 179, 180, 210, 212.
Greek Confederation of Labour, 85, 102, 105, 106.
Greek Maritime Union, 176.
Greek People, National Liberation Movement of, 34.
Greek, seamen, 176.
Greek Supreme Court, 85.
Greek Tobacco Workers' Union, 106.
Greene, Sir Hugh, 155.
Grierson, Edgar, 15.
Griffiths MP, James, 192, 197.

Gromyko, Andrei, 41, 188, 229.
Groza, Petru, 20.
Guardian, 152.
Guiterman, Helen (Sec. Youth Dept., BSFS, 1946), 51.
Gunther, John (USA), 227.
Gurkhas, 237.

Haldane Society, 170.
Hallsworth, Sir Joseph (General Council TUC), 96, 97, 98, 99, 100, 107.
Hamburg, Germany, 27.
Hancock, Florence, 171.
Hannington, Wally, 115, 116.
Han Su-whan, Lieutenant (South Korea), 228.
Hardy, George (Sussex District Secretary, CPGB), 180, 181.
Harrow College, 127, 143.
Harrow, London, 216.
Hassell, S.H. (Orpington DLP), 141.
Hayman, F.H. (Camborne LP), 61.
Haywards Heath, Sussex, 110, 111.
H-bomb, 221.
Herbison, Margaret, 15.
Hess, Rudolph, 52,
Hesse, Germany, 31.
Hewitson MP, M. (National Union of General & Municipal Wprkers), 204.
Higgins, Marguerite (*New York Herald Tribune*), 226.
Hiroshima, 55.
Hitler, Adolf, 10, 24, 26, 27, 28, 55, 63, 100, 102, 150, 169, 188, 224, 230, 236.
Holland, 150, 164, 174.
Hong Kong, 231.
Horinsky, B. (South Paddington LP), 59.
Horner, Arthur (National Union of Mineworkers), 69, 91.
Horner, John (Fire Brigades' Union), 177, 178, 242.
Horsham, Sussex, 113.
Horthy, Admiral, 19.
Hot Springs Conference (UNO), 75.
House of Representatives Appropriations Committee, USA, 189, 218.
House of Representatives, USA, 189.
Housewive's League, British, 76, 78, 79.
Hove, Sussex, 113.
Howey, General (USA), 220.
Hudson, Robert (Min. of Ag. and Fish), 75.
Hughes, Emrys, 198.
Hungary, 9, 16, 18, 19, 20, 24, 55, 150, 151, 169.
Hungary, Communist Party of, 16, 17, 18, 19, 20.
Hungary, National Independence Front of, 16, 17, 18.
Hungary, National Peasant Party of, 16, 18, 19.
Hungary, Smallholders' Party of, 16, 18.
Hungary, Social Democratic Party of, 16, 18, 19.
Hungary, Supreme Economic Council of, 18.
Hunter, G.B. (Union of Shop Distributive & Allied Workers), 90.
Hutchinson, H. Lester, MP, 34, 198, 216.
Hutt, Allen, 115.
Hynd, (Hackney Central DLP), 168.

INDEX

Iceland, 188.
If Russia Strikes? 190.
Imperial Chemical Industries (ICI), 196.
Imperialist War (Trory), 204.
Independent Labour Party (ILP), 66.
India, Communist Party of, 125.
India, Dominion of 9, 47, 48, 78, 119, 121, 123, 125, 197, 208.
India, Republic of, 208.
Indo-China, 34, 58, 117, 230.
Indonesia, 9, 33, 34, 35, 55, 58, 86, 117, 119, 123, 147, 197.
Industrial and Provident Societies Act, 45.
Information Research Department (IRD), 152, 166.
Institute of World Economy and Politics, Moscow, 149.
Inter-Allied Governing Authority in Berlin, 29.
International Federation of Trade Unions (IFTU) 83.
International Labour Conference in Montreal, 107.
International Postwar Settlement (LP), 132, 140.
International Seafarers' Union, 191.
Iran (Persia), 93, 240, 244, 245.
Iraq, 138.
Irish Democrat, 110.
Iron abd Steel Act, 245.
Iron Curtain, 36, 37, 50, 105, 152, 156, 215, 245.
Isaacs, George, 47, 92, 93, 94, 103.
Isle of Thanet, 79.
Islington, West, 161.
Italy, 9, 33, 34, 35, 49, 58, 70, 78, 85, 125, 150, 151, 157, 161, 174, 188.

Italy, Christian Democratic Party of, 49.
Italy, Communist Party of, 49, 125, 151.
Italy, Socialist Party of, 49, 125, 151, 166, 170.

Jackson, Andrew, 67.
Jackson, Nathan (Paole Zion-Jewish Socialist LP), 62.
James, G. (National Union of Railwaymen), 176.
Japan, 9, 33, 101, 123, 125, 142, 165, 187, 234, 239, 240, 241, 242, 246.
Japan, Communist Party of, 125.
Jefferson, Thomas, 67.
Jenkins MP, Roy, 194.
Jensen, 173.
Jodl, Alfred, 52.
Johnston, Ricard, 226.
Jones, Bill, 45.
Joyce, William (Lord Haw Haw), 51.

Kaltenbrunner, Ernst, 51.
Kansas, USA, 77.
Kartun, Derek, 53.
Keitel, Wilhelm, 51.
Kemsley Press, 76.
Kettering, Northampton, 78.
Kiel, Germany, 27.
Kiewe, Muriel (St. Marylebone LP), 60.
Kim I Sek (South Korea), 228.
King, Dr. William, 114.
Kirkpatrick, Ivone, 153, 154.
Klugmann, James, 149, 150, 151, 156.
Korea, 9, 33, 101, 165, 225, 234, 240, 241, 244, 245, 246, 248.

Korea, North, 225, 226, 227, 228, 229, 230, 231, 238.
Korea, North, People's Army of, 226, 230, 233.
Korea, South, 225, 226, 227, 228, 229, 230, 231.
Korea, South, National Assembly of, 226, 227.
Korea, South, Security Act, 226, 227.
Kosovo-Metohiba, Yugoslavia, 12.
Kremlin, Moscow, 130.
Kropotkin, Prince, 114.
Krupp, Alfred, 235.

Labour Believes in Britain, 195, 196, 198, 199, 201, 210.
Labour Directories, 113.
Labour for Higher Production (LP), 135.
Labour in Power, 1945-51 (Morgan), 199, 210, 231, 238.
Labour Monthly, 10, 26, 30, 46, 48, 49, 52, 53, 69, 108, 117, 146, 149, 156, 162, 172, 180, 190, 191, 198, 200, 206, 208, 216, 220, 224, 235, 239, 242, 246, 248, 250.
Labour, National Council of, 45, 46.
Labour Party, Annual Conferences of, 1940: 73 et seq; 1945: 49 et seq; 1946: 54 et seq; 1947: 129 et seq; 1948: 165 et seq; 1949: 192 et seq; 1950: 232 et seq; 1951: 243 et seq.
Lane, Mrs. H. (St. Pancras South-East DLP), 166.
Laos, 9.
Laski, Harold (NEC), 39, 54, 73, 134, 135.

Latin America, 101, 123, 174.
Lawther, William (National Union of Mineworkers), 174, 203.
League of Nations, Covenant of, 224.
Lease-Lend Act, 47.
Lee MP, Fred (Hulme), 136.
Leeper, Rex (Ambassador to Greece), 142, 143.
Leipzig, Germany, 26.
Lenin, Vladimir Ilyich Ulyanov, 250.
Leningrad, USSR, 112.
Leningrad Front, Military Council of the, 22.
Let Us Face the Future (LP Election Manifesto, 1945), 59, 72, 132, 140, 212.
Let Us Win Through Together (LP Election Manifesto, 1950), 210.
Lewes, Sussex, 113.
Lincoln, Abraham, 67.
Lindsay, Kenneth, 15.
Lippmann, Walter, 165, 208.
Liverpool, 94, 192, 198.
London, England, 11, 19, 23, 53, 102, 111, 190, 199.
London Trades Council, 84, 190.
London University, 134.
Looking Ahead (Pollitt), 126.
Lord Haw Haw, see under Joyce, William.
Lovelock, Irene, 78.
Lulcheu, 150.
Luxembourg, 164, 188.
Lyons, France, 51.
Lyttleton, Oliver, 248.

MacArthur, General, 187, 227.
MacDonald, Ramsay, 237.

Macedonia, 11.
Mackenzie-King, (Canadian Premier), 214.
Mainly about Books (Trory), 110.
Maisky, Ivan, 63.
Malaya, 101, 170, 172, 175, 180, 197, 212, 237, 238, 244, 246, 248.
Maldon, Essex, 79.
Manchester Guardian, 42, 186, 187, 207.
Manchuria, 165.
Manning, Leah, 198.
Marcouse, Irene, Holborn LP, 57.
Margate, Kent, 129, 180, 232.
Marshall Aid, 158, 161, 163, 165, 166, 175, 192, 202.
Marshall, General, 235.
Marshall Plan, 147, 152, 161, 163, 180, 190, 202, 235, 241.
Marxism and Reformism (Pollitt), 127.
Marx, Karl, 65, 110.
Masaryk, Jan, 15, 160.
May, Alan Nunn, 208.
Mayhew, Christopher, 152, 153, 154, 155.
May Day, 190, 191.
McCarthy, Mrs. Helen (Finchley and Friern Barnet CLP), 195,
McGree, L. (Amalgamated Society of Workers), 94, 95, 205.
McKerrow, C. (Transport & General Workers Union), 95.
McLennan, R. (Electrical Trades Union), 106.
McNeil, Hector, 186, 223.
Melbourne Sun, 226.
Merrells, S.J. (Fire Brigades' Union), 69.

Metaxas, 178.
Mid-Sussex Times, 110.
Middle East, 47, 85, 138, 142, 164, 197, 212, 237.
Mikardo, Ian, MP (Reading TC&LP), 57, 137.
Miklos, General, 17.
Millbank, London, 155.
Miller, F.M. (St. Pancras Borough LP), 130, 131.
Millington MP, Ernest (Chelmsford DLP), 132, 133.
Mollet, Guy, 152.
Mongolia, 9.
Montenegro, Yugoslavia, 11.
Monthly Journal (AEU), 111, 115.
Montreal, Canada, 107, 223.
Moore, L.F., Orpington LP, 57.
Moran, Lord, 76.
Morgan, Kenneth O., 199, 200, 210, 212, 231, 238, 243
Morning Standard, India, 37.
Morrison, Herbert, 38, 63, 65, 66, 67, 68, 71, 72, 73, 134, 135, 136, 138, 147, 170, 195, 210, 213, 235, 238, 247.
Moscow Conference (1945), 231.
Moscow, USSR, 10, 11, 15, 19, 21, 22, 26, 33, 84, 112, 124, 143, 144, 149, 158, 215, 225.
Mosley, Oswald, 45, 161.
Moulsecoomb, Brighton, 109.
Moutet, M.,
Mowbray, W. (Scottish Union of Bakers), 177.
Mr. Bevin and British Foreign Policy (Zilliacus) 34.
Munich, Germany, 16, 150.
Mussadiq, Dr., 238.
Mussolini, Benito, 102, 152, 169.

Mutual Defence Assistance Programme, 223.

Naesmith, A. (United Textile Factory Workers' Association), 139.
Nagasaki, Japan, 55.
National City Bank (USA), 225, 227.
National Coal Board, 83.
National Dock Labour Board, 200.
National Health Service, 56, 196, 217, 242.
National Insurance Bill, 56.
National Insurance Injuries Bill, 56.
National Service Act, 133, 138.
National Union of Mineworkers (NUM), 191.
National Union of Railwaymwen (NUR), 110.
Near the Sun (Tempest), 113.
Nelson and Colne, Lancashire, 56.
Nenni, Pietro, 151, 169.
Netherlands. See under Holland), 188.
Neurath, Constantin von, 52.
New Communist Party, 182.
New Corea Company, 225, 227.
New Foundations (Trory), 113.
New Light on Korea (Pritt), 229.
Newmarket, Suffolk, 79.
Newport, South Wales, 177.
News-Chronicle, 31, 213, 222.
New Statesman and Nation, 43, 52.
New York Herald Tribune, 30, 37, 165, 185, 188, 189, 190, 207, 208, 225, 226.
New York Nation, 236.
New York Times, 226.
New York, USA, 39, 43, 53, 226.
New Zealand, 54, 197.

Nicholas, W. (Union of Shop Distributive & Allied Workers), 175.
Nikitchenko,, Major-General I.T., 52.
Nixon, Russel A., 31.
No Easy Way, (Liberal Party Election Manifesto. 1950), 211.
Noel-Baker MP, Philip, 58, 62, 129.
Nordahl, 173.
Norden, Albert, 226.
North Atlantic Treaty, 186, 187, 189, 190, 196, 212, 223, 241.
North Atlantic Treaty Organisation (NATO), 188, 223, 240.
Northern Ireland, 79.
North Hammersmith, London, 216.
Norway, 22, 23, 24, 25, 173, 186, 188.
Norwegian Communist Party, 23.
Norwegian Government in London, 23.
Nottingham, Notts., 98.
Nuremburg Trial, 51, 52.

Observer, 124, 152, 202, 229.
Oder, River, 28.
O'Faolain, Sean, Editor, *The Bell*, 110.
Okinawa, 187.
Oklahoma, USA, 77.
Old Mechanics, 114, 115.
Old Town Square, Prague, 159.
One Way Only (Bevan, Wilson and Freeman), 239.
Ongjin, South Korea, 228.
Opel works, Germany, 52.
Open University, 152.
Oriental Consolidated Mining Company, 225.

INDEX

Our First Duty Peace (LP), 240, 241.
Overseas Information Department (OID), 156.
Overseas Press Club (USA), 226.
Oviedo, Spain, 112.
Owen, Dr. David, 156.
Oxford University, 127.

Pacific and Seventh Fleets (USA), 230.
Pacific Ocean, 123, 187.
Pact of Unity of Action refused in France, 152.
Pact of Unity of Action (Italy), 151.
Page, Barbara, 31.
Paine, Thomas, 67.
Pakistan, 197.
Palestine, 62, 117, 121, 123, 138, 142.
Pan-Hellenic Federation, 176.
Papen, Franz von, 52.
Papworth, A.F. (General Council TUC), 105, 107.
Paris, France, 19, 82, 102, 142, 223.
People's Press Printing Society, 44, 45.
Peru, 110.
Petit, F.W., West Lewisham LP, 57.
Petrescu, Titel, 150.
Peyer, Karolyi, 150.
Philippines, 9, 101, 165, 187, 230, 234.
Phillips, Morgan (Nat. Sec. LP), 130, 132, 160, 170.
Pieck, Wilhelm, 44.
Piratin, Phil, 216.
Platts-Mills MP, John, 169, 170, 216.

Podushkin, M. (Soviet Power Workers' Union), 222.
Poland, 9, 20, 55, 78, 95, 100, 101, 142, 143, 150, 158, 169, 185, 202.
Poland, Socialist Party of, 151.
Poland, Workers' Party of, 151.
Polish Corps, 93,
Polish Forces in Britain, 85, 93, 94, 95, 96, 97, 98, 99, 100, 117.
Polish Forces in Europe, 85.
Polish Provisional Government of National Unity, 20.
Polish Government in Exile in London, 20, 93.
Polish People's Democratic Government, 20.
Polish Workers' Party, 20.
Pollitt, Harry, 65, 66, 69, 70, 71, 108, 118, 119, 120, 121, 122, 123, 124, 125, 126, 172, 180, 217.
Political Affairs, 123.
Portugal, 188,
Potsdam Agreement, 43, 108, 123, 142, 144, 182, 187, 233, 235.
Potsdam Conference, 20, 30, 125, 143, 212.
Potsdam, Germany, 44, 55.
Prague, Czechoslovakia, 159.
Pravda, 38.
Price, G. Ward, 187.
Pritt, D.N., KC, MP, 108, 191, 198, 199, 210, 212, 216, 235, 237, 240, 244, 246.
Public Employees' Journal, 221.
Pyongyang, North Korea, 225.

Quæstor, 242.
Quin, Mabel (Sec. Women's Dept.,

British Soviet Society, 1946), 51.)
Quisling, Vidkun, 23.

Rabochy i Soldat, 250.
Radescu, General, 20.
Raeder, Erich, 52.
Railway Review, 110, 112, 113.
Ramadier, Paul, 157.
Ratner, H. (Salford North DLP), 166.
Razmura, General, 238.
Reimann, Max, 184.
Renner, Karl, 24.
Report of the Executive Committee (CPGB), 125.
Rhineland, Germany, 125.
Rhine-Ruhr, Germany, 31, 164.
Ribbentrop, Joachim von, 51.
Richmond, London, 216.
Right Road for Britain (Conservative Party), 201.
Rise Like Lions (Gallacher), 170, 198.
Robens, Alfred, 239.
Roberts, Bryn (National Union of Public Employees), 221.
Roberts, General (USA), 225, 226.
Romita, 170.
Roosevelt, Franklin D., 7, 53, 152, 220.
Rosenberg, Alfred, 51.
Rosling's, Messrs., 115.
Rotherham, South Yorkshire, 79.
Rothermere, Lord, 76.
Royall, Kenneth (Secretary for War, USA), 165.
Ruhr, 236.
Rumania, 9, 21, 55, 101, 150, 151, 169.
Russian Revolution (1917), 126.

Russia Today Society, 50, 110.
Rust, William, 45, 46, 49, 50, 68.
Ryukyu Archipelago, 187.

Saillant, Louis (Gen. Sec. WFTU), 83, 100.
Samuel, Sir John, 237.
Sanatescu, General, 20.
Santander, Spain, 112.
Saragat, Giuseppe, 150, 168, 170.
Sargeant, Tom (Hampstead DLP), 136.
Sargent, Sir Orme, 153.
Sauckel, Fritz, 51.
Savoy, House of (Italy), 49.
Saxony, Germany, 44.
Scandinavia, Social Democratic Party of, 166.
Scarborough, (North Yorkshire), 180, 243,.
Schacht, Hjalmar, 52.
Schaffer, Gordon, 50.
Schumacher, Dr. Kurt, 44, 149, 150, 161, 167.
Schuman Plan, 236.
Scotland, 96, 99.
Scott, J.R. (AEU), 105, 106.
Scottish TUC, 222.
Seoul, South Korea, 225, 226.
Serbia, 11.
Seventy Years of Trade Unionism, 80.
Severing, Karl, 191.
Seydlitz, General von, 27.
Seyss-Inquart, Artur, 51.
Shawcross, Sir Hartley, 48, 161, 239.
Sheffield, South Yorkshire, 79.
Shinwell, Emanuel, 57, 91, 165, 166, 218, 238.
Shirac, Baldur von, 52.

INDEX

Shop Assistants' Union (National Amalgamated Union of Shop Assistants Warehousemen & Clerks), 111.
Shuffeldt, Margaret (Chelsea DLP), 141.
Siam (See Thailand).
Siberia, USSR, 23, 165.
Silverman MP, Sidney (Nelson & Colne DLP), 56, 133, 134.
Simon Lord, 109.
Sinclair, Sir Archibald, 113.
Singapore, 248.
Slovakia, Communist Party of, 13, 14.
Slovakia, Democratic Party of, 158.
Slovakia, Freedom Party of, 14.
Slovakia, Labour Party of, 14.
Smith, Ellis, 15.
Smith, Lyn, 152, 153, 154, 155, 156.
Smith, Sir Ben, 47.
Smithfield Market, 76.
Social Insurance and Allied Services (Beveridge), 81.
Society for Cultural Relations with the USSR, 50.
Sofia, Bulgaria, 21.
Solley, Leslie, 198, 216.
South Africa, 78, 86, 125, 197.
South Africa, Communist Party of, 125.
South America, 100.
Southampton Docks, 76.
Southern Railway, 112.
Soviet-German Pact of Non-Aggression, 204.
Soviet Military Administration in Germany, 29.
Soviet Union, See under USSR.

Spain, 34, 55, 58, 60, 84, 86, 112, 118, 119, 123, 125, 212.
Speer, Albert, 52.
Squibb, E.J. (Southampton DLP), 130.
Stalin, Joseph, 8, 10, 28, 30, 42, 130, 185, 213, 215, 220..
Stalingrad, USSR, 26.
Stalingrad, Battle of, 94.
Stanley, Jack (Constructional Engineering Union), 193.
Stepney, London, 216.
Stettin (See under Szczecin.)
Stilwell, F' (Transport & General Workers' Union), 242.
Strachey, John, 77, 78
Streicher, Julius, 52.
Stross, Barnett, 15.
Stuttgart, Germany, 32.
Suez Canal, Egypt, 138, 237, 238.
Sullivan (*New York Times*), 226.
Sunday Express, 30.
Sunday Express, 52.
Sussex Daily News, 78, 114, 115.
Sussex Federation of Trades Councils, 111.
Sussex University, 152.
Sussex Weald, 113.
Sweden, 90.
Symington, (Secretary for Air, USA), 165.
Syngman Rhee, 225, 226, 228.
Syn Sung Mo, 225.
Szalasi, Ferenc, 19.
Szczecin (formerly Stettin), Poland, 20, 37, 63.

Taft, Senator, 218.
Tanner, Jack (Amalgamated Engineering Union), 68.

Tarazov, MP, 86, 87.
Tass, 42.
Teheran Conference, 212.
Telegraf (West Berlin), 183, 229.
Tempest, Victor, 113.
Tewson, Victor, 172, 173, 179, 205, 206.
Texas, USA, 77.
Thailand, (Siam), 47, 58.
The Bell, 110, 111.
The British Road to Socialism (CPGB), 125, 126, 127, 201.
The Hague, Holland, 168,
The Labour Government 1945-1951 (Pritt), 210, 235, 240.
The Labour Party in Perspective (Attlee), 61.
The Librarian, 110.
The Margate Conference (Pollitt), 180.
The Sacred Band (Trory), 114, 115.
The Socialist Road for Britain (CPGB Election Manifesto, 1950), 201, 210.
The Times, 11, 30, 35, 60, 118, 161, 163, 183, 188, 201, 207, 224, 235.
This is the Road (Conservative Party Election Manifesto), 211.
Thomas, Graham (Monmouth DLP), 196.
Thompson, Dorothy, 41.
Thorpe, J. (Brightside DLP), 194.
Thuringia, Germany, 26.
Thus Wars Are Made (Norden), 226.
Thyssen works, 28.
Timber Control, 90.
Tito, General, 241.
Tokyo, Japan, 227.
Tomkins, A.G. (National Union of Furniture Trade Operatives), 90, 204.
Torode, A. (Sign & Display Trade Union), 99.
Tracey, Herbert, 154.
Trades Disputes Act (1927), 48, 71, 104. Trades Disputes and Trade Unions Bill (1946), 48, 72.
Trades Union Congress, General Council of, 83, 84, 85, 95, 96, 97, 98, 100, 106, 107, 108.
Trade Union Law Amendment Act of 1927, 54.
Trafalgar Square, London, 51, 84, 190.
Transport and General Workers' Union, 39, 63, 94, 199.
Transport House, London, 62, 167.
Tribune, 241.
Tribunite, Left, 210.
Trieste, on the Adriatic coast, 123..
Trojan Star (British ship), 199.
Truman Doctrine, 147, 161, 241.
Truman, Harry S., 7, 29, 30, 36, 152, 163, 164, 165, 167, 185, 187, 188, 207, 208, 214, 215, 223, 233, 234.
Truman's Economic Report to Congress, 164.
Trygve Lie, (Gen. Sec. UN), 187.
Turkey, 186.
Turner, E.J. (Electrical Trades Union), 178, 179.
Twickenham, London, 216.

Ulbricht, Walter, 28.
"United Europe" Committee, 132.
United Nations Association, 133.
United Nations Balkan Committee, 179.

INDEX

United Nations, Charter of, 40, 41, 98, 102, 103, 139, 140, 211, 212, 224, 232.
United Nations, General Assembly of, 84, 102, 123, 188.
United Nations [Organisation], 10, 27, 33, 35, 39, 71, 75, 84, 102, 117, 118, 119, 125, 129, 133, 134, 139, 169, 185, 187, 211, 214, 222, 228, 241, 243, 245.
United Nations Security Council, 34, 40, 41, 43, 117, 123, 139, 185, 186, 229.
United, Press, 225.
United States Air Force, 165, 166.
United States, Communist Party of, 66, 67, 68, 123.
United States, Communist Political Association of, 67.
United States Information Agency, 155.
United States of Europe, 124, 169.
United States Senate Military Affairs Committee, 31, 76.
United World Economic Report (1848), 202.
Unity in Action (CPGB), 75.
Unity Pact (Poland), 151.
Unsan gold mines, Korea, 225.
Usher Hall, Edinburgh, 212, 213.
Ural mountains, 22, 71.
US News & World Report, 183.
USSR, All-Union Central Council of Trade Unions of, 86.

Varga, E., 149.
Vienna, Austria, 24.
Viet Minh Front, Liberation Army of, 59.

Vietnam, Democratic Republic of 9, 25, 59, 117.
Vistula, River, 28.
Vosvodina, 12.
Vyshinsky, A.Ya., 208.

Walker, Gordon, MP for Smethwick, 73.
Wallace, Henry, 186, 187.
Wandsworth, London. 138.
Wandsworth Prison, London, 51.
Ward, Fred (Waterloo TC&LP), 142.
Warner, Christopher, 153.
Washington, DC, USA, 19, 40, 55, 101, 102, 185, 186, 201, 206, 214, 218, 225, 229, 233, 235, 248.
Washington, George, 67.
Wenceslas Square, Prague, 16.
Werner, Dr. Arthur, 28.
Werth, Alexander, 42.
West Fife, Scotland, 216, 246.
White House, Washington, 207, 233.
William, Francis, 233.
Williams MP, Tom (Co-operative Party), 221.
Williams, T.H. (USDAW), 168.
Wilson, Dr. Henry, Bishop of Chelmsford, 51.
Wilson, G.P. (Cannock DLP), 138.
Wilson, Harold, 239, 241.
Women's British-Soviet Committee, 50.
Wood, Councillor A. H. (Pres. Brighton Trades Council), 80.
World Federation of Trade Union (WFTU), 48, 82, 83, 84, 204, 205, 206.

World News, 240.
Worrall, John S. (Attercliffe DLP), 133.
Württemburg, Germany, 31.

Yalta Conference. (See under Crimean)
Yates, MP, V.F. (Ladywood DLP), 133.
Young, Sir George, 50.
Young, Jimmy (Association of Engineering & Shipbuilding Draughtsmen), 82.
Yugoslavia, 9, 11, 12, 158.
Yugoslavia, National Liberation Front of, 11, 12.
Yugoslavia, Federative People's Republic of, 12, 55, 78.

Zeeland, Mr. Van, 169.
Zhdanov, A.A., Colonel-General, 22.
Zhukov, Marshal, 29.
Zilliacus MP, Koni, (Gateshead LP&TC), 61, 132, 133, 139, 140, 142, 166, 198, 207, 216.
Züricher Zeitung, 227.

Mail Order Catalogue of
BOOKS AND BOOKLETS BY ERNIE TRORY

Available from CRABTREE PRESS
4 Portland Avenue, Hove, East Sussex BN3 5NP

ABOUT THE AUTHOR

IN THE PERIOD from 1939 to 1946, Ernie Trory published two pamphlets and three books: *Sussex for the People* (1939); *Sussex and the War* (1940); *Mainly about Books* (1945); *New Foundations* (1946); and *The Sacred Band* (also 1946). He was expelled from the Communist Party (CPGB) in 1942 - see *War of Liberation* (1987), pages 73 *et seq* - and ceased to write on political subjects after 1946. He took to studying postal and philatelic history and contributed widely to magazines catering for these subjects. He started to write, in parts, *A Postal History of Brighton* and *A Philatelic History of the Olympic Games*. Only one part of the former appeared but six parts of the latter were published.

All of these books, both the political and the philatelic, are long since out of print and turn up only occasionally in second-hand book lists; but *Sussex for the People* (1939), Ernie Trory's report to the Second Sussex County Congress of the CPGB, of which he was then full-time organiser, as well as *Sussex and the War* (1940), his report to the Third Sussex County Congress of the CPGB, were reprinted in an appendix to his *Imperialist War*, published in 1977.

In the course of his researches into the philatelic history of the Olympic Games, he amassed a collection of rare philatelic items relating to the Olympic Games from 1896 to 1952, which won several international awards. On the strength of these, he was asked to sit on a panel of seven judges at the International Exhibition of Olympic Games and Sports Stamps in Rimini (*Verso Tokyo*) in 1964; and again in Riccioni (*Verso Mexico*) in 1968.

His visit to Rimini with his wife in 1964 was his first venture abroad since the end of the Second World War but he made amends with subsequent visits to the continent, taking in first Greece and then Yugoslavia and Albania and eventually all the socialist countries in Europe except Rumania.

This led to an in-depth study of the countries he had visited and rekindled his enthusiasm (it had never really died) for the communist cause. He applied to rejoin the CPGB but then thought better of it and withdrew his application. It had moved so far to the right by then that he was no longer interested in becoming a member. In 1977 he became a foundation member of the New Communist Party, to which he still belongs, writing occasionally for the *New Worker*.

Between 1974 and the present time, Ernie Trory has written and published a further seventeen books and pamphlets, of which fourteen are still available. Some of these booklets and pamphlets are not readily available from booksellers as their prices, which are the same as when they were published, are so low that the trade discounts do not always cover the postages involved. If you are interested in any of these, you should order now while the stocks last. It is true that all but two or three of the following were written before the collapse of the socialist system in Europe but the facts contained in them are still valid and the warnings given about imperialist-sponsored counter-revolutionary activities have been justified by subsequent events.

ALL THE FOLLOWING PRICES INCLUDE POSTAGE

SOVIET TRADE UNIONS AND THE GENERAL STRIKE
An Example of International Solidarity
48 pages Price: 80p ISBN 0 9503503 3 8

THE ENTHUSIASM with which the Soviet people greeted the news of Britain's General Strike is carefully recorded by the author. Using extracts from speeches at factory meetings throughout the USSR, he captures the feeling of international solidarity of the Soviet workers who levied themselves a day's wages each week to support the British workers. A cheque was presented to the TUC who, fearing the taunts of Moscow gold from Fleet Street, turned it down. - Derek Clarke in UNIONEWS (University of Sussex Union).

On the 13th May, 1926, Violet Lansbury, daughter of the Labour leader George Lansbury, wrote to her father from Moscow: "The refusal of the General Council of the TUC to take the money collected by the workers here is disgusting." The letter was published in full in *Lansbury's Labour Weekly*, and is quoted in *Soviet Trade Unions and the General Strike*, an excellent pamphlet by Ernie Trory. - **BRITISH-SOVIET FRIENDSHIP**.

SOCIALISM IN GERMANY
A Short History of the German Democratic Republic
80 pages   Price: £1.35p   ISBN 0 9503503 5 4

BOURGEOIS HISTORIANS conveniently forget to mention that Hitler's first victims were communists and trade union activists leading the anti-fascist struggle. But the Communist Party of Germany carried on the fight underground and abroad, rallying the progressive forces against Hitler and his Nazi thugs.

In 1944, when, with the help of the Soviet Army, the end of the war was in sight, the Party began to plan the coming peace. The people of eastern Germany found the benefits of socialism - rising living standards, no unemployment, free education and health services. Ernie's pamphlet tells the whole story, simply and clearly. - Renee Sams in the NEW WORKER.

Ernie Trory reminds us of much that is too readily forgotten about the Cold War in Germany, the overturning of the Potsdam Agreement, the division of Germany and the arming of the Federal Republic. He recalls the other side of the story of the Berlin "blockade" and airlift, the 1953 uprising and the building of the Wall. - H.J.Fyrth in the BULLETIN OF THE SOCIETY FOR THE STUDY OF LABOUR HISTORY.

The second half of this booklet concentrates on three key events: the strikes of the 17th June, 1953, the building of the Berlin wall on the 13th August, 1961, and the Warsaw pact intervention in Czechoslovakia in August, 1968. These last two, Trory considers, "will go down in history as the two events that saved Europe from becoming the centre of a third world war." - MEMBERS' BULLETIN (Britain-GDR Society).

This booklet is extremely valuable in the wealth of historical detail it compresses into a few pages on this hidden chapter of workers' history. The author shows how the division of Germany was connived at by the imperialist forces who refused to implement the agreements on democratisation at Yalta. - Dónal Ó Leannáin in the IRISH SOCIALIST.

This short survey should do something to counter the hostile propaganda in the media. - Gordon Schaffer in LABOUR MONTHLY.

HUNGARY 1919 AND 1956
The Anatomy of Counter-Revolution
88 pages   Price: £1.90   ISBN 0 9503503 7 0

INDEFATIGABLE activist Ernie Trory contributes another well-researched booklet on recent history. He studies the two counter-revolutions in Hungary, using Hungarian sources and, in the case of 1956, eye-witness accounts from Charlie Coutts who was reporting for the *Daily Worker* at the time and in a telling passage wrote: "I couldn't help feeling that the old politicians were coming out to reap the benefit of the struggle of the youth and students."

The role of the Soviet Union is clearly brought out, and the whole is useful when coming up against the "What about Hungary?" argument by those questioning Soviet motives and the need for closer British-Soviet relations. - BRITISH-SOVIET FRIENDSHIP.

The four main causes of the counter-revolution in 1956, which attempted to turn Hungary off the road to socialism, were sectarianism in the Party, opportunism in opposition to it, the activities of the avowed enemies of socialism, and imperialist interference.

Ernie's account of Nagy's refusal to arm the workers demanding the right to defend socialism against the armed counter-revolutionaries, his legalisation of the fascist organisations, and his illegal formation of an "inner cabinet" including at least one open enemy of socialism should should all provide food for thought for opponents of the Soviet assistance to Hungarian socialism in 1956.

This book is a clear indicator that it was János Kádár's government, and those of the fraternal socialist countries, that really stood for freedom in Hungary. - NEW WORKER.

The uprising, regarded by *Daily Express* foreign correspondent Sefton Delmar as one of the great events in history, is described by Mr. Trory as a counter-revolution by reformist factions in the Communist Party backed by foreign imperialists and émigré reactionaries. He says Marxists-Leninists should take heed of what happened in Hungary, both in 1919 and in 1956, and beware of any activities directed towards isolating the Party from the people - Adam Trimingham in the Brighton EVENING ARGUS.

POLAND IN THE SECOND WORLD WAR
The Background to its Present Problems
120 pages   Price: £2.55   ISBN 0 9503503 8 9

THIS BOOK from Ernie Trory sheds welcome light on the past few years' events in Poland. It seeks to trace back to their roots some of the poison berries that have emerged recently in Polish society. The book is written with Ernie's usual attention to detail - at times you feel almost overwhelmed with facts and references. - NEW WORKER.

Another interesting aspect of Polish history is the million-pound financing, by the British government, of the Polish government-in-exile. In the end it became clear that the activities of this government with its underground links with dubious elements in Poland was hindering the war effort. The British government withdrew its recognition but did not send them packing. Since the end of the war there is evidence that consistent efforts have been made to make Poland a wedge between Russia and the West. - Desmond Greaves in the IRISH DEMOCRAT.

Ernie Trory's work is not well known to many Canadians, but should be. His writing is mainly historical and *Poland in the Second World War* is a valuable, though brief, introduction to the early background of Poland's recent problems. He treats of such key topics as British-Soviet relations during the war, the role of the London-based government-in-exile, the Katyn murders, the Warsaw uprising, the formation of the Polish Provisional Government, and the settlement of Poland's post-war borders. These are big subjects, but Trory does a good job in raising the reader's awareness of the imperialist nature of British policies towards Poland and of the treacherous activities of the Polish government-in-exile. - DL in the CANADIAN TRIBUNE.

CHURCHILL AND THE BOMB
A Study in Pragmatism
128 pages   Price: £2.55   ISBN 0 9503503 9 7

THIS IS ANOTHER valuable book from the pen of the indefatigable Ernie Trory to whose meticulous research in the cause of peace the entire progressive movement is indebted.
    Churchill's attitude to the Soviet Union changed many times. When

he thought it was weak - above all when the USA had the monopoly of atomic weapons - he was prepared to resort to pressure and political blackmail. When he realised the military strength of the Soviet Union he was prepared to come to terms.

In the short time that America had a monopoly of the atomic bomb he never ceased to call for its use in a "preventive war" against the Soviet Union. After the Soviet Union exploded an atomic device Churchill changed his tune and called for a summit meeting with Stalin. - Harry Cousins in BRITISH SOVIET FRIENDSHIP.

Hypocrite or pragmatist? About Churchill, the author leaves it to us to decide. But in providing us with such a detailed and informative study of this complex and forceful character he has given us a handbook that can be of great help to all engaged in today's greatest activity, the struggle for peace. - Ian Gunn in EDUCATION FOR TOMORROW.

Much of what the author has to say has never been revealed to the general public in the Western countries. A great deal, though publicly acknowledged at the time, has since been forgotten by many people. - R.J.M. Tolhurst in SURVEY (Australia).

POLITICS AND THE OLYMPICS
The Story of Los Angeles
With an Introduction by Andrew Rothstein
40 pages   Price: £1.40   ISBN 0 9513020 0 0

ALL WHO ARE ANXIOUS for the Olympic movement to flourish in its true spirit should read this booklet to understand how the breaking of the Olympic charter caused the Soviet withdrawal from the games. The threatened interference by the United States authorities with the entry to the United States of Soviet athletes and the refusal to allow Soviet planes and ships to bring the Soviet team to the United States are well documented. - William Wilson in BRITISH-SOVIET FRIENDSHIP.

LA held the Olympics in 1932, and Ernie opens by contrasting the high ideals of the first LA games with those of 1984. The second time round, philosophy and principles were non-starters. The race was for a fast buck. In his introduction, Andrew Rothstein stresses that the reason why the Soviet Union and all the socialist countries except Rumania were forced to pull out was consideration for the personal safety of the athletes in the socialist teams. - NEW WORKER.

CALGARY AND SEOUL
The Games of the XXIV Olympiad
84 pages Price: £3.00 ISBN 0 9515098 0 2

ERNIE TRORY gives a lot of detail about the political background to the Seoul games and indeed to the Korean Peninsular as a whole. This is a very useful account and will be of interest even to the most non-sporting of readers. The period leading up to these games was full of political incident. The South Korean leaders hoped to gain international prestige from the games; they hoped for trade agreements and to use the world's media to denigrate the Democratic Republic of Korea.

They spurned its offer to sponsor the games jointly. They even accused the North Koreans of deliberately bringing down a South Korean passenger liner, killing 115 people. The young woman they produced before the world's press as the alleged perpetrator of the crime seemed more and more unlikely as time went by. The whole business had the hallmarks of a CIA-style operation.

Large anti-government demonstrations by students and workers were brutally suppressed by security forces. An *Observer* correspondent, Peter McGill, wrote that "up to the 10th June, 1988, an average of 2,500 rounds of tear-gas has been fired every day this year."

Commercialism reached a zenith of greed and vulgarity at the Los Angeles Olympics. The Calgary Winter Games were also infected particularly over rival bids to obtain television "rights." Connected to the high money stakes involved in top-level sport is drug abuse, a particular feature of the 1988 Olympics. These unwelcome trends are well discussed in this book. - Ann Rogers in the NEW WORKER.

Ernie Trory, who has a lengthy political background, has a very uncomplicated view of the Olympics. In his introduction to this lively account he points out that he has always endeavoured to present the Olympics as reflecting the economic and political struggles of the period during which they are being held. Korea is a divided country like Germany. Anyone who doubts the author's outlook might consider at length why the USA is in favour of ending the division in Germany but not in Korea. - Harry Cousins in BRITISH-SOVIET FRIENDSHIP.

THE SOCIAL WAGE
Its Role under Capitalism and in
the Transition from Socialism to Communism
48 pages   Price: £2.45   ISBN 9515098 1 0

IN 1984, Ernie Trory was invited to give the Tommy Jackson Annual Memorial Lecture at the Amalgamated Engineering Union Hall in Crawley. Tommy Jackson, who died in 1955, was a founder member of the Communist Party (CPGB). The bulk of the pamphlet consists of Ernie's address, which looks at the question of state welfare. He details its origins from the Poor Laws and the workhouse system to national insurance and the post-war construction of the Welfare State. The post-war Labour government introduced sweeping reforms, setting up a National Health Service, which was then described as the best in the world. What they actually set up is examined in part by Ernie in this booklet which deserves a wide audience.

The rest consists of four articles and speeches covering problems in the socialist states, the role of the social wage during the construction of socialist society, and Gorbachev's revisionism.

The Social Wage is a thought-provoking essay on a question which is often ignored but which underlies the thinking of much of the Labour Party's strategy even today. - Andy Brooks in the NEW WORKER.

I expected this to be heavy going but it is articulate and compelling. The first part, *The Welfare State*, which the author prefers to call *state welfare*, outlines the history and failings of the present system in Britain - the *social wage* being public services, health, housing, benefits etc. as distinct from the *money wage*. In the second section, *Material and Moral Incentives*, the collapse of the socialist system in the Soviet Union is examined with a view to stimulating discussion on the implications for the rise of Marxist-Leninist socialism here - "When the people realise that the social wage is more important than the money wage, they will have raised their conscious desire for the transition to communism to a level that will make it possible. To work for others as for oneself is absolutely essential before mankind can move on from socialism to communism."

The appeal of this booklet is primarily moral, and I think anyone with an open mind will find it rewarding reading - even if they are not committed Marxist-Leninists. - Neil K. Henderson in NEW HOPE INTERNATIONAL REVIEW

HOW DID IT HAPPEN?
The Dialectics of Counter-Revolution
84 pages   Price: £4.25   ISCB 9515098 4 5

TRORY OUTLINES the root causes of the debacle that transpired in the former USSR, analysing from a Marxist point of view all the currents, outward and hidden, that went towards this disintegration. His delving into the programme and consequences of the 20th, 21st and 22nd Congresses of the CPSU are very enlightening. - Michael Lucas in NORTHSTAR COMPASS (Canada).

Many readers will already have seen *The Social Wage*, which Ernie Trory wrote in 1992. His latest work takes off where the other one ends, and pulls no punches in its conclusions. Written in the author's easy style, it takes the debate a notch further on - and deserves to be read. - Andy Brooks in the NEW WORKER.

"The people of the Soviet Union and the former socialist countries of Europe will soon find out, if they have not already done so, that capitalism will not work the second time round," writes Ernie Trory.... He is quite certain that socialism will come again, even if it is difficult to know how soon.
Ernie Trory is an erudite writer, extremely well versed in Marxist and Leninist doctrine. His explanation of historical materialism and dialectics is clear and valuable to the ordinary reader. We may not accept all his current applications of it but this provocative booklet will certainly merit our attention. - Frank Allaun in the MORNING STAR.

Trory's earlier book, *The Social Wage*, dealt with the growth of money wages at the expense of the social wage under "real socialism" and the disastrous consequences this had morally. Now he examines the related issue of commodity production under socialism. The renewal of the forces of commodity production meant in turn a greater role for the law of value, which began to play the role of economic lever as under capitalism, replacing the law of balanced development as articulated by Stalin.... These are just some of the questions raised by Ernie Trory's stimulating book. Review in POSTMARK PRAHA (Czech Republic).

BIOGRAPHY

CRADLED INTO POETRY
The Life and Times of Percy Bysshe Shelley
264 pages   Price: £6.95   ISBN 0 9515098 3 7

PROMOTING AN AWARENESS of Shelley's political views equal to the appreciation of his poetry is the stated aim of this book. It is therefore the longer poems which receive the most attention, both as victims of unmerited neglect and as vehicles better than the shorter lyrical pieces for political themes.

A substantial but sprightly digest of the causes and course of the French Revolution, recounted with some of the tone of the old-fashioned school text book - and none the worse for that - sets the scene for some reactions from the British intelligentsia of the time to both Revolution and Terror. Such is the background of earthy politics and economics to a poet much etherialised.

The engaging *Preface* alludes to the circumstances in which the book was written and, forty-three years later, re-written. *Cradled into Poetry* is plainly a labour of love. Love as the best fuel for labour is a most Shelleyan idea. - David Hicks in ORBIS: INTERNATIONAL QUARTERLY REVIEW OF POETRY AND PROSE.

Oh that Shelley were living in these turbulent times! One cannot help being struck by the many historical similarities between the time of the poet and the daily news of the present: the huge tax demands, the rise of new "nation states,", the reckless extravagance and profligacy of members of the Royal Family and, as always, the unceasing exploitation of the poor. *Cradled into Poetry* is a deeply interesting and necessary book. - Sheilah Grubb in EDUCATION FOR TOMORROW.

Trory takes cognisance of the many momentous happenings in an eventful period of our history and commands respect with his clear impartial style. Had school history primers been as interesting, there would be far more people about today enjoying an active interest in history and poetry. Not just for the lovers of Shelley but for the general reader too, this book is highly recommended. - Ken M. Ellison in NEW HOPE INTERNATIONAL REVIEW.

TRUTH AGAINST THE WORLD
The Life and Times of Thomas Hughes
Author of *Tom Brown's School Days*
280 pages Price: £9.50 ISBN 0 9515098 2 9

THOMAS HUGHES, a little-known Christian socialist and radical reformer, is given a new appraisal in Ernie Trory's latest biographical endeavour. It would be more accurate, perhaps, to see the author's portrayal of Hughes's life as a springboard for accounts of contemporary political events.

The background and sidelights are frequently rewarding. Taken in this sense, there are some valuable insights into the condition of labour, agitation and organisation of the working people. A case can always be made for historical studies which bring to life the struggles of the working class and the inter-play of class forces. In many of the author's descriptions this is what we get - and it is the book's main strength.

Clearly a considerable amount of research has gone into this study, and amassing the Hughes literature is quite an achievement. A book like this is well worth digging into. - Steve Lawton in the NEW WORKER.

This is in fact a splendid history of the last century, especially of its political and economic events, written from a Marxist viewpoint. Thomas Hughes was deeply involved in most of them and nearly always on the right side.

In the clothing trade, men and women worked in small workshops or sweatshops for scandalous wages and excessive hours. Hughes reported the horrific experiences of young girls forced into prostitution to supplement their pay. He was involved in many causes, for example when the Amalgamated Society of Engineers suffered the big lockout of 1852 he spoke on their platform and wrote regularly for their union journal.

In the US there was civil war between the North and the slaveowners of the South, with the British ruling class supporting the latter and the industrial workers the former. Hughes, as an opponent of slavery, was with them all the way and was the main speaker at huge meetings in the campaign.

The biography of this pioneer shows us what one man can achieve in his lifetime. - Frank Allaun in the MORNING STAR.

A TRILOGY OF CONTEMPORARY HISTORY

BETWEEN THE WARS
Recollections of a Communist Organiser
160 pages   Price: £2.60   ISBN 0 9503503 0 3

MORE THAN AT ANY OTHER TIME in this century, the 'thirties contrasted class against class and polarised society in such a fashion that one class could not even begin to comprehend the life style of the other. In his *Between the Wars*, Ernie Trory describes life in the Communist Party and his role as an organiser of the unemployed. His account of unemployed marches, demonstrations and raids on mayoral banquets provides a rare glimpse into how the politically motivated individual fought the depression. - Stephen Kelly in TRIBUNE.

The author of this book is a Brighton man who was an AEU Shop Steward during the war. *Between the Wars* was written in 1940 when he was in the army. Parts of it are about his adventures in the mid-thirties in Northern Spain, the Soviet Union and the Netherlands. He was active in the NUWM and in the Shop Assistants' Union, being elected a delegate to its National Conference three times. He was also active in the fight against fascism and war; and in 1938 was appointed Sussex County Organiser of the Communist Party. - AUEW JOURNAL.

Once Ernie Trory became convinced of the need to organise the working class in struggle, he took part in the many aspects of that activity with intelligence, courage and ability. All these experiences and activities developed his understanding and stature in the movement. The descriptions that Ernie Trory gives of his efforts to guide and lead the developing movement will be read by future historians as a valuable source of material at "grass roots" level. - Edumnd & Ruth Frow in the BULLETIN OF THE SOCIETY FOR THE STUDY OF LABOUR HISTORY.

IMPERIALIST WAR
Further Recollections of a Communist Organiser
244 pages   Price: £5.95   ISBN 0 9503503 0 3

ERNIE TRORY was a district organiser of the CPGB when the war broke out in 1939, and gives a vivid description of the problems and trials of working-class organisations in his area during the next two years. More important, he fits this into the general picture of the difficulties encountered by the Communists and a widening circle of working-class organisations of that period, faced with the immediate issues of the war and the ultimate question: what kind of war was it during the first two years? This narrative is set in an account of the international situation before and during the war - with British and French imperialism fearful of German preparations for armed redivision of the world, yet clutching at the dream that, if kindly treated, the Nazis would turn against the Soviet Union. - Andrew Rothstein in LABOUR MONTHLY.

If you like your history well-spiced with personal reminiscences, you will find *Imperialist War* fascinating reading. It is an unusual combination of personal experiences and painstakingly researched history giving an almost day to day account of the Second World War from September 1939 to June 1941. The author states in his introduction that it was Hitler's apparent decision *not* to go to war with the Soviet Union that caused Chamberlain to declare war on Germany; and I think he proves his point. The perfidy of the ruling class of Britain with their policy of appeasement is clearly shown and well illustrated with quotations from documents of the time. That perfidy is contrasted with the principled stand taken by the Soviet Union whose role in the Battle of Britain saved us from almost certain annihilation. - Renee Sams in the NEW WORKER.

In his previous volume, *Between the Wars*, Trory presented a fascinating account of the growth of the Brighton CP in the 1930s. This local history is now carried forward. Sussex was not a typical area for the Party. The two largest occupational groups among the delegates to the 1940 County Congress were teachers and shop assistants. Nevertheless historians will learn a good deal from Trory's detailed accounts of the grass-roots working of the Party, accounts which draw upon and extensively reproduce local records in his possession. There is local evidence here for the view that the adoption of an anti-war line in the Party in October 1919 was accepted by the membership with relief and even enthusiasm, and that it had little adverse effect on the membership. - James Hinton in the BULLETIN OF THE SOCIETY FOR THE STUDY OF LABOUR HISTORY.

WAR OF LIBERATION
Recollections of a Communist Activist
395 pages   Price: £11.40   ISBN 0 906917 27 1

THE PRESENT WORK gives a lively account, stage by stage and usefully providing precise dates, of the war on the various fronts, of the diplomatic activities of the Western Allies and the Soviet Union respectively, and of political struggles in Britain at the most critical periods of the war, notably over the question of a second front in the West. Churchill's correspondence with Stalin and his contrasting private letters to President Roosevelt, as well as his discussions with Foreign Secretary Anthony Eden on how to frustrate the Soviet Union are so fully quoted that readers who do not have the time or the opportunity to go through the many relevant volumes published after the war are very well served.

Later, Trory quotes striking examples of how Churchill, by January 1942, was already speculating on the Soviet Union's probably emerging exhausted after the war, and the advantage this would give to Britain and the US.

The author accompanies his narrative with a modest account of his own war work as an engineer and his political activities throughout. - Andrew Rothstein in the MORNING STAR.

Ernie Trory lived in Burgess Hill during part of the last war. When he joined Caffyn's, the company was working under government contract rebuilding army lorries and, says Trory, had always been notoriously anti-union. "When I started working there," he recalls, "I was the only employee with a union card in my pocket. Naturally, I did not immediately make this fact known." Later, Trory was able to take up the case of a member of his union who had been ordered to give up possession of his home in 15 days. Trory's efforts were rewarded and a large flat was found for the man who had previously lived with his wife and four children in a tied cottage. In this book, Trory relates the great international and national events of the period under review to life in the trade unions and political parties in his own locality, and to his own political experiences. - MG in the MID-SUSSEX TIMES.

There is plenty of meat in this book, a well-written and fascinating account of world events by a former member and organiser of the

Communist Party of Great Britain who was expelled from the Party in May, 1942. The author does not apologise for including his own recollections of his experiences with the Communist Party. It all adds up to the making of an interesting and readable book. - Albert Bowbrick in the AEU JOURNAL'

For those like myself, who lived through the war but were too young to understand the politics, *War of Liberation* has the value of recalling and putting into perspective many things that I did not understand at the time. For those born since the war, the wealth of detail makes those momentous times come to life again, giving an understanding of that period which changed the world.

Interestingly, Ernie notes that the seeds of the later revisionism of the CPGB were already being sown: "During the imperialist stage of the war, the membership of the CPGB had comprised people of deep convictions, men and women who were prepared to make sacrifices for their beliefs. After the change in the character of the war, new people came into the party in large numbers, many of them with no strong class convictions, just people who wanted to help win the war and saw the Communist Party as the driving force to that end. The party failed to educate its new members in the principles of Marxism-Leninism and, as a consequence, many of them left when the cold war began while others stayed in to lay the foundations of the revisionist and reformist policies that led to the CPGB's programme, *The British Road to Socialism*. - Renee Sams in the NEW WORKER.

All our publications are available by order from most booksellers, though only a few will have them in stock. If you have any difficulty in obtaining copies, please order direct from us. All the prices quoted on previous pages include a small charge for packing and posting. **ORDER NOW FROM CRABTREE PRESS, 4 PORTLAND AVENUE, HOVE, EAST SUSSEX BN3 5NP.**

USUAL TRADE TERMS FOR BOOKSELLERS

NO SALE OR RETURN

IN COURSE OF PREPARATION

PEACE AND THE COLD WAR
Part Two: 1952-1964
The Tories Take Over

Note: Will all customers (trade and personal) please notify us when they change addresses, so that we can continue to send notifications of new publications.

In the meantime, the author would be pleased to hear from any readers of his books who have comments to make - good or bad! He can be reached c/o Crabtree Press.